The Western Literary Canon in Context
Part III

Professor John M. Bowers

THE TEACHING COMPANY ®

PUBLISHED BY:

THE TEACHING COMPANY
4151 Lafayette Center Drive, Suite 100
Chantilly, Virginia 20151-1232
1-800-TEACH-12
Fax—703-378-3819
www.teach12.com

ISBN 1-59803-471-5

John M. Bowers, Ph.D.

Professor of English, University of Nevada, Las Vegas

John M. Bowers is a Professor of English at the University of Nevada, Las Vegas, where he has served as chairman of the Department of English. In 1971 he received his B.A. from Duke University, and he went on to earn an M.A. in 1973 and a Ph.D. in 1978 from the University of Virginia. In 1975 he was awarded a Master of Philosophy degree from The University of Oxford, where he was a Rhodes Scholar with a specialty in medieval English literature.

Professor Bowers has published four books: *The Crisis of Will in "Piers Plowman"*; *The Canterbury Tales: Fifteenth-Century Continuations and Additions*; *The Politics of "Pearl": Court Poetry in the Age of Richard II*; and *Chaucer and Langland: The Antagonistic Tradition*. He is the author of more than 30 articles and essays on authors, including Saint Augustine, Marie de France, and William Shakespeare, as well as seven entries in the 2006 edition of *The Oxford Encyclopedia of British Literature* on writers such as William Caxton and works such as *The Travels of Sir John Mandeville*. He has championed scholarship on Chaucer's contemporaries Thomas Usk and Sir John Clanvowe as well as the 15th-century Chaucerian poets Thomas Hoccleve and John Lydgate. His current book projects concern Chaucer, William Langland, and the *Gawain* Poet.

He has been a visiting research fellow at Merton College, University of Oxford, and a resident scholar at the Rockefeller Foundation's Study Center in Bellagio, Italy. He has lectured widely, with presentations in New York, Los Angeles, London, and Berlin. He has taught at the University of Virginia, Hamilton College (now Kaplan University), California Institute of Technology, and Princeton University. His regular teaching assignments include Chaucer, Shakespeare, literary theory, and world literature.

Professor Bowers has received numerous awards for his scholarship and teaching, including fellowships from the Andrew W. Mellon Foundation, the National Endowment for the Humanities, and the Solomon R. Guggenheim Foundation. Among his many teaching recognitions, he is the recipient of the Nevada Regents' Teaching Award.

Table of Contents
The Western Literary Canon in Context
Part III

Professor Biography i
Course Scope 1
Lecture Twenty-Five   Nationalism and Culture in Goethe's *Faust* 4
Lecture Twenty-Six   Melville's *Moby-Dick*
and Global Literature 19
Lecture Twenty-Seven   Cult Classic—*The Charterhouse of Parma* 35
Lecture Twenty-Eight   East Meets West in *War and Peace* 51
Lecture Twenty-Nine   Joyce's *Ulysses* and the Avant-Garde 67
Lecture Thirty   *The Magic Mountain*
and Modern Institutions 82
Lecture Thirty-One   *Mrs. Dalloway* and Post-War England 98
Lecture Thirty-Two   T. S. Eliot's Divine Comedy 114
Lecture Thirty-Three   Faulkner and the Great American Novel 130
Lecture Thirty-Four   Willa Cather and Mosaics of Identity 146
Lecture Thirty-Five   Tolkien's *The Lord
of the Rings*—Literature? 162
Lecture Thirty-Six   Postcolonialism—The Empire
Writes Back 178
Timeline 194
Glossary 202
Biographical Notes 205
Bibliography 215

Credits:

Excerpts from the poem "Chard Whitlow" used by kind permission of the
Henry Reed Estate.

The Western Literary Canon in Context

Scope:

Why read *Moby-Dick*? These thirty-six half-hour lectures on *The Western Literary Canon in Context* ask what are the great books that every educated person should know, and why have these literary works—not others—achieved this status within an official list of masterpieces? Why do some bestsellers stand the test of time? Why do some obscure authors steadily increase their standing? We will examine the context: Did the political elite champion an author? Did great historical events such as World War I effect the literary climate? Did the spread of literacy and technology bring the work to a wider audience? Canon formation becomes a complicated, untidy, and sometimes random process, always in the state of being revised. Why these thirty-six authors and titles, not others? Mostly because they retain canonic status in university courses, in textbooks like *The Norton Anthology*, and in paperback series like Penguin Classics. We'll look at how the academic curriculum perpetuates—and changes—the development of the canon.

Lectures One and Two begin with the Bible as the epitome of what "Western," "literary," and "canonic" mean to us. An official list of which works went into the Bible—and which were excluded—emerges as the operative principle for canon formation. Canonic books are honored with translation and subject to scholarly interpretation. The Bible defines how books are written, how they are organized and edited, and even what they look like.

Lectures Three through Eight examine the earliest works of the Western canon. Rediscovered in the 19th century, the Mesopotamian *Epic of Gilgamesh* poses a problem, crossing the boundary between East and West. Ancient Greek culture offers a new starting point, giving rise to genres that become canonic: the epics of Homer; the histories of Herodotus and Thucydides; the tragedies of Aeschylus, Sophocles, and Euripides; and the philosophic writings of Plato and Aristotle. "Firstness" sometimes insures inclusion in the canon.

Lectures Nine through Twelve cover imperial Rome. Virgil's *Aeneid* appropriated the achievements of the Homeric epics as propaganda for Emperor Augustus. Ovid grafted Greek mythology to Roman literature in his *Metamorphoses*. Boethius synthesized the best of Plato and Aristotle into Latin literature. And as the Church replaced the Empire, Saint Augustine interpreted pagan poetry allegorically to rescue literary classics for later Christian readers.

Lectures Thirteen through Seventeen examine medieval literature. *Beowulf* extolled the heroic virtues of the northern Europeans in the first surviving English vernacular epic. Something revolutionary happened as a result of religious reforms in 1215; Dante's used his native Italian language to create Europe's first canonic masterpiece: *The Divine Comedy*. *Sir Gawain and the Green Knight* shows how Arthurian literature reflected local courtly values. Boccaccio's *Decameron* invented "fiction" for the new middle-class audience, including women. Chaucer built upon this experiment in his *Canterbury Tales*, while he pursued the goal of making himself famous as "the father of English literature."

Lectures Eighteen through Twenty-One focus on the Renaissance. Sir Thomas More's *Utopia* exploited the new technology of the printing press when Europeans were first exploring the Americas. Shakespeare's tragedies and comedies traveled the globe, following Englishmen on their voyages of discovery and colonization. Cervantes filled a comparable role for Spanish-language culture; his *Don Quixote* established the novel as the new prestige genre in the Western canon, despite the fact his novel was sometimes banned. One recurring question becomes how "dangerous" books, once censored, eventually become classics.

Lectures Twenty-Two through Twenty-Four mark the transition to the Romantic era. After the English Civil War, John Milton composed *Paradise Lost* as a capstone to the entire classical and Christian traditions. The Western canon is becoming its own determining context: As writers become more prolific, canon formation begins to operate within the output of individual authors. Voltaire produced huge volumes of writing, but only *Candide* became universally read. Commercial publishing, with its demand for instant bestsellers, means that great authors were not immediately acclaimed. *Pride and Prejudice* only slowly gained recognition as a literary classic, showing how women like Jane Austen entered the literary pantheon.

In Lectures Twenty-Five through Twenty-Eight, Western literature expands to include new national cultures. Written in German, Goethe's *Faust* redrew the cultural map of Europe in the wake of the Napoleonic Wars. In America, Herman Melville widened these horizons to create a global, "multicultural" stage upon which the drama of *Moby-Dick* plays out. The French writer Stendhal explored national character within the old Europe by setting his novel *The Charterhouse of Parma* in northern Italy. Tolstoy's *War and Peace* is "about" Russia across an entire generation, from before the Napoleonic Wars, when aristocrats spoke French, to afterward, when people spoke Russian.

Lectures Twenty-Nine through Thirty-Six bring this series to a close with the 20th century. The First World War asserted the single most powerful context. James Joyce published *Ulysses* in 1922, but the novel's action is set in 1904, when Europe was still peaceful and cosmopolitan. As an allegory for the rush to self-destruction, Thomas Mann's *The Magic Mountain* told the story of a young German who emerges from a sanitarium only to face certain death in the trenches. In the mid-1920s, Virginia Woolf's *Mrs. Dalloway* told two stories: one of a veteran with "battle fatigue," and the other of the older generation overseeing the decline of the British Empire. In the war's wake, T. S. Eliot depicted Europe's cultural desolation in *The Waste Land*, while his later works sought consolation in Christianity. As a battlefield veteran, J. R. R. Tolkien embraced a different consolation: *The Lord of the Rings* reaches back into an ancient heroic past, before *Beowulf*, to imagine a world where warriors fought bravely for a cause worthy of their sacrifice.

Like other European languages, English becomes the literary medium of authors who are not English. In the mosaic of American culture, Faulkner's *The Sound and the Fury* dramatizes the issues of race in Southern literature, while Willa Cather's *Death Comes for the Archbishop* explores the multiethnic character of New Mexico. At the end of the 20th century, the Western canon is enriched by writers whose origins lie in the East. Tracing the history of India's independence, Salman Rushdie's *Midnight's Children* epitomizes the new postcolonial novel. Immigrant and transnational authors use the language of the former imperial rulers. As the boundaries of "context" expand to encompass the whole world, the Western literary canon is hardly recognizable as "Western" anymore—or even narrowly literary, as film adaptations of novels like Ondaatje's *The English Patient* boost the prestige of the original books.

Lecture Twenty-Five
Nationalism and Culture in Goethe's *Faust*

Scope:

The early 19th century witnessed the collective aspirations of nationalism captured in Goethe's two-part dramatic epic *Faust*. As a German-language writer, Goethe felt responsible for creating a national culture long before the unification of Germany in 1871. Reaching back into the medieval past, *Faust* traces the adventures of an insatiable spirit willing to sell his soul for the totality of human experience. In an age dominated by Napoleon and Lord Byron, titanic human ambition was no longer a moral failing but something compelling. Gigantic yearnings, like Beethoven's, fostered a new aesthetic of the colossal and the sublime, while the cult of the scientist looked forward to figures like Einstein.

Outline

I. Johann Wolfgang von Goethe spent nearly his entire working life in the German city of Weimar and as a writer helped to create a distinctly German literary tradition, even before Germany was a nation-state.

   A. By this point in the early 19th century, other European nations felt this need to have a great national poet. As a great reader of Shakespeare, Goethe positioned himself to become the great author of German-language literature.

   B. Like Sir Thomas More, Goethe trained to become a lawyer but neglected his legal career to pursue a literary career.

   C. His epistolary novel *The Sorrows of Young Werther* became the first international bestseller of the German literary tradition.

II. There was no real German nation-state until Bismarck's 1871 victory in the Franco-Prussian War. Unlike England, Germany had a culture long before it had a nation.

   A. It was a culture deeply invested in music and very much rooted in the medieval past.

B. It is significant, then, that Dr. Faust, the hero of Goethe's great masterpiece, was a German magician, necromancer, and charlatan said to have died around 1540.

III. Goethe's *Faust* was also related to a phenomenon in vogue in the 19th century: Gothic fiction.

A. Gothic novels explored the demonic, sinister, superstitious, and supernatural aspects of medieval culture.

B. Mary Shelley's *Frankenstein* dates from this period, as does the novel *The Vampyre* by Lord Byron's personal physician, John William Polidori.

C. Goethe's *Faust* was very much in line with this vogue and was centered around the real-life figure of Lord Byron, a literary and cultural icon that obsessed Goethe throughout his career.

IV. Goethe became a champion of the northern Germanic traditions and cultures of Europe, which is somewhat ironic because he invented the term World Literature (*Weltliteratur*).

A. He was wide ranging in his reading and writing. He actually did an imitation of the Persian poet Hafez in his collection *West-Eastern Divan*.

B. He had also traveled to Italy and had been exposed to early Greek culture when in Sicily.

V. His career, then, evolved in such a way that there was constant contrast between the northern Germanic culture and the southern European culture.

A. This idea of a German-Mediterranean split continued to obsess later thinkers such as Nietzsche in his *The Birth of Tragedy*.

B. We will also see this tension in the work of Thomas Mann and in the differing approaches of J. R. R. Tolkien and C. S. Lewis.

VI. As he emerged as a romantic figure in the early 19th century, Goethe was a champion of a new aesthetic based on artistic inspiration, the sublime, and the cult of genius.

A. Romantic inspiration as the source of authentic art and poetry was very much in the air at this time.

B. The problem with art based on inspiration alone is that the source of inspiration can fade away.

C. *Faust* contains numerous fragments and dead ends. In fact, Goethe described his overall body of work as "fragments of a great confession."

VII. Goethe participated in an aesthetic tradition that drew heavily upon a late classical literary critic, Longinus, who produced a treatise we call *On the Sublime*.

A. Longinus emphasized the spectacular, claiming that the experience of it "raises us toward the spiritual greatness of god."

B. This idea of an intense, overwhelming aesthetic experience lined up with the German movement of Sturm und Drang, which was represented in Goethe's *Prometheus*.

VIII. Longing for the transcendent became a marker of the German tradition after Longinus.

A. In the 13th and 14th centuries, Meister Eckhart and Wolfram von Eschenbach wrote tales about the quest for the spiritual and the god-like.

B. Later, the same theme would be played out in the works of Friedrich Nietzsche, Richard Strauss, Hermann Hesse, and Rainer Maria Rilke.

IX. German art, especially opera and other music, would constantly embrace the colossal after Goethe. This can be seen in the works of Richard Wagner and Gustav Mahler and in the use of majestic German music to mark momentous political changes in the nation.

X. Longinus also gave the Western tradition the sense that certain great writers are geniuses.

A. Longinus put Homer and not too many others in this category, but it would become the gold standard, the great test for any writer.

B. After World War I, Oswald Spengler would define the genius of the West particularly in terms of this Faustian spirit: the yearning for the infinite and the cult of great men of action with their insatiable ambitions.

XI. This spirit as embodied in Faust creates a peculiar theological paradox: Though he has committed every sin, he is taken up to Heaven.

  A. The restlessness that underlies his sin also underlies his salvation. What was a crime in traditional Christianity has now become a heroic virtue.

  B. Bonaparte was seen as a real-life embodiment of this Faustian urge to reach impossible heights of power. Even his defeat was colossal and spectacular.

XII. What is the answer to the challenge of this German idealism? Try harder, aim higher.

  A. This ideal of the power of the will became a kind of obsession throughout later German culture, reaching its sinister conclusion in the Nazi era.

  B. Faust himself is addicted to willful actions, yet his passivity toward the end of the story looks forward to the spectator mentality of Modern characters like Leopold Bloom.

XIII. With the rise of Romantic figures like Goethe and Lord Byron, the cult of genius moved beyond military and political men and toward the artist and the scientist.

  A. These two types are observers, watching the world so that they can represent it correctly in their art and theory.

  B. Goethe had a very charismatic presence and was in a strong position to foster this cult of the genius, and particularly the cult of the scientist.

  C. Goethe himself was a scientist. His research on comparative botany and plant morphology actually influenced Charles Darwin decades later.

  D. Faust, as a character, ends his long, worldly career as an engineer. His willingness to trample an elderly couple for the sake of his project establishes progress as a justification for any means.

XIV. Hereafter we get a familiar cultural icon: the German genius, specifically the German scientific genius.

  A. Einstein became the epitome of the 20th-century cult of the scientist, with his constant striving beyond relativity toward a unified field theory.

B. Einstein also made a Faustian bargain: He urged the creation of the atomic bomb but was a passive observer of its consequences.

XV. Since Aristotle, the Western tradition has been invested in a sense of progress, and that progress has been entrusted to the scientific community in our own day. But there is a sinister side that Goethe was already contemplating: that the science of progress rolls over anyone who gets in its way.

Suggested Readings:

Goethe, *Faust*.

Bloom, "Goethe's *Faust, Part II*: The Countercanonical Poem," in *The Western Canon*.

Boyle, *Goethe*.

Heller, *The Disinherited Mind*.

Questions to Consider:

1. Like authors and literary works, canonic genres have their ups and downs over time. The 19th century was the age of the novel, not drama, and yet Goethe chose to write *Faust* as a play that is almost impossible to imagine staging. Can you think of a single Romantic or Victorian play that is still read, studied, and holds the stage?

2. It is remarkable how many canonic authors wrote for fame, not money. Though a celebrity writer, Goethe made his livelihood as a court official at Weimar. Can you think of any great authors who wrote primarily for money and achieved lasting fame only as an unexpected consequence?

Lecture Twenty-Five—Transcript
Nationalism and Culture in Goethe's *Faust*

Johann Wolfgang von Goethe spent his entire working life in the German City of Weimar, even turning down an early job offer in France. He also spent his entire career as a writer, helping to create a distinctly German literary tradition even before there was a Germany as a nation-state.

Now remember, literature always starts off locally, beginning way back when, with the Greek city-states. Herodotus identified himself with Halicarnassus. The Greek tragic playwrights all identified themselves as Athenians. Dante, Petrarch, and Boccaccio would have self-identified as Florentine writers. Interestingly, though, when we get to Chaucer, he doesn't identify as a Londoner—but that's where he lived and worked—because his aspiration was to become the father of English literature, a national writer.

By this point in the early 19th century, other European nations feel this need also to have a great national poet, such as Shakespeare, who had emerged in England. Shakespeare also had worked hard to establish his credentials as a national writer, with wonderful patriotic expressions like this great description of England from his play *Richard II*:

> This royal throne of kings, this sceptred isle,
> This earth of majesty, this seat of Mars,
> This other Eden, demi-paradise …
> This precious stone set in the silver sea …
> This blessed plot, this earth, this realm, this England.

As a great reader of Shakespeare, Goethe positioned himself to become the great author of the German-language literature.

Like Sir Thomas More and many others before him, Goethe trained to become a lawyer. He even published his thesis, but like Ovid much earlier, he neglected his legal career instead to pursue a literary career. His epistolary novel *The Sorrows of Young Werther* in 1774 became the first real bestseller of a German literary text throughout Europe. It is an epistolary novel. Remember, the letter writing has been a sort of separate genre, very dignified in Europe since Cicero. There were translations of *The Sorrows of Young Werther*, and it even influences Jane Austen's *Sense and Sensibility*, where the young heroine Marianne, when she is jilted by Willoughby, is perfectly willing to die for love; this is what happens to Werther.

But there is no real German nation-state until much later: 1871 is usually reckoned as the founding date, after Bismarck's victory in the Franco-Prussian War. So unlike England, which is very far ahead in the creation of a nation-state, the Germans had a culture long before they had a nation. It was a culture deeply invested in music, for example, with the great composers Bach, Beethoven, and Brahms. German cultural history, as it began to be understood, was also very much rooted in the medieval past—that is, in an era before the rise of the nation-state, when it was a level playing field and all of these cultures were equal.

It is significant, then, that Dr. Faust, the hero of his great masterpiece, was a German magician, necromancer, and charlatan said to have died around 1540—that is, in the medieval period. Dr. Faust's exploits were collected in a book that had wide currency in Europe, the *Faustbuch*, which described him as an occult scholar in league with the devil. It's the *Faustbuch* that then becomes the source for Christopher Marlowe's great play *Tragicall History of D. Faustus* in 1590. The figure of Faust as a conjuror and a sorcerer continues to lurk in the background of Shakespeare's own wizard character Prospero in *The Tempest*.

Goethe's *Faust* was related also to a vogue in the early 19th century—also the late 18th century—in Gothic fiction. These are the novels exploiting the demonic, sinister, dark, superstitious, supernatural aspect of medieval culture. Remember, Jane Austen's *Northanger Abbey* actually pokes fun at the Gothic novel; specifically Ann Radcliffe's *The Mysteries of Udolpho*, with its gloomy castles and powerful but menacing male figures. Mary Shelley's *Frankenstein* dates from the same period, 1818, as well as their friend, Lord Byron's personal physician, Dr. Polidori, with his memorable novel *The Vampyre*. And so there is a great sort of vogue in these Gothic novels at this time, and Goethe's *Faust* fits very much into that vogue, very much centered around the real-life figure of Lord Byron, a literary and cultural icon that very much obsessed Goethe throughout his career.

Goethe becomes a real champion of the northern Germanic traditions and cultures of Europe, and this, in a way, is ironic, because he invented the term World Literature—*Weltliteratur*. He also was very wide ranging in his reading and his writing; he actually did an imitation of the Persian poet Hafez in his *West-Eastern Divan*. This is a translation of a Persian poet that anticipated other enterprises like Edward FitzGerald's the *Rubáiyát of Omar Khayyám* and then, in our times, the translations by the Persian-language poet Jalal al-Din Rumi. So Goethe had a very wide-ranging curiosity about this world literature and had actually been to some of the places. He had his famous tour of Italy in the 1780s, where he discovered Sicily. In Sicily, he felt that he really got in touch with original, authentic, primal Greek culture, those Greek colonies that had been established in Sicily at a very, very early time.

His career, then, would evolve in a way that there was constant contrast between the northern Germanic culture of his homeland and the southern European culture. For example, in *Faust*, Part I there is a Germanic *Walpurgisnacht*, with the Germanic characters of witches and goblins. In *Faust*, Part II, there's what we call the classical *Walpurgisnacht*, with the mythological characters of nymphs and satyrs. This idea of a sort of German-Mediterranean split continues to sort of obsess later thinkers such as Nietzsche in his *The Birth of Tragedy*—Nietzsche very much championing what he sees as the northern virtues embodied in a character like Prometheus, the hero who suffers because he has knowingly disobeyed divine law for the betterment of mankind.

Later on, we're going to see this all over again in the writings of Thomas Mann. His *Death in Venice* will be all about that southern Mediterranean culture, and then his companion piece, *The Magic Mountain*, set in the Germanic Alps—again a north-south contrast in the works of Thomas Mann. Even in the English literary tradition, we will see this particular split. J. R. R. Tolkien was trained as a Germanic philologist, and so his Middle Earth is populated with characters from the Germanic tradition: elves and goblins. However, his friend C. S. Lewis was trained as a classicist, and so when Lewis writes his "Chronicles of Narnia," what do we find here? We find fauns and centaurs out of the Mediterranean mythological tradition.

As he emerges as a romantic figure in the early 19th century, Goethe is going to be very much a champion of a new aesthetic that will be based on, one, artistic inspiration; two, the sublime as an aesthetic effect; and finally three, the cult of the genius, ultimately the artist and the scientist.

Now, romantic inspiration as the source of authentic art and poetry was very much in the air; the English poet William Wordsworth spoke of "the spontaneous overflow of powerful feelings." Goethe had his own phrase, "the spontaneous work of active nature." The problem with art based on inspiration alone, though, is that the source of inspiration can fade away. The artwork can fade away and flag as well. The famous example is Coleridge's "Kubla Khan," a poem that he began in a fit of inspiration—also after smoking a little opium—but he was interrupted, and he could never get back to the source of inspiration that had produced the poem "Kubla Khan." A later author, Stendhal, is also going to be a writer who works in the heat of inspiration, but as a result, his career is littered with unfinished novels and books that simply flagged because his inspiration failed him.

Faust itself contains numerous fragments and dead ends and bits and pieces very much characteristic of what we call the Romantic fragment poem. It is an assembly of brilliant sketches, many of which never really cohere into that organic wholeness that had been so much the aesthetic standard since Aristotle's *Poetics*. In fact, Goethe described his overall career and his writings as "fragments of a great confession." He saw everything as the bits and pieces of a total expression of himself as the artist.

He is going to line up in an aesthetic tradition that will draw heavily upon a late classical literary critic Longinus, who produced a treatise we call *On the Sublime*. This is all very mysterious; we don't know who Longinus is; we don't even know that that's his name; we don't know when it was written. It's one of these works that only surfaced in the Renaissance, when they were rediscovering many other Greek manuscripts. But it perfectly described the sort of aesthetic intentions very much characteristic of this period, especially with an emphasis on the spectacular. Longinus says what really catches our attention are great rivers, mighty oceans, violent lightning storms, a fiery volcanic eruption. One thinks immediately of the explosion, eruption of Mount Doom at the end of *The Lord of the Rings*, a really spectacular moment, sublime in the sense of Longinus. This is what Longinus says about these spectacular events: "It is the unusual that always excites our wonder. … Sublimity raises us toward the spiritual greatness of god." So Longinus's idea of this sort of great, spectacular, intense, overwhelming aesthetic experience very much lined up with the German movement of Sturm und Drang, sometimes translated as "storm and stress" or, better, "storm and impulse." Sturm und Drang is very much represented in Goethe's own early tragedy, *Prometheus*. He wrote his own *Prometheus*.

Longing for the transcendent is going to become a marker of German artistic creation ever since then. It actually has antecedents in the medieval period. The 14th-century Christian mystic Meister Eckhart was very much a character who wrote about the longings for something beyond the human—the spiritual, the godlike—though also you had Wolfram von Eschenbach in the 13th century writing his *Parzival* quest for the Holy Grail. This would eventually become the source work for Richard Wagner's last sublime opera, *Parsifal*.

There's also a posterity within German cultural production that preserves that Faustian yearning for the transcendent of the great, the receding, that thing that you were always reaching for—Longinus's sublime that he says raises a man toward the spiritual greatness of God. We're going to see this in Nietzsche's *Thus Spoke Zarathustra*. This is the great literary work that will inspire Richard Strauss's tone poem that then Stanley Kubrick would use for the sublime music in his film *2001: A Space Odyssey*, very much about the transcendence of mankind going to the next level of consciousness. Perfect choice.

You find it also in Hermann Hesse's novel *Siddhartha*, about the man becoming aware as the Buddha, the Awakened One. You find it in Rainer Maria Rilke's *Dueno Elegies*, these wonderful poems always sort of reaching for the angelic presence just beyond the material world. There's a great film from 1987, Wim Wenders's classic *Wings of Desire*, very much inspired by Rilke's poems, where angels inhabit the divided city of Berlin; the humans and the angels live side-by-side, and—the lovely twist—the angels envy the human experience of passion and sorrow. And so again the sense that there's some other reality just beyond the seen reality. We'll also get it in Thomas Mann; his *Death in Venice* is very much about the aesthetic and the erotic longing for something more than is immediately available.

Okay, so back to Goethe's *Faust*. Partly inspired by Mozart's opera *Don Giovanni*, with its hero's insatiable pursuit of sexual conquest, the tragedy of Faust is always more of an opera than a stage play, with all the characteristic excesses and failings of an opera libretto. The German art after Goethe will constantly embrace bigness, described with the term *kolossal*—the colossal, the big. And where are we going to see this? In other operas, especially Richard Wagner's great monumental operas. We see it in the symphonic tradition, especially at the end. Gustav Mahler wrote his 8th Symphony, nicknamed *Symphony of a Thousand*, and what is the subject of the 8th Symphony? It's a musical setting of the conclusion of Goethe's *Faust*, Part II.

Thomas Mann, when he comes to write his novels, writes colossal novels like *The Magic Mountain*; he even gets around to writing his own *Dr. Faustus*, and so there is this sort of German appetite for the colossal, the big—even if it's destructive—as long as it's huge. There is this haunting story about how the Nazi German general staff went to attend a performance of Wagner's *Götterdämmerung* ("the downfall of the gods") even as the Soviet Red Army was closing in on Berlin. It is that one fall of the gods paralleling the real-life fall of Nazi Germany going on at the same time—a chilling, chilling story. On a more upbeat note, we have the fall of the Berlin Wall in 1989, and what happened to celebrate this? Berliners came out—and in the background, a performance of Beethoven's Symphony No. 9, the "Ode to Joy" at the Brandenburg Gate as the wall came down—a great sort of longing for the majestic, the sublime.

One of the other things Longinus would give to the Western tradition is the sense that certain great writers are geniuses. That word "genius" has a special category. Longinus would put Homer and not too many other people in that category, but it becomes the gold standard. It becomes the great test for any writer—is he or she a genius? In the wake of World War I, Oswald Spengler, in his *Decline of the West*, would define the genius of the West particularly in terms of this Faustian spirit; it is sort of a marker of Western art and achievement. And what is it that will mark the kind of particularly romantic genius? A yearning for the infinite and a sort of cult of these great men of action with their insatiable ambitions.

There's a peculiar sort of conclusion to the overall Faust drama. Faust ought to be damned to Hell; he's committed every crime, every sin, and yet he is taken up into Heaven. He is saved at the end of the story. The critic Eric Heller summed up this theological paradox at the end of *Faust*, Part II. This is how he explained it: "What is Faust's sin? Restlessness of spirit. What is Faust's salvation? Restlessness of spirit." And so the thing that sets him apart from mere man is this titanic restlessness of spirit—never satisfied, always striving, always wanting more, more, more. This is no longer a sin as it would have been in traditional Christianity; it is now a heroic virtue.

Remember, too, that the composition of the *Faust* poem, especially Part II, extended throughout the period of the Napoleonic Wars. Bonaparte would have been seen as a real-life embodiment of this Faustian urge to reach impossible heights of power, and the French emperor's tyranny—and finally his defeat—actually was, in a way, a fulfillment of this, because it was spectacular; he failed in a huge, colossal manner, especially with his comeback and his defeat at the Battle of Waterloo.

So if that's the challenge to this sort of romantic idealism of the Germans and others, what is the answer? Try harder. Aim higher. Goethe had an aphorism: "What can we … call our own except the energy, the force, the will!" This idea of the power of the will becomes a kind of obsession throughout later German culture. Nietzsche would write a work called *The Will to Power*, which takes the *Übermensch*, the superman, beyond good and evil. This ultimately has a very, very sinister and evil conclusion in the Nazi era. One thinks of Leni Riefenstahl's 1935 Nazi propaganda movie entitled the *Triumph of the Will*.

Faust himself, as a character, is addicted to willful actions; whatever he wants, he does. And yet, especially toward the end, he becomes a very odd character. He's more like a sports fan; he wants to watch others. He wants to observe the intensity of the action, but only as a spectator, a bystander. There's a scene in *Faust*, Part II of a great battle, but Faust takes no part in the battle. He doesn't even offer strategy to the rulers; he simply watches from a safe distance. It's a kind of voyeuristic excitement, watching the spectacle go on before him. In a sense, this looks forward to modern man, modern characters like Leopold Bloom in James Joyce's *Ulysses*, who is no Ulysses. He's not even an Aeneas; he is simply a common man watching the passing parade of politics and life in Dublin in 1904.

There is a movement here from Goethe, Lord Byron, and other Romantic figures, including Napoleon—the cult of the man of genius, individual men of action. And yet, as it moves forward, these men don't need to be military, they don't need to be statesman. There's a new kind of cult of genius invested in the artist and the scientist. Notice that these two types are like Faust themselves:

observers. They are watchers. It is part of a sort of Aristotelian notion of theory. Remember the word *theory* originally meant to *look carefully at something*, and this is what the artist does—watches, observes things so that he can represent them correctly in his art. This is also what the scientist does: scientific observation to get the phenomenon, the evidence correct in order to move forward to a hypothesis.

There are two types of artists, when you think about it: There are artists like Shakespeare and Jane Austen, who lived rather shadowy, colorless lives. We know almost nothing about them, always trying to probe their identities and personalities through their works. Then there are artists like Petrarch and Lord Byron, who were celebrities in their own right, and Goethe was of this kind. He was an artist who had a charismatic presence, in some ways more interesting than any single work that he ever wrote. He is very much in a position to foster this cult of the genius, and particularly the cult of the scientist.

John Milton had mentioned Galileo in *Paradise Lost*, but it is in this period that Galileo becomes a kind of culture hero. He is the scientist who overcame superstition to rise above this to a new level of awareness of the scientific realities. Goethe himself was a scientist. He prided himself on his research; he actually thought that he would be best known in the future for his work in optics. Goethe's own research in comparative botany and plant morphology actually influenced Charles Darwin a generation or two later. And so, he puts this into his work as well, especially *Faust*, Part II. Dr. Faust has a student, Wagner, who produces the world's first test-tube baby—a "homunculus," he's called—sort of a medieval version of Mary Shelley's Frankenstein monster. So already Goethe is thinking about genetic engineering and a kind of test-tube baby that actually stays within the test tube in which it was created.

Faust, as a character, ends his long, worldly career as a scientist himself, an engineer. He's obsessed at the end of his life with reclaiming dry land from the ocean, using the most advanced techniques actually being used in Holland at this time to bring back dry land from the ocean. But part of the point of this story is that progress—so much a virtue in Western civilization since the Greeks—the idea of progress means justifying anyone who stands in your way, rolling over anyone or anything.

At the end, as Faust is trying to reclaim ocean, his great construction site going on, there's an elderly couple whose home is in the way of progress. They have interesting names: Baucus and Philemon, and immediately you recognize those are not Germanic names. One more time Goethe has automatically reached into the classical literary grab bag, and these are characters from Ovid's *Metamorphoses*. It's a famous story about Baucus and Philemon. They were visited by two poor beggars looking for a handout. The two poor beggars were actually the gods Zeus and Hermes, but Baucus and his wife Philemon were very hospitable, generous, brought them in, gave them a great welcome, and as a result they were rewarded for their hospitality by being the only two people saved from a great flood that the gods brought to punish the other neighbors.

What you see here at the very end of his career is Goethe doing an interpretation of Ovid. This was a great industry of Western literature almost since Saint Jerome and Saint Augustine, interpreting the classics to keep them alive. His interpretation of Ovid is even reminiscent of what Dante had done in the fable of the poets. And here the moral of the story is pretty transparent—that Baucus and Philemon in classical times had offered hospitality, been generous, and they were rewarded, and they were saved from the flood. Here, though, the elderly couple and their little cottage stand in the way of the new gods, science and engineering, and they are trampled so that the ocean, instead of flooding the land, can be held back with the latest techniques of dike and pump engineering.

Hereafter, then, we get an also-familiar sort of cultural image, a cultural icon—the German genius, and specifically the scientific genius. In the 20th century, Albert Einstein would fulfill this, become the epitome of the 20th-century cult of the scientist. And like a Goethe character, he is reaching beyond the amazing achievements of his relativity theory; he spends the entire life on that kind of quest for something even greater: the unified field theory, or what we sometimes call the theory of everything. He never quite reached it, but it's that wonderful striving and yearning and never quitting— truly a sort of triumph of the will on the part of the scientist.

Einstein's interesting also because he made his own Faustian bargain; this is built into the way culture works now. Einstein, in 1939, sent a letter to President Roosevelt urging him to develop the atomic bomb, which led to the Manhattan Project, which led to the bombing of Hiroshima and Nagasaki. But notice, like Faust, Einstein is a bystander; he is a passive observer. He never actually worked on the Manhattan Project. He got it going, he was the sort of figurehead, and yet he stood back and watched the results of this bargain that he had made with political power.

Back in the 1950s, many of us will recall that the German rocket scientist Werner von Braun was very much a kind of spokesperson for the American space program. Even Walt Disney would bring him onto television to introduce space travel to the audience: very much the image of the trusted German scientist. Now this wasn't always to remain this way. We now have also the much more sinister figure of Dr. Strangelove in Stanley Kubrick's classic black comedy by the same name, and it is not at all an accident that Dr. Strangelove has that very, very heavy German accent. He is the scientific genius to whom people turn for answers. Some people have even identified Dr. Strangelove as a reflection of Dr. Henry Kissinger as well—not a scientist in the old sense, but now a political scientist. Henry Kissinger actually came to this country at age 15 but never lost his German accent. Interesting: after all these years, still has a very thick German accent. You really wonder if this isn't part of his credibility, because of that image of the German scientist—somebody who can be trusted because they are smarter, more ingenious with things, that they get things right.

And so here we have it: Since Aristotle, the Western tradition has been invested in a sense of progress, and that progress, that sense that things get better and better, has been very much entrusted to the scientific community into our own day. It is science, it isn't superstition. But there is that sinister side that Goethe is already looking at; that is, the science of progress, engineering, and so on rolls over anyone who gets in the way of progress. We're going to see this very interestingly fulfilled in Thomas Mann's *The Magic Mountain*, where the hero actually becomes a victim of medical science. Hans Castorp actually turns out to be a threat to his Swiss doctors. Why is he such a problem to the scientific community? Because he's completely healthy.

Lecture Twenty-Six
Melville's *Moby-Dick* and Global Literature

Scope:

Consumerism and the Industrial Revolution meant a worldwide search for resources to supply 19th-century homes and factories. Melville's *Moby-Dick* describes the technical process of whaling, almost like a how-to manual, while Captain Ahab's obsession with avenging himself upon the great white whale parallels this unquenchable commercial thirst for the raw materials of oil and ambergris. The multiethnic *Pequod* becomes a microcosm of this new global community. Published first in London, Melville's American novel typifies the reach of the Western literary tradition beyond the old European homelands. Melville's whaling novel, with its forbidden eroticism, represents another good example of a work more often listed as canonic than actually read.

Outline

I. In 1848, exactly when Melville was sitting down to write *Moby-Dick*, Marx and Engels were laying out in their *The Communist Manifesto* a clear idea of what world literature would mean in a world of global commerce.

   A. They predicted that "intellectual creations of individual nations [would] become common property" and, by extension, national cultures would unify into a global culture.

   B. Indeed, during the 19th century the imperial nations of Britain, France, Spain, and the United States were largely unified in their commercial values and global ambitions.

II. *Moby-Dick* is really about the global search for whale oil and ambergris for the consumer economy created by the Industrial Revolution.

   A. In the course of the novel, the ship does cross the world, starting in Nantucket and ending in the Pacific Ocean east of Japan.

   B. The whaling ship itself is a microcosm of the new global community: One harpooner is a Pacific Islander, one an African, and one an American Indian.

III. In this novel, Melville does what any writer who wants to get into the game does: He attaches his writing to the Western canon itself.

    A. He clearly aligns himself with the biblical traditions of Jonah and the Whale and Noah's Ark.

    B. There is also a background of the epic sea voyages of the *Odyssey* and the *Aeneid*.

    C. Captain Ahab is a wonderful gathering of all the great characters of Western literature: Prometheus, Oedipus, Satan, Hamlet, and Prospero.

IV. Harold Bloom has claimed that "To become canonical, any new work must have the countercanonical built into it," and we see this in Melville.

    A. Melville built the plot of his masterpiece on basic historical facts from nautical history.

    B. But the storyline is not what interested Melville most. He was aiming to create a counter-canonical work—the antinovel.

V. *Moby-Dick* very clearly belongs to the New England Puritan culture.

    A. The Puritans were practical, and they were drawn to useful books like encyclopedias.

    B. In the 18th century, there was a boom in encyclopedia writing, with the purpose of combating superstition and fueling revolutionary opinion.

    C. Melville absorbed the encyclopedic tradition for another purpose. Great American literary classics of the frontier and pioneer culture resembled the how-to manuals with which Americans are obsessed even now.

VI. But there is something strange going on in *Moby-Dick*: It is encyclopedic, it looks like a how-to manual, but it doesn't really function like one.

    A. There is a disconnect from the pragmatics of how-to books. The novel starts to read like a computer manual written by an English professor schooled in French critical theory; you can't exactly learn whaling from it.

B. This points to another aspect of the Puritan tradition: the use of practical material as a starting point for philosophical or spiritual reflection.

VII. The Puritan tradition emerged in America but had an earlier history as a counter-tradition in England. To understand *Moby-Dick*, we need to look at the great literary works produced in the age of Chaucer.

    A. *Piers Plowman*, a vast spiritual allegory by William Langland, was written during this time and had tremendous early influence on England.

    B. The urge of the Langlandian hero, a shadowy character wandering the world and experiencing spiritual wonders, reemerges in Melville's protagonist Ishmael, as well as in the works of Nathaniel Hawthorne and Walt Whitman.

    C. The Langlandian tradition of allegorical symbolism dominates every page of *Moby-Dick*. Any common shipboard item assumes complex allegorical meanings.

VIII. The parallel counter-tradition of Puritan literature in *Moby-Dick* is revealed in the first line: "Call me Ishmael."

    A. In the Bible, Ishmael is the first (but illegitimate) son of Abraham, and Abraham later fathers a legitimate son, Isaac.

    B. These twin genealogies appear in the literary tradition, with the "legitimate" Chaucerian line and the "outlaw" Langlandian line.

    C. With the novel's first words, Melville is signaling that he is following the outlaw tradition, and the novel form fits this aim perfectly since it is an outsider's genre.

IX. Following the Puritan tradition, *Moby-Dick* engages in a sort of satire and pushback from official church religion.

    A. The novel was first published in London to rave reviews, so the American publisher rushed it into print without reading the manuscript.

    B. American church writers were outraged by the anti-Christian elements that they found in the book.

X. In modern times, we are beginning to realize the outlaw quality of this novel in terms of its sexual content.

A. Through his earlier novels, Melville had established a reputation for himself as a literary sex symbol in the manner of Lord Byron.

B. In *Moby-Dick*, he pushed the envelope even further. Literary critic Leslie Fielder has pointed out the undercurrent of homosexual themes in American literature. The question is, how innocent is the homosexuality in *Moby-Dick*?

    1. Ishmael and Queequeg actually meet each other naked in bed and very soon enter into a formal betrothal agreement.

    2. Though not much is said throughout the rest of the novel, it is clear that the rest of the crew recognizes them as a couple.

C. Many people would doubt that Melville understood such a relationship, but while he was writing in 1849, he was also reading Thomas Hope's *Anastasius; or, Memoirs of a Greek*, which provided the details of male-male bonding in Greek culture.

XI. Notice that, in the creation of his antinovel, Melville has done everything that a writer is not supposed to do.

A. He has confused who the protagonist is: Captain Ahab or Ishmael.

B. He has neglected the Aristotelian directive of telling a linear story with a beginning, middle, and end.

C. He has thumbed his nose at the Ovidian directive that there has to be a love interest, generally a heterosexual one, in the story.

D. Melville is pushing back from the English tradition in a type of postcolonial revolt, using the genre of the novel to create a different kind of literature.

XII. So the question is, why don't we recognize the odd qualities in *Moby-Dick*?

A. It has been famous for so long that we don't exactly see the novel that Melville wrote anymore.

B. The canon is so fixed, we tend to acknowledge the naming of the books more than the reading of them.

Suggested Readings:

Melville, *Moby-Dick*.

Bercaw, *Melville's Sources*.

Fiedler, *Love and Death in the American Novel*.

Questions to Consider:

1. Context counts. If *Moby-Dick* had been written 10 years later, Melville would have found himself in the run-up to the Civil War. Can you imagine how the novel's international outlook and attitudes toward racial identities would have become very different if the book had been written in the midst of America's greatest national crisis?

2. *Moby-Dick*'s debt to the ghost story looks like an embarrassment. But many literary classics have their roots in "subliterary" genres of popular culture. Can you think of other canonic works that grow out of fairy tales, boyhood adventures, children's stories, and other unlikely mainstream writings?

Lecture Twenty-Six—Transcript
Melville's *Moby-Dick* and Global Literature

Europeans and their books had taken to the seas three centuries before Herman Melville wrote *Moby-Dick*. Remember, Thomas More's *Utopia* was very much inspired by early voyages of discovery recounted by Amerigo Vespucci. *Don Quixote* was smuggled into Mexico in those crates of brandy. Shakespeare's *Hamlet* had the first recorded production on an English merchant ship in 1607 off the coast of Sierra Leone. And then later on, Shakespeare's *The Tempest*—very much rooted in early accounts of the English colony of Virginia.

Goethe had already coined the phrase World Literature, *Weltliteratur*, but in 1848, at exactly the time when Melville was sitting down to write *Moby-Dick*, off in Germany Karl Marx and Friedrich Engels are publishing their *The Communist Manifesto*. In this work, they have a clearer idea of what world literature will mean in a globe of international, inter-oceanic trade and commerce. Listen to what Marx and Engels say:

> The intellectual creations of individual nations become common property. National one-sidedness and narrow-mindedness become more and more impossible, and from the numerous national and local literatures, there arises a world literature.

Here he is really tackling what has been the mainstay of the Western tradition from the beginning, starting with local literature in Athens, and then more recently the national literatures of nations like England and Germany. They are now predicting a world literature, a kind of global commerce in the European books that have become the mainstays of Western civilization. And indeed, during the hundred years from the end of the Napoleonic Wars to the outbreak of World War I, the imperial nations of Britain, France, Spain, and United States were really unified in their commercial values and global ambitions. And indeed, this commitment to industrial wealth and technological prowess meant that these Western nations ended up controlling 84 percent of the surface of the planet by the outbreak of the First World War. This would include the Belgian Congo, opened up for colonial exploitation by Henry Stanley with his 180 pounds of books trekked into the interior.

Melville's *Moby-Dick* is really about the global search for whale oil and ambergris for the consumer economy created by the Industrial Revolution, and in the course of the novel, they really go round the world. They start off at Nantucket, cross the Atlantic, round South Africa, cross the Indian Ocean, and end up in the Pacific Ocean somewhere to the east of Japan. There's also a wonderful sense that the whaling ship itself is a kind of microcosm of the new global community; it's a gathering of nonwhite, non-English characters who man the whaling ship the *Pequod*. Take, for example, the three harpoonists, really the important guys on the ship. One is a Pacific Islander, another is an African, and the third is an American Indian. It is really appropriate to say that *Moby-Dick* is the original multicultural novel in the American literary tradition.

Melville in *Moby-Dick* does the work of any writer who wants to get into the game, and so he attaches his writing to the Western canon itself. Very clearly, he aligns himself with the biblical tradition with Jonah and the Whale but also the story of Noah's Ark, bringing one of everything or two of everything on board—a real kind of microcosm on the *Pequod* as it was on the Ark. There is also in the background the epic sea voyages of the *Odyssey* and the *Aeneid*. Captain Ahab is a wonderful sort of gathering of all the great characters of Western literature. He is the tormented Prometheus; he is the crippled Oedipus; he is the lightning-scarred Satan. He is a wonderfully sort of Shakespearean character. He is Hamlet brooding on the wrongs committed against him; he is even Shakespeare's Prospero, plotting vengeance on those enemies of his on the sea.

Harold Bloom makes an interesting statement about Goethe's *Faust*, Part II, which he describes as that most grotesque masterpiece in the Western canon. This is what he says about *Faust*, Part II: "To become canonical, any new work must have the countercanonical built into it."

Melville started his own grotesque masterpiece with really just two basic, simple, historical facts from nautical history. First of all, there really was a white whale named Mocha Dick spotted in the South Pacific in the early 1800s. And second, there really was a Nantucket whaling ship, *The Essex*, rammed and sunk by a whale in 1820. So there it is. That is the bare bones of the story.

Many readers have often said that this would be a really, really good novel if Melville just got rid of all the whaling stuff in the book. But clearly, the stuff that isn't this storyline, the bare bones of the plot, was really what interested Melville most, because he was aiming for that counter-canonic status for this novel that really isn't quite a novel. If you think back throughout the tradition, so many of the masterpieces really set out to set themselves against the canonic standards of the time. Remember, Ovid's *Metamorphoses* is an anti-epic, sets itself against Virgil's *Aeneid*. Boccaccio's *Decameron* is the anti-*Divine Comedy*. *Don Quixote* is the anti-chivalric romance. Goethe's *Faust* is an antitragedy, one that has a happy ending.

And so *Moby-Dick* really is an antinovel, and to appreciate this you only need to look back to Jane Austen's *Pride and Prejudice*, with its great economy of plot and incident and character, never anything out of place, never anything superfluous. It's almost as if everything in *Moby-Dick* is superfluous. And it is also as if here we have the prototype of the kind of novel we will see increasingly into the 20th century and beyond, what we're going to call the postcolonial novel. The whole purpose of the postcolonial novel is to talk back, write back to the dominant genre of the imperial tradition that imposed that genre on colonies. And remember, the Americas started off as an English colony.

Moby-Dick also very clearly belongs to the New England Puritan culture. One of the things about Puritans is they're very practical, they like things that are useful. This would eventually lead to a whole philosophical outlook of pragmatism best voiced by William James at Harvard University, brother of the novelist Henry James. And this means that people like really sort of practical books like encyclopedias.

Back in the 18th century, Chambers's *Cyclopaedia* of 1728 really inspired a kind of boom in encyclopedia writing, leading to the famous 35-volume French encyclopedia, with its famous contributors like Voltaire. The purpose of Voltaire and others was to expand human knowledge, to combat superstition and fuel revolutionary opinion. But there are other purposes to the encyclopedia, and Melville sort of has absorbed this tradition into this novel. He's done his research; he's based his knowledge of whaling on books like Frederick Bennett's *Whaling Voyage round the Globe*. What is this other purpose of the encyclopedic tradition? The critic Hugh Kenner made an interesting observation that the great American literary classics, as part of a frontier and pioneer culture, resemble how-to manuals. It's kind of related to the boom in reference books as well as encyclopedias. And if you think about it, if you go into a bookstore, Americans are still particularly obsessed with how-to books of various kinds—how to have a relationship, how to succeed in business, how to do yoga, even those books like *Jane Austen for Dummies*. We want to know how to do something; we want it all in one volume. Now I mentioned that Thomas Jefferson had a copy of the 35-volume French encyclopedia at his home at Monticello, and this wasn't only about fueling revolutionary zeal; it was also helping him run his plantation. Monticello was isolated, out in the frontier, and the encyclopedia provided him with the great how-to book for his farming enterprises.

But there is something kind of weird going on in *Moby-Dick*. It's encyclopedic, it looks like a how-to book, and yet it doesn't really function like one. The tip-off comes early on, where Ishmael, the narrator, tells us that he was a schoolmaster before he became a sailor. That means there's a disconnect from the pragmatics of the how-to books. *Moby-Dick* starts to read a little bit like a computer manual written by an English professor schooled in French critical theory; it just doesn't really hang together, doesn't really make sense. In fact, if you look closely, you can't really learn much practical about whaling by reading *Moby-Dick*.

There's another string, then, of the Puritan tradition that is really sort of shaping what is truly going on in the novel, and that is a use of the practical material as a starting point for something much more philosophical—and even spiritual—meditation. Look at Thoreau's *Walden*. Here you have living in the wilderness, but it's a meditation on the spiritual challenges and lessons of living in the wilderness. Or look at another more recent classic, *Zen and the Art of Motorcycle Maintenance*. In the beginning, the author, Pirsig, actually tells the reader not to expect any really practical information on maintaining their Harley-Davidson.

So the Puritan literary tradition will emerge in America, but it has an earlier history; it starts in England. What we find in the Puritan tradition in England is a counter-tradition, a parallel tradition to the official Chaucerian tradition that comes down from the late 14th century from the father of English literature. What is this other tradition? We get a hint of it in Father Mapple's sermon, early in the novel. It is a sermon on Jonah and the Whale, but in delivering that sermon, Father Mapple, and of course Melville himself, is reaching back into this tradition, the tradition of Jonathan Edwards, of *Sinners in the Hands of an Angry God*, which itself reaches back deeper into a literary tradition mostly invisible to modern readers.

I always say that to understand *Moby-Dick*, we need to go back to the 14th century and look at the other great literary work produced in the age of Chaucer. This would be a poem called *Piers Plowman* by a writer we call William Langland. This was a vast spiritual allegory written by a contemporary of Chaucer's in London, and it was also the first real national bestseller in England. But it's again one of these hard, non-narrative, unfunny stories, not much love interest—a great kind of metaphysical allegory, a spiritual quest of a book.

It had tremendous early influence in England. *Piers Plowman* inspired the leaders of the Peasants' Revolt of 1381; it was adopted as a kind of canonic text by the early Protestant followers of John Wycliffe. It survives, though, in more than 54 manuscripts from the medieval period; that makes it second only to the *Canterbury Tales* in the number of literary manuscripts that survive for *Piers Plowman*. It really had quite a readership in England and then was finally printed for the first time in 1550 by radical Protestants during the reign of King Edward VI. So this is the work that has been there in the English tradition. It's been read by people for generations; it gets into what I call the DNA of the literary tradition in England and surfaces in other literary works—very clearly in John Bunion's *Pilgrim's Progress*, even to some extent in Milton's *Paradise Lost*, later on in William Blake's prophetic books and Wordsworth's self-searching poem the *Prelude*.

We know that *Piers Plowman* not only had its long-staying presence in England, but *Piers Plowman* actually migrated to America with the Puritan fathers themselves. The first copy of *Piers Plowman* arrived in Massachusetts in 1630, brought over by a man who had become the father of Anne Bradstreet, the first American poet. I call this the smoking gun. It really traces direct connection of the *Piers Plowman* tradition into America and into that first named American poet, Anne Bradstreet.

The urge of the Langlandian hero, then—a protagonist, a shadowy character—to wander wide in the world and experience wonders of a spiritual kind survives, as I say, in a DNA to reemerge in Melville's protagonist Ishmael. Listen to how Ishmael describes his own restless wandering out into the wilds: "I am tormented with an ever-lasting itch for things remote. I love to sail forbidden seas and land on barbarous coasts."

So this restless self-examining, questing, a kind of semi-allegorical approach to literature, comes through this Langlandian tradition into the Puritan tradition, and we find it in evidence throughout especially the New England tradition in the novels and short stories, for example, of Nathanial Hawthorne, to whom the novel *Moby-Dick* is dedicated. We also find it in Walt Whitman in his *Leaves of Grass*, actually published four years after *Moby-Dick*, and it continues. You can even look at T. S. Eliot as the New England Puritan re-imported back into England, his homeland, and you can even read his *The Waste Land* as a sort of 20th-century equivalent or counterpart to Langland's *Piers Plowman*.

The Langlandian tradition of allegory and symbolism really dominates every single page of *Moby-Dick*. Any common shipboard item—a coin, a harpoon, a compass needle—suddenly assumes complex allegorical meanings that generate even larger and all-encompassing oceans of symbolic meaning. Captain Ahab is especially addicted to these kind of metaphysics. Listen, for example, as he compares his obsession with getting the white whale to a steam locomotive on its iron rails. This, of course, is brand new technology—the steam locomotive and the rails and the tunnels and the trestles and all the rest. But he immediately adapts this practical, technical imagery to his own mania for getting the white whale:

> Swerve me? The path to my fixed purpose is laid with iron rails, whereon my soul is grooved to run. Over unsounded gorges, through the rifled hearts of mountains, under torrents' beds, unerringly I rush! Naught's an obstacle, naught's an angle to the iron way!

The tip-off to the sort of parallel counter-tradition of Puritan literature even begins in the very, very first line of the poem, that mysterious introduction of the narrator, "Call me Ishmael." Who is Ishmael? In the Bible, he is the son of Abraham, not by his wife but by the Egyptian slave woman. Abraham couldn't have a child for so long, so he fathered a son by his Egyptian slave, and his name was Ishmael. Later on, Abraham would father a legitimate son with his wife, Sarah, who would be named Isaac. And so here you have it. Here, of the twin genealogies: the legitimate genealogy of Isaac—

you can call that the mainstream Chaucerian tradition in English literature—and then that outlaw genealogy, the outcast son Ishmael, part of that Puritan tradition, the Langlandian tradition going back to *Piers Plowman*. And so Melville signals that he is doing this outlaw, outcast, underground tradition by naming his hero, his narrator, Ishmael.

So the novel itself is perfect for this sort of tradition, because from its beginnings the novel is an outsider's genre. It is for the minority and the marginalized people. The Puritans themselves had been that marginalized minority in England before crossing the Atlantic. Remember, even the English Bible was a banned book; you could be burned for heresy for reading the English Bible. Benjamin Franklin in his autobiography actually tells an interesting anecdote from his family history. He recalls how his great grandfather back in England had to conceal the family English Bible, strapping it under a footstool so they could read it. But if the church warden or someone came by, they could strap it back, turn the stool over, and the church official would never find it. The Puritan tradition, especially certain English writings, had that kind of banned status for generations in the English tradition.

Indeed, *Moby-Dick* engages in this sort of satire and the sort of pushback from official church religion all the way through, that assault upon the hypocrisies of churchmen made famous first by Langland's poem *Piers Plowman*. It is interesting: *Moby-Dick* was actually published first in London and got great reviews in London. The reviews were so glowing that the American publisher in New York rushed the book into print without even reading the manuscript. The publisher didn't realize the content of the book until the reviews started coming out in the American magazines, which were very often church magazines. The church writers were outraged by what they found in Melville's novel. They found Melville's anti-Christian harangues. They found Captain Ahab's blasphemies, his parodying and mocking the sacrament of Baptism. He even does a kind of sinister, demonic parody of the sacrament of the Eucharist in the novel. Also, they were appalled, these early church magazine reviewers, by Melville's open-mindedness to non-Christian religion. There is the cannibal Queequeg, who has a kind of heathenism, and even Ishmael joins his friend worshipping a little black idol, and this really outraged the Christian magazines at the time.

Now in modern times we're beginning to realize the outlaw quality of the novel in terms of its sexual content. Melville had established a reputation for himself in his prior novels, *Typee* and *Omoo*. They had won him a reputation as a literary sex symbol, sort of the American equivalent of Lord Byron back in Europe, because Melville had sailed to the South Pacific—he had visited the Polynesian women on these islands. He was very much like Gauguin on Tahiti, only two generations before Gauguin on Tahiti.

But when he gets to *Moby-Dick*, he's doing something even kinkier. Back in the 1960s, there was a literary critic named Leslie Fiedler who published a really landmark literary study called *Love and Death in the American Novel*. He shocked the reading public of that time by pointing out that the classics of American literature—books studied in high school—actually contained homosexual love stories. This is how he put it anyway; he pointed out "The failure of the American fictionist to deal with adult heterosexual love and his consequent obsession with death, incest and innocent homosexuality." This got people very outraged. He pointed out these themes in *Huckleberry Finn*, for example. There's something more going on between Huck and the runaway slave, Jim.

This has become fairly routine. It has been naturalized in our literary discussions; my students routinely talked about "Oh, the gay sex scene in *The Great Gatsby*." Now I'm sure that *The Great Gatsby* wasn't read that way for a very long time, but now we tend to spot those things in the novels. The question is, as Leslie Fiedler would have put it, how innocent is the homosexuality in *Moby-Dick*? Ishmael and Queequeg actually meet each other naked in bed. The film adaptations of *Moby-Dick* have real trouble with this scene; they really can't picture it the way Melville describes it. But after meeting naked in their common bed, they very soon become what Melville calls "bosom friends," and they even enter a formal betrothal agreement that modern contemporary readers would recognize as what we now call gay marriage. Listen to how it's actually described in the book. This is Ishmael talking:

> I found Queequeg's arm thrown over me in the most loving and affectionate matter. You had almost thought I had been his wife. ...

> ... He pressed his forehead against mine, clasped me round the waist, and said that henceforth we were married. ...

> … Thus, then, in our hearts' honeymoon lay I and Queequeg—a cozy, loving pair.

Not much is said about this later on in the novel, but it's very clear that the rest of the crew recognized Ishmael and Queequeg as a couple. They are treated that way; they share a bunk. It isn't otherwise talked about, but that's the point.

You're going to say—many people would say—Melville could not have understood such a relationship as we are talking about a same-sex union, but actually he had read about such a thing. He got a hold of a book by Thomas Hope entitled *Anastatius; or, Memoirs of a Greek*. He actually bought it twice in the year 1849, just when he was writing *Moby-Dick*. He had to buy it a second time because his first copy was confiscated as obscene by English customs authorities. But Hope's book, *Memoirs of a Greek*, had actually described this ritual, this practice, this custom of male-male relationships, a real sort of betrothal, a bonding, in a recognized sort of union between two men in that particular culture. Melville had read about it; he knew about it exactly when he's writing *Moby-Dick*, and so he is able to bring this really sort of strange ingredient into his novel— again, making it much more of a kind of outlaw piece than before.

Notice that, in the creation of his antinovel, he has done everything that a writer is not supposed to do. He has confused who the protagonist is, for example. When you think about *Moby-Dick*, you think about Captain Ahab, but is that really the protagonist, or is it Ishmael? Ishmael has his goal of desire to take to the sea, to visit those barbarous lands. He wants adventure, and he gets adventure. And at the end, he is the one who survives; he is the one who is found floating on what had been Queequeg's casket.

Interesting kind of side note—when *Moby-Dick* was first published in London, the printer actually omitted the very, very last part of the manuscript, and so the very end of the novel has the whaling ship *Pequod* go down, end of story. He had omitted the section where Ishmael actually survived to tell the story. It is an interesting case that if that had been the only printed version of *Moby-Dick*, that would be our version. As we'll see later on, it is very often the editors and the publishers who will determine the shape of the novel as it will descend to us as a kind of classic that's very often tampered with by other people who actually get it into print.

And so there is a confusion in this antinovel about who the protagonist really is. Melville neglects the primary directive coming down from Aristotle of telling a linear story with beginning, middle, and end. It is very hard to find the plotline in *Moby-Dick*; there's so much else; there's information, and yet it's information that turns out not to be terribly practical. You couldn't actually learn the art of whaling from reading *Moby-Dick*. It is information almost for information's sake, creating this grotesque masterpiece that defines it within the Western canon. And finally, it thumbs its nose at that prime directive descending from Ovid that there has to be love interest in the story—and even Ovid would have probably suggested the love interest should be between a man and a woman. If you imagine that Jane Austen is setting the standard for what the English novel is supposed to look like in the 19th century, then the imperative of marriage between men and women is absolutely central to the novel tradition as it comes down in the English tradition. But Melville is pushing back from that. He's an American; he has that kind of revolt of the postcolonial, uses the novel as a genre to create a different kind of literature—different from the English genre that had been that of the parent culture homeland in England.

So the question is, especially in terms of the same-sex relationship between Ishmael and Queequeg, how come we have never noticed this? *Moby-Dick* was another one of those books on the list given out by my high school librarian, Ms. Cunningham. I am sure that when I read this book in high school, this is not something that I noticed.

Here's an interesting comment made by the Argentine writer Borges, and he's actually talking about *Don Quixote*. And what Borges said is, "Fame is a form of incomprehension, perhaps the worst." And so here it is: Why don't we recognize the odd qualities in *Moby-Dick*? Because it has been so famous for so long that we accept it exactly the way it is and we don't see exactly the novel that Melville wrote anymore. The queerness (if you'd call it that) in the novel becomes like what we call the rhinoceros in the living room; we've lived with this book for so long that we don't actually notice its exact contents. And because the canon is such a sort of fixed entity, we tend to acknowledge it more in the naming than we do actually in the reading of books. Not long ago, there was an advertisement in magazines for a credit card company, and they list all the things that you ought to do before you die. And one of the things they list is to read and finish *Moby-Dick*. Notice the presumption there is that most people have not finished *Moby-Dick*.

I want to end now by recalling that story from before, contained in Woody Allen's wonderful film *Zelig*. Remember, this is the story about a man who becomes a pathological liar, and under hypnosis we find out that he assumed this pattern in his life because at school, some very bright people asked him if he'd read *Moby-Dick*, and he was ashamed to say that he hadn't. This started his life of lying and pretending, dodging and weaving, because he'd lied about reading *Moby-Dick*. At the end of the movie, he's been cured of his status as a human chameleon, somebody who blends in and falsifies his whole life. And yet, at the very end of the movie, he says his only regret is that he never finished *Moby-Dick*.

Lecture Twenty-Seven
Cult Classic—*The Charterhouse of Parma*

Scope:

A veteran of the Grand Army, Stendhal embodied the Romantic ideals of Bonaparte set against the harsh realities of the greedy, conservative post-Napoleonic era. As a "cult classic" admired by every later novelist, even Hemingway, *The Charterhouse of Parma* takes a humorous attitude toward its upper-class characters but with a political agenda missing from Jane Austen's novels. Stendhal introduces a realistic style perfect for describing his Italian characters exactly as they might have been. Readers feel that they really know the romantic Gina del Dongo, her handsome nephew Fabrizio, and the cynical politician Count Mosca. The "pursuit of happiness" becomes the new driving force.

Outline

I. I've spoken quite a lot about the phenomenon of genius recognizing genius in the creation of the Western literary canon. But certain individual works are particularly dear to other writers, like Stendhal's *The Charterhouse of Parma.*

    A. Balzac and Gide both expressed their admiration for the perfection of *Charterhouse.*

    B. Simone de Beauvoir singled Stendhal out as one writer who could depict female characters "without mystery."

    C. Even Ernest Hemingway admitted that he "fought two draws with Stendhal."

II. A canonical work has to extend its influence beyond its home country, and *Charterhouse* clearly achieved this.

    A. Italo Calvino described it as one novel containing many novels.

    B. Its vast timeline particularly influenced Tolstoy in his writing of *War and Peace.*

III. The action of the book starts in 1796, but the novel was actually written in 1838. This affords the novelist another kind of time perspective: the ability to look back over several decades.

A. This perspective allowed Stendhal to realize the failure of Napoleonic idealism.

B. The knowledge of this failure prompted him to open the novel with a kind of sad irony that would be mimicked by Tolstoy.

C. It is worth noticing other interesting influences from Stendhal to Tolstoy, such as their heroes' shared characteristics of illegitimacy and cluelessness in battle.

IV. We have in *Charterhouse* a wonderful case of what we call the Stendhalian narrator.

A. This is an omniscient narrator who knows more than any of the characters in the novel.

B. The Stendhalian narrator shares information with the reader from the beginning, so that there are wonderful moments in the plot that only the reader can appreciate.

V. Despite Stendhal's claim, especially through *Charterhouse*, to a position within the Western canon, he has a slippery footing for several important reasons.

A. "Stendhal" was one of more than 200 pen names used by Marie-Henri Beyle. Too many pen names can begin to erode an author's status.

B. Stendhal dabbled in almost every conceivable genre. By the 19th century, categories of literary profession were starting to harden, and if you wrote in all genres, you wouldn't be known for them.

C. Stendhal wrote during a great age of nationalism in literature, yet he disassociated himself from his native France, falling in love with Italy instead.

VI. Stendhal actually dictated *The Charterhouse of Parma* in 52 days of creative outpouring in November and December of 1838.

A. As a result of this rapid-fire, effortless production, the story has this extraordinary pace, lightness, and sense of surprise.

B. Because he dictated this book so quickly, Stendhal qualifies less as a craftsman than other great writers who revised.

C. Unlike these writers who agonized over revisions, Stendhal was more of an embodiment of the Romantic aesthetic of inspiration. His inspiration sometimes flagged, and his output is littered with unfinished books.

VII. Stendhal was not much respected in his homeland, or even in his lifetime. There is often a sense that the reading public needs a lag time to catch up with a great writer.

  A. Stendhal knew this and predicted that he would be famous "around 1880," a prediction that turned out to be accurate.

  B. As a result of this posthumous recognition, many of his works were published after his death. In this respect, he joins the ranks of Thucydides, Chaucer, Shakespeare, and Tolkien.

VIII. The cult classic *The Charterhouse of Parma* has many peculiarities about it. In some sense, it can be compared with *Moby-Dick* as an antinovel.

  A. Stendhal starts the book with a famous battle scene, instead of following convention and placing the battle at the end.

  B. The book is woven together with recognizable clichés—it can even be seen as a bodice-ripper kind of novel.

  C. The title is not explained until the final three paragraphs of the novel, where it is revealed as a monastery, though it suggests a mood of Gothic gloom.

  D. There is also a funny punning going on in the French version of the title that alludes to both intoxication and the hero's "greenness."

IX. Another novel set at the time of the Napoleonic Wars, William Makepeace Thackeray's *Vanity Fair*, has the famous subtitle *A Novel Without a Hero*. In a sense, the same thing could be said about Stendhal's novel.

  A. Throughout the book, Fabrizio del Dongo is called "our hero," and yet he isn't even born when the novel begins and he drops out at various points in the narrative.

  B. In a sense, Gina del Dongo is the true protagonist, as she is the character with motive. Yet she too is missing during long stretches of the novel.

  C. Stendhal's refusal to organize his novel around a single protagonist is again a kind of pushback against tradition.

X. In a sense, Stendhal espoused the Aristotelian idea of mimesis, that artwork should imitate and represent everything around it. Yet *Charterhouse* does something different: It is highly politically engaged.

    A. Stendhal has been credited as the founder of the artistic idea of man embedded in a total cultural reality.

    B. This means that every little detail assumes meaning in a cultural context, even the powdering of hair.

    C. Stendhal was no armchair historian; he had been an active participant in Napoleon's campaigns. After Napoleon's fall, he developed a great contempt for the ruling nobility.

    D. What he foregrounds in the book is a political commitment, an emerging strain in the 19th-century novel.

XI. At the heart of *Chaterhouse*, however, is something not quite so political: the pursuit of happiness.

    A. When you read the novel, you are struck that the word "happiness" appears on nearly every single page.

    B. There is a bittersweet sense throughout the book that happiness is fleeting; no one gets to enjoy it for very long, especially given the rapid demise of the characters at the end of the book.

    C. Stendhal showed lighthandedness and subtlety in handling the canonic works of the past on the topic of happiness. Late in the novel, Gina del Dongo is linked by name to Boethius, introducing the sense of Fortune's Wheel turning and happiness falling away.

    D. It would remain to Tolstoy to pursue the great question: Where and what is happiness?

Suggested Readings:

Stendhal, *The Charterhouse of Parma*.

Auerbach, "In the Hotel de la Mole," in *Mimesis*.

Calvino, "Guide to New Readers of Stendhal's *Charterhouse*," in *Why Read the Classics?*

Greaves, *Stendhal's Italy*.

Questions to consider:

1. Though the 19th century was a great age for nationalism in the arts, the Frenchman Stendhal lived in Italy and his finest novel is set in Italy. Can you think of other canonic authors whose works were set in countries different from their native lands?

2. "Cult classics" often enter the Western canon almost by accident. For example, Petrarch would have been astonished that his sonnets became his most famous literary works. Voltaire would have felt the same about *Candide*. Can you think of other literary classics that achieved a degree of lasting fame that would have surprised their authors?

Lecture Twenty-Seven—Transcript
Cult Classic—*The Charterhouse of Parma*

I've spoken quite a lot about the phenomenon of talent recognizing talent—genius recognizing genius—in the creation of the Western literary tradition. But there are certain individual works—I'm calling them cult classics—that are particularly dear to other writers, and none quite so much perhaps as Stendhal's *The Charterhouse of Parma*. Even in its own day, the great novelist Balzac devoted a very lengthy review, a very positive review of the novel. "One [finds] perfection in every detail," said Balzac. *Charterhouse* "often contains a whole book in a single page."

Later on, André Gide expressed his admiration of Stendhal's agility: "He doesn't need to put on his track shoes before he starts running." Marcel Proust's *Á la Recherche du Temps Perdu* can actually be looked at as a 4,000-page update to this sort of social novel that Stendhal had created before him. Simone de Beauvoir, in her feminist manifesto *The Second Sex*, actually singled him out for praise as one writer who would depict female characters "without mystery … to recognize in woman a human being is not to impoverish man's experience." Even Ernest Hemingway, who spent a lot of his career in Paris, admitted, "I've fought two draws with Stendhal."

Notice that he thinks of the literary competition literally in the sense of a boxing match, climbing into the ring, slugging it out with another author. There's a very interesting case of this sort of male rivalry built into the Western canon. Now the two draws that Hemingway figured he had reached with Stendhal would have been in his own novels: *The Sun Also Rises*, a kind of social novel, and then *Farewell to Arms*, a military novel. He truly admired that scene in *Charterhouse of Parma* in the Battle of Waterloo—the fog of war, the confusion. It is an episode that actually comes early in Stendhal's novel, because he really wants to depict the post-Napoleonic period in Italy and elsewhere in Europe.

I have to admit that, in terms of a great affection to a particular novel, when I planned this trip back East to record these lectures, I stood before the bookcase in which I had assembled all of the titles reviewed in this course, deciding which one to bring with me as travel literature, and the one book I instantly selected was *The Charterhouse of Parma*.

Now the influence obviously needs to reach beyond its home country. Remember, a book always has to travel beyond its homeland. And so in the 20th century in Italy we find the writer Italo Calvino describing *Charterhouse* as one novel that contains many novels and sometimes a book that impresses first-time readers as just so amazing that this must be the best novel ever written. But the particular influence of *Charterhouse of Parma* beyond its home culture is going to be with Tolstoy, in his writing of *War and Peace*. One of the things that Tolstoy was really going to be impressed by was the fact that the story extends over three decades of time and actually creates what Tolstoy and others would recognize as something rather new in fiction, and that is time perspective. He actually watches characters mature and even grow old. This is something that E. M. Forster would admire in Tolstoy himself, this ability—willingness—to let his characters grow old before the reader's eyes, but it was something originally achieved by Stendhal.

The action starts in 1796, but the novel is actually written in 1838. There's another kind of time perspective: The novelist can look back over several decades. This gives Stendhal a position to realize the failure of Napoleonic idealism, the liberalism, the imperial designs to unite Europe under one heroic ruler. He knows that this has come to nothing by the time he writes, with a kind of sad irony, the opening lines of the novel. Let me quote the opening line of *Charterhouse of Parma*:

> On May 15, 1796, General Bonaparte entered Milan at the head of that young army which had lately crossed the Lodi bridge and taught the world that after so many centuries Caesar and Alexander had a successor.

I wanted to quote that line because Tolstoy is thinking about that line when he decides how to begin his novel *War and Peace*. Listen to the opening line of *War and Peace*: "Well, Prince, so Genoa and Lucca are now just family estates of the Buonapartes." That is, *War and Peace* starts with that same statement that Napoleon's armies had entered Italy and had taken possession of these towns like Genoa and Lucca. In fact, that opening sentence in *War and Peace* is actually spoken in French by the hostess of the party, and so Tolstoy is acknowledging this influence by actually using Stendhal's own language.

It is worth noticing, then, the other interesting influences from Stendhal to Tolstoy. The battle scene, for example—Tolstoy's sort of chaotic fog-of-war battle scene at Borodino has his rather hapless hero, Pierre Bezukhov, sort of clueless on the field of battle, exactly like Stendhal's hero Fabrizio was at Waterloo. In fact, the first thing that we are told about Pierre when he enters that party in chapter 1 is that he is the illegitimate son of Count Bezukhov. We're actually told he's an illegitimate son; this is suggested to Tolstoy by the fact that Stendhal's character Fabrizio is also an illegitimate son.

The difference is this: Fabrizio's illegitimate parentage is known only to the author and to the reader (and the mother, of course, and she keeps that secret). What we have here is a wonderful case of what we call the Stendhalian narrator, the super-omniscient narrator who knows everything and knows actually more than any of the characters in the novel. The fact that Fabrizio is the natural son of the Marchese del Dongo's young wife and a French officer, Lieutenant Robert, billeted at the del Dongo palace during the French occupation in Milan turns out to be one of these things that the Stendhalian narrator shares with the reader from the very beginning; we know throughout the course of the story, and yet none of the main players within the plot knows this.

There are these wonderful moments, then, that only the reader can appreciate. For example, Fabrizio at Waterloo actually encounters his real biological father, who is now a member of Napoleon's general staff. In fact, Fabrizio involuntarily provides his father with a fresh horse after his father's original horse had been shot out from under him. And yet at this moment—the father being helped by the son—neither of them knows their real identity and their real relationship to each other. Only the reader, because apprised of this by the narrator, can enjoy that.

It also informs the plot complications that run throughout the novel—this blood kinship between Gina del Dongo and her nephew Fabrizio—because she loves him, he loves her, but it is impossible for them to take this mutual attraction any further because of the incest taboo between aunt and nephew. But the reader knows that there is no conflict here, because the real father is this French lieutenant, Robert. So if you could say that the tragedy of *Oedipus the King* results because of the unknown kinship between the king and his mother, Jocasta, the tragic comedy (you might call it) of

Charterhouse is the fact that the characters don't know a lack of an incest taboo (that is, a lack of any kind of prohibition) that would have kept Fabrizio and Gina from pursuing their romance with each other.

Despite Stendhal's claim, especially in *Charterhouse*, to a position within the Western canon, he really has a very slippery footing for several important reasons. First of all, it's his name, Stendhal. It is a pen name, but it's one of more than 200 pen names used by the writer Marie-Henri Beyle. Now it's okay for a canonic writer to have a pen name, like Voltaire, but stick to just one. If there are too many, this really begins to erode an author's status. For example, Homer is mostly just a name to us; no real biography attaches itself that we can rely on, but at least we have Homer's name. With Stendhal, we have over 200 names drifting around in the literary marketplace.

Also, Stendhal didn't write only novels. He was an extraordinarily versatile writer who wrote for money, dabbled in every conceivable genre—rather reminiscent of Voltaire in that way. In the 19th century, these categories of the literary profession were beginning to harden, almost like in ancient Athens, so that you are a novelist or a poet or a biographer or a historian, but you don't do all of those things. And if you do, you won't be known for them. For example, Melville wrote poetry, but nobody reads Melville's poetry because to us he is a novelist.

Writing novels is only one thing that Stendhal did. He published only two by the time he wrote *Charterhouse*—one of them also highly regarded: *The Red and the Black*, in 1830. But he wrote other things. He was very fond of music, so he wrote biographies of Haydn, Mozart, and Rossini. He even wrote a biography of his hero, Napoleon. He published a two-volume history of painting in Italy, plus travel guides to Rome, Naples, and Florence. There is a wonderful sort of side note: Stendhal, when he first went to Florence, was so overwhelmed by the Giotto frescoes that he saw that, to this day, there is actually a sort of psychological condition called the Stendhal syndrome. It applies to anybody who has an overwhelming emotional reaction to their first visit to the magnificent Renaissance city of Florence.

Another reason that Stendhal's standing in the tradition is rather slippery is that he wrote in the early 19th century, a great age of nationalism in literature. Remember, this is what Goethe was so much about, and yet Stendhal dissociated himself from his homeland, France. He had fallen in love with Milan and northern Italy. He had settled there as a diplomat, and then he remained there and actually sets the action of his novel in Italy. Because it's Italy, he can sort of draw upon various native Italian traditions. He can engage in this sort of religious satire of Boccaccio's *Decameron*, for example.

Writing in Italy, about Italy, in French, he uses the occasion also to criticize his homeland from overseas. This is never thought to be particularly patriotic, and he says over and over again, for example, that, unlike the French, the Italians are still willing to die for a great love. So many of the virtues, so many of the aesthetic characteristics of this novel are actually best described with Italian words that we still have in our language—*brio*, *gusto*, and especially *sprezzatura*. That is a wonderful word, *sprezzatura*; it means "effortless excellence." It is just this wonderful sort of ease of brilliant production.

In fact, this so much points to another phenomenon about *Charterhouse of Parma*. Stendhal actually dictated this novel in 52 days during this huge creative outpouring in November and December of 1838. As a result of this rapid-fire, effortless production, the story has this extraordinary pace. It's light, it's fast-moving, filled with sudden surprises. It is what the translator Richard Howard calls "grasshopper prose."

In mentioning this translation, it's worth reminding ourselves that a great novel, a great work of literature, needs translation if it wants to move from its native land and have a wider international and even global readership. Stendhal has been especially blessed in recent years with this translation by Richard Howard. It caught on, it's beautiful, it's elegant, it seems to catch the spirit of the original. There was even a point after its publication in 1999 that Howard's translation of *The Charterhouse of Parma* was a book that New Yorkers were actually reading on the subway.

Because Stendhal dictated this book so very quickly, he qualifies less as a craftsman, who revises. This is one of the things that we have come to expect from writers, that they take considerable care over their writing; they revise, revise, revise. Shakespeare was said by his rival Ben Johnson never to have blotted—that is, Shakespeare didn't revise. However, we do have that one scene that Shakespeare contributed to the play *Sir Thomas More*, and in that, in Shakespeare's own handwriting, we see lots of cross-outs, lots of insertions. And so the evidence of that one scene in the play *Sir Thomas More* serves as evidence that, yes, even Shakespeare was a careful craftsmen; he revised.

Later on, of course, we know that Jane Austen revised her first draft of *First Impressions*. She "chop'd and crop'd" until it became *Pride and Prejudice*. Later on, Stendhal's heir (as it were), Tolstoy, was a compulsive reviser. Believe it or not, he put *War and Peace* through eight separate revisions, and each time his faithful wife made a fair copy—copied out everything in a clear hand, provided her husband with the new fresh copy—and then he proceeded to start tearing it apart and revising it again. In the 20th century, James Joyce is actually revising *Ulysses* in the galley proofs themselves. He isn't over, even when it's in press; he's still revising.

Stendhal, on the other hand, is more of an embodiment of this Romantic aesthetic of inspiration. Remember, both Wordsworth and Goethe are talking about that spontaneous overflow of feeling. And so here you have somebody who was invested with that inspiration in those 52 days and completed this amazing, amazing novel. However, sometimes for Stendhal, inspiration flagged, and so his output is littered with unfinished books. In fact, in his output we have three novels that he wrote, all of them unfinished.

He wasn't much respected in his homeland or even during his lifetime. There is often this sense of a lag time that needs to catch up with a great writer. We saw this to some extent with Jane Austen already; she had that sort of small circle of fans in London but not nearly the kind of notoriety and fame that her contemporary, Sir Walter Scott, did. Stendhal himself recognized this. He proclaimed, "I will be famous around 1880," and indeed it was a prediction that turned out to be accurate. It took about four decades after his death for his reputation really to take off. As a result, there was a lot of posthumous publication of his works, including his autobiographical writings.

Again, it is worth pausing for a moment to appreciate how many of the classics of our literary tradition were actually published after the author's death. Of course, we know that Thucydides never finished the *Peloponnesian Wars*; it ends in mid-sentence, we presume, because he died. The *Aeneid* was left unfinished when Virgil died after returning from that research trip to Greece. Chaucer's *Canterbury Tales*, left unfinished when he died in 1400—it was up to his son, Thomas Chaucer, and others to patch it together after the author's death. And if you really want to look carefully, all of Shakespeare's plays were published after his death without any participation by the playwright himself. And it goes on. A great deal of Tolkien's work was published after his death—*The Silmarillion*, for example, and his translations such as his (really pretty good) English rendering, poetic translation, of *Sir Gawain and the Green Knight*. And so here you have this interesting phenomenon where the reputation, the full output of a major author, will very often result from these publications after the writer's death himself.

The cult classic *Charterhouse of Parma* has a lot of peculiarities about it. In some sense, it is another antinovel. You can even compare it a bit with *Moby-Dick* in breaking so many of the rules. For example, that famous battle scene at Waterloo is actually near the beginning of the novel. You're not supposed to do that. The battle scene is supposed to come at the end of the novel, but Stendhal thumbs his nose at that convention and puts it near the beginning, so that everything else follows in the wake of the defeat of Napoleon.

Stendhal knew the novel tradition very well. He even knew the English novel tradition. There is a wonderful story that he had memorized the opening chapters to Oliver Goldsmith's novel *The Vicar of Wakefield*. This is a really wonderful 18th-century novel, and so to improve his English and to get to know the craft of the genre from the inside, Stendhal memorized *The Vicar of Wakefield*. And this, again, is something in the modern world that we don't often appreciate, and that is learning by memorizing. Our education system has tended to neglect that, but throughout history we have examples of writers, artists of various kinds, learning the real innards of their art and their craft by memorizing the works of the masters.

Charterhouse of Parma is also a novel that is woven together by what we recognize as clichés, some of the really hackneyed ingredients of the novel as it's emerged to him. You can actually look at *The Charterhouse of Parma* as a run-of-the-mill potboiler, even a bodice-ripper kind of novel. It has all of those tawdry ingredients. There is court intrigue, secret boudoir romance, saber-rattling heroics, and this exquisitely frustrated love triangle that emerges in the course of the novel. Another quirky thing about this book is that the title never explains itself until the final paragraphs. In the final three paragraphs of the book, we finally find out what is the Charterhouse of Parma. And even English readers might need a little footnote to know what a charterhouse is. "Charterhouse" is a Carthusian monastery, such as the one that Sir Thomas More lived in early in his career. In fact, the London Carthusian house is still there; it has become a boy's school—very good boy's school—and is called Charterhouse School. So, Charterhouse is a monastery in which the hero Fabrizio retires at the very, very end of the novel. But there is something else going on here. It is almost as if we're being given a setup for one of these Gothic novels. *Charterhouse of Parma*—it sounds like a spooky monastery, the sort of Gothic novels that Jane Austen is making fun of in her own *Northanger Abbey*, a title that also suggests a sort of Gothic gloom and mystery and sinister events going on.

There is also a kind of funny punning going on in the title, because the French word for charterhouse, Carthusian, is *chartreuse*. That is the French word for Carthusian or charterhouse. That word itself has other meanings. Many of us know chartreuse is also a liqueur; it was made by the Carthusian monks, and so this liqueur is called Chartreuse. It is also a color, and the color chartreuse derives from the color of that liqueur produced by the Carthusian monks—that rather light green, distinctive color that we call chartreuse, from the liqueur from the name of the monks. And so a first-time reader of this book, not seeing any monasteries until the last three paragraphs, might think that this might actually be *The Liqueur of Parma*, and in fact, so many of the characters are intoxicated with love along the way. Or it might be *The Light Green of Parma*, and in fact, Fabrizio the hero is in fact the kind of greenhorn—green behind the ears—and so that too sort of has a wonderful kind of resonance.

There is another novel set at the time of the Napoleonic Wars, William Makepeace Thackeray's wonderful novel *Vanity Fair*. It has the famous subtitle *A Novel Without a Hero*. In a sense, the same thing could be said about Stendhal's novel. It is very hard to figure out who is the hero of *Charterhouse of Parma*. All the way through, Fabrizio del Dongo is constantly called "our hero," and yet he isn't even born when the novel begins and drops out at various parts in the narrative. He is like one of those characters not even born when his story begins, later on, like Saleem Sinai in Rushdie's *Midnight's Children*.

In a sense, the true protagonist is Gina del Dongo; she is the one who has motive. She schemes, she plots, she manipulates all for the good to get what she wants, and yet she too drops out and is missing during long stretches of the story (unlike, for example, Elizabeth Bennet, who is present in every scene almost of *Pride and Prejudice*). So Stendhal's refusal to organize his novel around a single protagonist is again a kind of pushback, a rejection of the whole Great Man view of history that Tolstoy will bring to culmination.

Stendhal had a famous statement that "a novel is a mirror strolling down the highway." That is, it reflects everything around it. In that sense, he is very much in the Aristotelian idea of mimesis, that an artwork should imitate, reflect, and represent everything around it. This is a sort of aesthetic that even Dr. Johnson would approve of when he talked about the novel. And yet *The Charterhouse of Parma* is doing something quite different. It is also a political novel, highly engaged. The tip-off is that Voltaire's name appears on the second page, and so we know that we're dealing with a novel that is going to engage with the politics of the time and especially its fight back against tyranny in Europe.

The great critic Erich Auerbach wrote about Stendhal's artistry and credits him with this idea of a total reality encompassed within a novel. Listen to what Auerbach says in his book *Mimesis*:

> Insofar as the serious realism of modern times cannot represent man otherwise than as embedded in a total reality, political, social, and economic, which is concrete and constantly evolving—as is the case today in any novel or film—Stendhal is its founder.

That means that every little detail in the cultural context, the total reality, assumes meaning. One of my favorite ones is whether a man powders his hair or not. Powdering your hair was an indication that you were a monarchist; however, not powdering your hair indicated you had liberal, progressive views. There is a point in the novel where Count Mosca actually stops powdering his hair to please Gina, the woman he loves, but by doing so, he risks the displeasing his lord, the Prince of Parma.

Now Stendhal was no armchair historian here; he wrote about the things he knew about. At age 16, he was a cavalry dragoon in

Napoleon's army during the invasion of Italy. He remained as an aide-de-camp during the campaigns in Germany and Austria and actually experienced firsthand the invasion of Russia. After Napoleon's fall, though, he saw France being driven by greed and bourgeois self-interest, and those holding liberal views, like himself, found it best to take exile in another country. Like Jane Austen, in a little bit of a way, he has a cast of characters who are mostly part of the lesser nobility—the gentry class in her case—and he shows great contempt for those who are at the upper, ruling end of the nobility, like Marchese del Dongo and Prince Ernesto of Parma—a contempt far beyond the kind of petty tyranny exercised by Lady Catherine de Bourgh in *Pride and Prejudice*.

So what he is going to foreground is a kind of political commitment nowhere seen in Jane Austen's novels, much stronger as an emerging strain in the 19th-century novel. These political novels actually had impact on their times—for example, Charles Dickens's *Nicholas Nickleby* led to the reform of private boys' schools in England. There is a famous story: When Harriett Beecher Stowe, author of *Uncle Tom's Cabin*, visited the White House in 1862, President Abraham Lincoln is supposed to have remarked, "So you're the little woman who wrote the book that started this great war!"

At the heart of *Charterhouse*, though, is something not quite so political; it is the pursuit of happiness, the part of the liberal idealism of America's founding fathers. When you read the book, you are struck that the word "happiness" appears on almost every page. Gina del Donga, for example, early on when she is widowed, returns to the countryside of her girlhood, and she thinks, "Life is fleeting, do not be so hard on the happiness which offers itself to you, make [fast] to enjoy it!" Part of the bittersweet quality of this novel is that nobody gets to enjoy happiness for very long, and certainly not at the end. There is a kind of breathless conclusion to the novel; everybody is killed off in rapid order. There is a legend that the publisher wanted it shorter, and so he ended it quicker. But this rapid dispatching of characters really sort of fits into this sense that nothing happy really lasts. Fabrizio dies soon after his love Clélia, who had succumbed shortly after the death of their biological son. Gina dies soon after Fabrizio, and then Count Mosca is said to become enormously rich, but without the woman that he loved.

Now love—we know, of course, from the ancient tradition—is one of the gifts of Fortune, according to the *Consolation of Philosophy*. And here's one final example of Stendhal's lighthandedness in handling the epics, the great canonic works of the past. Remember, Milan, where he sets so much of the action, was the home of Boethius, and Boethius became a saint: Saint Severinus Boethius. In northern Italy, he was called simply San Severino. Late in the novel, Gina has remarried, and she is now the Duchess Sanseverina. So here you have a kind of tip-off—a very subtle, almost subliminal clue now that she is the Duchess Sanseverina—that there is this sort of Boethian mechanics going on, that happiness does not last very long. The Wheel of Fortune turns, and all of these characters will come to the sad fact that what they had sought in life eludes them and slips away. It would remain, then, the challenge of Stendhal's great successor in Russia, Tolstoy, to pursue, in his great novel *War and Peace*, the great questions: Where, and what, is happiness?

Lecture Twenty-Eight
East Meets West in *War and Peace*

Scope:

War and Peace is "about Russia" in the far-reaching sense that a literary work represents a whole people and creates a sense of nationhood. Originally, Tolstoy wanted to write a trilogy of novels centering on the failed liberal movement of the 1820s, but he first needed to trace these political currents back to the period of the Napoleonic Wars. Challenging Aristotle's cause-and-effect storytelling and the Great Man view of history, Tolstoy describes how the whole Russian people contribute to their nation's destiny. Hence *War and Peace* needs hundreds of characters with a variety of self-interests over a whole generation to address the universal question: What is life *for*? Tolstoy steadily imagines the Napoleonic Wars as a great East-West conflict, with Russia's traditions rooted in her Oriental past and Eastern Orthodox Christianity.

Outline

I. Tolstoy claimed that *War and Peace* was "not a novel," a shocking claim because this is one of the great novels of the Western tradition. This invites us to question the status of the genre and even the status of the "Western-ness" of Tolstoy's writing.

　　A. Looked at in this way, *War and Peace* becomes another example of an outsider novel, even an antinovel.

　　B. It fulfills Harold Bloom's expectation of a kind of subversiveness built into the real masterpieces within an individual genre.

II. Believe it or not, Tolstoy intended *War and Peace* to be a society novel like some of the great English novels of the period.

　　A. The work starts out with a party—a great tool for writers, because it allows them to assemble all of the characters in one place and begin the interaction that will follow over the rest of the story.

　　B. Here Tolstoy has done something we have seen with so many great masters: He has taken the standard features of a genre and then stretched them to the breaking point.

III. Tolstoy allows his society novel to evolve into a family saga, then a historical chronicle, and finally a national epic. Tolstoy is giving us what will become a political novel.

    A. Tolstoy originally wanted to write about the men who were involved in the Decembrist uprising of 1825. He planned a continuation of the story in which Pierre, a member of the Decembrists, returns from exile in Siberia.

    B. Before he got either project off the ground, he decided he needed to start further back, in the period of the Napoleonic Wars.

    C. In this way, he arrived at *War and Peace*—the poster child of the big novel originally meant as the first part of a trilogy.

IV. It is worth pausing to appreciate the status of the trilogy in the Western literary canon.

    A. The trilogy legacy can be seen in the Greek tragedies, in Dante, in Tolkien, and even in the novels of Jane Austen.

    B. It is easy to see why the trilogy would embed itself in the Western tradition, because it conforms to Aristotle's notion of beginning, middle, and end.

    C. Tolstoy may have decided against a trilogy because he was dissatisfied with this Aristotelian concept.

V. *War and Peace* is a kind of national epic, with titanic figures confronting each other. Tolstoy did exhaustive research to be sure that he got everything right.

    A. When Napoleon and Czar Nicholas appear in the novel, they act and speak exactly as Tolstoy's research had indicated.

    B. Like Cervantes and Stendhal before him, Tolstoy had personal experience with warfare. He had been an artillery officer in the Crimean War.

VI. Because of his war experience, Tolstoy knew that generals did not win battles. He appreciated the role of small forces in big events.

    A. History for Tolstoy became the self-interest of millions of people drawn to a vast national drama.

    B. *War and Peace* introduces some 580 characters whose actions or inactions drive great historical events. In a way, it was a trick that he had learned from Stendhal.

VII. Since Tolstoy's history is not based on the Great Man view of history like Thucydides, there cannot be a single plotline running throughout the novel.

  A. The truth for Tolstoy was not clear-cut and could not be described in the single, coherent, plausible plotline suggested by Aristotle.

  B. Tolstoy's view of history as open-ended to factors and contingencies has much more in common with our modern notion of chaos theory.

  C. As a result, Tolstoy rejected the Aristotelian idea of beginning, middle, and end.

  D. The ultimate goodness that Pierre and Natasha find is not contingent upon recognizing a universal truth but upon accepting the complex and coincidental texture of life as a whole.

VIII. As an old joke says, *War and Peace* is about Russia.

  A. In this way, Tolstoy is more like Herodotus than Thucydides. He is an anthropologist encompassing the totality of the Russian people.

  B. The only unity of place is the wide-flung borders of the Russian nation itself.

IX. When Tolstoy said that *War and Peace* was not a novel, he was setting himself, his novel, and his culture against the European tradition. This raises the question of East versus West and even poses the question of whether Tolstoy belongs in the Western literary canon at all.

  A. Russian literature stands on the Eastern side of the historic divide between Roman Europe in the West and Byzantine civilization in the East, from which Russia derives its culture, religion, and alphabet.

  B. Tolstoy resembled Herodotus in defining his people by contrast with the foreign—in Tolstoy's case, the French.

    1. This was a great assault on the Eurocentric thinking that had dominated Western literature for so long.

    2. This can be seen in the gradual disappearance of the use of the French language in the novel as its characters identify their Russianness.

C. Unlike the foolish characters in European novels, Tolstoy's Pierre demonstrates a type of strength in his simplicity, emblematic of the Eastern Orthodox concept of the Holy Fool.

D. One of the most prominent and important geopolitical fault lines in the last 100 years has been the divide between the Catholic West and the Orthodox East.

X. We in the modern world bring an expectation to our writers; we want to see them develop and make progress.

A. We want to see quick learning, and Tolstoy is a terrific case of this.

B. He wrote society novels early on, *War and Peace* in the middle of his career, and spiritual and religious writings late in life.

C. Tolstoy gives us a surprise at the end of his career—the short historical novel *Hadji Murád*.

  1. This is the tale of a Chechen tribal warrior fighting against the Westernized Russian military occupation of his homeland.

  2. In *The Western Canon*, Harold Bloom singles this book out as the "best story in the world."

  3. The narrative has a spare kind of realism that anticipates Hemingway.

  4. *Hadji Murád* looks forward to postcolonial novels like Rushdie's *Midnight's Children*, where the European genre becomes the vehicle for non-Western writers and their non-Western heroes.

Suggested Readings:

Leo Tolstoy, *War and Peace*. (NB: No single translation is definitive, and readers vary in their preferences, with recent audiences preferring translations by Briggs or Pevear and Volokhonsky over Maude).

Bayley, *Tolstoy and the Novel*.

Berlin, *The Hedgehog and the Fox*.

Bloom, "Tolstoy and Heroism," in *The Western Canon*.

Forster, *Aspects of the Novel*.

Maude, *The Life of Tolstoy*.

Questions to Consider:

1. *War and Peace* raises a question that goes back to the earliest Greek historians: Where does factual history end and literary storytelling begin? Do Herodotus's digressions into cultural anthropology discredit him because he does not tell a straightforward narrative? Does Thucydides's focus on "Great Men" discredit him because he leaves out the common foot soldiers and civilians? Big as his novel is, what does Tolstoy leave out that might undercut his status as a historical truth teller?

2. Tolstoy cannot resist the novelist's urge to include a "love interest" among his main characters. Not since Homer's *Iliad* have Western writers managed to tell a war story without including some romantic plotline. Can you think of a single great war novel that refuses to include some ingredients of a love story?

Lecture Twenty-Eight—Transcript
East Meets West in *War and Peace*

When asked, "What is *War and Peace*?" Tolstoy replied, "It is not a novel." This is a shocking reply from the author himself, because this is one of the great novels of the Western tradition. It really invites us to question the status of the genre, and even the status of the "Western-ness" of Tolstoy's writing.

Looked at in this way, *War and Peace* becomes another example of an outsider novel, even an antinovel, much like *Moby-Dick* was. Its author is writing back from the fringes toward the European homeland of the genre of the novel and therefore also doing something with the genre that is a sort of full-scale response, artistically and even politically, to the homeland of the genre itself. Remember, Harold Bloom said about *Faust*, Part II that to become canonical, any new work must have the counter-canonical built into it. *War and Peace* fulfills this particular expectation of a kind of subversiveness built into the real masterpieces within an individual genre.

Believe it or not, Tolstoy intended *War and Peace* to be a society novel like some of the great English novels of the period, such as those by Anthony Trollope. In fact, in another novel, Anna Karenina is on a train reading a novel, and we're told it's about fox hunting and other things, so we know she's reading a novel by Anthony Trollope.

And what is *Anna Karenina* itself about? The famous opening line says it all: All happy families are alike, but each unhappy family is unhappy in its own way. It is a social novel; it's about a family— why some families are happy, why some families are not happy. This had been an early theme in Tolstoy's fiction. He had actually written a novel in 1859, a decade before publishing *War and Peace*, and the title of that novel was *Family Happiness*. In fact, this carries over into *War and Peace*. The three main characters, Pierre, Andre, and Natásha, return in their own personal lives to that question left hanging at the end of *Charterhouse of Parma*: What and where is happiness?

Because he imagined it as a society novel originally, *War and Peace* actually starts off at a party. A party is a really great tool for a writer, because it allows him to assemble all of the characters in one place and begins the interaction that will follow out over the story. Virginia Woolf's *Mrs. Dalloway* is all about having a party; the entire novel is about throwing the party and then having the people in her circle, and even the people from her past, show up. The party is a wonderful way of focusing characters and narrative. Natásha Rostov's house, as it gets ready for its own kind of parties and dances, sounds very much like the giddy, boisterous Bennet household expecting the arrival of Mr. Bingley in *Pride and Prejudice*. Listen to what Tolstoy says about them: "Love was in the air at the Rostovs' at this time, as it always is when there are very young and very charming girls around." This whole sort of society world sounds very much like the world of Jane Austen—girls looking for boys, dances, balls, parties, all the rest.

So Tolstoy has done something with *War and Peace* that we see with so many of the great masters: He's taken the standard features of the genre and then stretched, and packed, and stretched some more, right to the breaking point. It's almost like with *Hamlet*; *Hamlet* is a revenge tragedy, but Shakespeare has loaded it with three different plots and a huge amount of material, including the famous eight soliloquies that you wouldn't necessarily find in the standard genre of the revenge tragedy.

Tolstoy continues to allow his society novel to evolve as it unfolds for the reader, starting off with the world of parties and social gaiety. It evolves into a family saga (actually, the saga of several families), then it becomes historical chronicle and eventually assumes the scale of national epic. Yet it is not a national epic serving as propaganda for the existing power structure. It is not meant to flatter the czars as originally Virgil's *Aeneid*, as a national epic, was specifically designed to flatter Emperor Augustus.

So Tolstoy is giving us what will become a political novel. This is so much a part of the grain of 19th-century fiction—a political novel. But he actually started to write a different political novel. Tolstoy originally wanted to write about the men who were involved in an abortive coup, or uprising; it was called the Decembrist uprising of 1825. This was a group of liberals who wanted to impose a constitution on the czar. That was the core idea that Tolstoy had, to talk about the Decembrist uprising. But then he was thinking he really needed a sequel to this, and so he planned a continuation of the story in 1856, where Pierre, who had been a member of the

Decembrists, comes back from his Siberian exile, a broken old man who's learned from his suffering. But before he got either of these novel projects off the ground, Tolstoy decided that really to understand the men involved in the Decembrist uprising, he needed to go back to the period of the Napoleonic War. That is really the roots of their political commitments: during the Napoleonic period. And so here he arrived at this extraordinary revelation: *War and Peace*—the poster child, as it were, of the big, big novel—was actually meant originally as the first volume of a trilogy.

It is worth pausing for a moment to appreciate the status of the trilogy in the Western literary canon. Remember, back in Ancient Athens, tragedies were never written as single, free-standing plays; tragedies were always part of a trilogy, of three plays. The only complete one that survives is Aeschylus's *Oresteia*. Dante writes his *Divine Comedy* as a sort of trilogy of Hell, Purgatory, and Paradise. The English novel, as it began to be published and popularized, was always published in three volumes; this would include Jane Austen. These novels are very often now all together in one volume, but if you notice the divisions, they were always in three volumes. They came to be nicknamed "triple-deckers," because novels were done in those three volumes. Indeed, Tolstoy's early career as a novelist featured an autobiographical trilogy of novels entitled *Childhood*, *Boyhood*, and *Youth*. And of course, in more recent times, Tolkien wrote a very, very big novel, an adventure fantasy that his publisher insisted on splitting into three volumes. This, of course, is *Lord of the Rings*, always intended by him as one big book, but now separated into those three books that we actually call the trilogy.

It's easy enough to see why the trilogy would embed itself in the Western tradition, because it so much conforms to Aristotle's idea of a story having beginning, middle, and end. This suggests also why Tolstoy jettisoned the idea of putting *War and Peace* as part of a large trilogy, because he is very dissatisfied with this Aristotelian organization of narrative into beginning, middle, and end. Tolstoy liked to compare himself (or have himself compared) to Homer, and indeed, *War and Peace* is a kind of great national epic with these sort of titanic figures confronting each other—Emperor Napoleon and Czar Nicholas I. And he did exhaustive research, Tolstoy did, to be sure he got everything right. He went through the military chronicles, the plans of the battle, looked at everything. He made the statement, "Wherever in my novel historical persons speak or act, I have invented nothing." And so when Napoleon or Czar Nicholas appears, what they do—what they say—is exactly what the chronicles told him. In this case, he is unlike the Athenian historian Thucydides; remember, he invents speeches such as Pericles's famous funeral oration, just puts words into the mouth of historical characters.

Now, like Cervantes and Stendhal before him and Hemingway and Tolkien later, Tolstoy actually had personal experience of warfare. He had been an artillery officer during the Crimean War. Therefore, he appreciated the reality on the ground. He knew that generals did not win battles. There is the old saying, "For want of a nail, the shoe was lost. For want of a shoe, the horse was lost. For want of a horse, the battle was lost." This is the sort of thinking that Tolstoy appreciates so much, and so when he tells this story, he's just as likely to be focusing on the horse that throws a shoe as he is on General Katúzov praying before a holy icon on the brink of the great Battle of Borodino. History for him, therefore, is not the product of a single Nietzschean superman; history for Tolstoy becomes the self-interest of millions of ordinary people drawn into a vast national drama that is sometimes called the swarm-like existence of mankind.

As a result, *War and Peace* introduces some 580 characters whose actions or inactions drive great historical events. In a way, it was a trick that he had learned from Stendhal, again. Stendhal introduces these minor, low-class characters sometimes. For example, at the Battle of Waterloo, Fabrizio is helped repeatedly by a woman who has a canteen wagon, and she gives him advice on how to be a soldier, how to dress, how to behave, how to talk. And when you think about it, the only reason Fabrizio survives the battle and goes on to be hero of the novel is because he was helped by that woman at the canteen wagon. Later on, of course, Tolkien will carry this forward. The most important characters in his trilogy are the little people, the Hobbits of the Shire, but it is on their actions, the little people, that the entire destiny of Middle Earth turns.

So Tolstoy is giving us a history that is not the Great Man view of history descending from historians like Thucydides, and therefore there cannot be a single plotline running throughout the novel. This is something that will bother other writers. Henry James, the American-turned-British novelist, had a real objection to Russian novels. He described them as "loose baggy monsters with their queer elements of the accidental and the arbitrary." But that is exactly what

Tolstoy was going for. He didn't want a novel like Jane Austen with three or four families in a country village. The truth of history is not simple and clear cut. It's not describable in that single, coherent, plausible plotline such as suggested by Aristotle. There are accidents. There are coincidences. It's open-ended to factors and contingencies. His view of history is much more like our modern notion of chaos theory. Some minor thing happens—like the butterfly's beat—and many major things follow from that.

As a result, Tolstoy will abandon the Aristotelian formula for Western storytelling for 2,000 years. There is no obvious beginning, middle, and end to his story. The opening chapter is at Anna Pavlonda's party in Saint Petersburg in 1805, but in a way, it's arbitrary. It's a starting point that he has to choose out of many possible ones, preventing a kind of infinite regression into prior events, prior events, prior events.

The ultimate goodness and happiness that Pierre and Natasha finally find isn't contingent on recognizing some sort of universal truth, the master narrative of providence, some unifying principle in the world, or a kind of divine explanation, a theodicy—that is, the explanation that all is for the best in this best of all possible worlds. Their happiness comes by accepting the complex and coincidental texture of life as a whole—what Tolstoy's great admirer the Cambridge philosopher Ludwig Wittgenstein would describe: "The world is everything that is the case."

There's a joke about the man who took a speed-reading course, and the first book he tackled was *War and Peace*. Asked after reading the book in one day what it was about, he said, "It's about Russia." It's a joke, but like so many jokes, it has a very, very good point to it. *War and Peace* is about Russia. One of the first Russian reviewers of the complete novel in 1869 grasped exactly Tolstoy's achievement. This is what he said:

> The picture of human life is complete.
> The picture of the Russian of those days is complete.
> The picture of what we call history and the struggle of nations is complete.
> The picture of everything that people considered to be their happiness and greatness, their sorrow and their humiliation, is complete. That is what *War and Peace* is.

And so in this case, Tolstoy is actually more like Herodotus than he is like Homer. He is an anthropologist encompassing the totality of the Russian people—at peace at the beginning, then at war against French, and then at peace at the end. So there is no unity of place in that Aristotelian sense, except the entire wide-flung borders of the Russian nation itself.

E. M. Forster was a very great admirer of Tolstoy. In his wonderful series of lectures published as *Aspects of the Novel*, he had already admired what we call the time perspective, rolling out a great tapestry of generations. But he also admired this particular vastness of the novel's setting. Here is how he described the extraordinary effect:

> After one has read *War and Peace* for a bit, great chords begin to sound, and we cannot say exactly what struck them. … They come from the immense area of Russia, over which episodes and characters have been scattered from the sum-total of bridges and frozen rivers, forests, roads, gardens, fields, which accumulate grandeur and sonority after we have passed them. … Space is the lord of *War and Peace*, not time.

A wonderful sort of way at looking at the novel if we aren't any longer looking for those plot elements that we would find in a traditional novel.

Why don't we visit our classic critic Erich Auerbach? Toward the end of his study *Mimesis*, he mentions in passing that he's not going to write about Russian novelists, because he said he can't read them in the original language. I suspect, though, that one reason he turned away from Russian novelists like Tolstoy is that he sensed that they did not really fit in his title, Western literature. Western literature—there was something about the Russians that wasn't quite Western.

When Tolstoy said that *War and Peace* wasn't a novel, he was very clear that he intended a deviation from European forms. He's setting himself—and his novel, and his culture—over and against the European tradition. This raises the entire question of East versus West, and it even poses the question of whether Tolstoy belongs in the Western literary canon at all. *War and Peace* reminds us that Russian literature stands on the Eastern side of that great historic divide between Latin, Roman Europe in the West and Greek,

Byzantine civilization in the East. Russian culture—and its religion, and even its alphabet—derive from the Eastern Byzantine Empire. To the extent that Tolstoy recognized himself as the heir of Homer and Herodotus, he was very aware that both of those writers lived east of the Bosporus in Asia Minor.

Tolstoy actually studied Oriental languages as a university student, and when he returned from his grand tour of Europe, he was actually very disdainful of the Westernizing impulse of fellow writers like Turgenev. In this sense, again, Tolstoy resembles the writer Herodotus—historian, defining his people by contrast with that foreign other. For the Greek historian Herodotus, that foreignness, that alien presence, was represented by the Persians, who invaded under Xerxes. For Tolstoy, that alien otherness will be represented by the French, who invade under Napoleon. How do you know that you are Russian? You're not French. This is an extraordinary turnaround; it's a great assault on that sort of Eurocentric thinking that has dominated for so long. It is shifting the center of things to a non-European culture.

One of the things any reader notices is how much of the dialogue in the novel is French; it totals up to about 2.5 percent of the text is actually in French. The opening line of the novel is spoken in French. This was the courtly language, an import language to Russian society. But over the course of the novel, the French language itself decreases and fades away. By the end of the novel, people are eating Russian food, they are wearing Russian native dress and even dancing native dances.

I want to look for a moment at one of my sort of favorite episodes; it is where Pierre arrives at the Battle of Borodino, and he's dressed in a white hat and green swallowtail coat, this gentleman who has come out to observe the battle. In a way, he's motivated by the same chivalric idealism as Don Quixote, but he really comes off as clueless and fumbling as Fabrizio at the Battle of Waterloo. Listen to this great definition of the description of the fog of war:

> Everything Pierre saw on either hand looked so indistinct that glancing left or right over the landscape, he could find nothing that quite lived up to his expectations. Nowhere was there a field of battle as such, the kind of thing he had expected; there was nothing but ordinary fields, clearings, troops, woods, smoking camp-fires, villages, mounds, and

little streams. Here was a living landscape, and try as he might he could not make out any military positioning. He could not even tell our troops from theirs.

Pierre has a kind of simplemindedness about him that puts us in mind of an actually positive statement that Tolstoy made elsewhere. Tolstoy said, "There is no greatness where there is not simplicity." And so Pierre's fumbling, naïve simplicity is quite different from other literary morons like Candide and especially Fabrizio, who is frustratingly stupid in most of his life, particularly at Waterloo.

But Tolstoy is doing something different; he is in a different culture, and the simplicity of Pierre actually makes him look like the Holy Fool, a particularly prominent and sacred figure in the Eastern Orthodox tradition. And he isn't alone in this. In the same year that the last installment of *War and Peace* was published, Dostoevsky publishes a book whose hero is also a kind of Holy Fool: Prince Myshkin. The title of the novel usually is translated as *The Idiot*, but a much better translation would be *The Simpleton*, because Prince Myshkin, too, also fits into this Orthodox, Eastern tradition of the Holy Fool.

So what we see here developing in the 19th century anticipates something that modern political theorists like Samuel Huntington will discuss in his well-known book *The Clash of Civilizations*, that there are these fault lines that run throughout the world, and they're not so much geopolitical fault lines having to do with the borders of nations. In fact, borders of nations often cut across these cultural and ethnic fault lines. And here is one of the great and important fault lines that has been prominent certainly in the last hundred years, and that is between the Catholic West and the Orthodox East. This has been very much at heart of the problems in the former Yugoslavia. That country was a country that created its borders across many of these cultural fault lines—religious, ethnic, and so on. So, when the country dissolved, you had countries like Catholic Croatia fighting with Orthodox Serbia, very much at that particular fault line in miniature that Tolstoy is describing in large scale between Russia and France in his own time.

It is a wonderful observation that a great author is more than one author. If he lives long enough, a great author becomes somebody different over the course of his career. Look at Shakespeare, the playwright who gave us *Romeo and Juliet* and *The Taming of the*

Shrew early in his career, during the reign of Elizabeth I. He would become a different playwright, a different Shakespeare, when he would write *King Lear* and *The Tempest* later, during the reign of James I. In fact, this becomes an expectation that we in the modern world bring to our writers; we want to see them develop, we want to see them make progress.

By the 20th century, there is going to be an extraordinary imperative that we will see, for example, in James Joyce's career, that we expect the writer to create a brand new style, even a brand new language, every time he writes a new book. We want to see quick learning; we want to see a steep learning curve for a writer, and so we almost insist upon this as a kind of modern standard for the growing, developing, achieving writer. Tolstoy is a terrific case of this. He wrote those sort of society novels early on; he writes *War and Peace* sort of midway through his career. But then the older Tolstoy becomes almost a completely different writer. He becomes deeply invested in religious and spiritual questions. His books are now entitled *Resurrection* and *The Kingdom of God is Within You*. He actually becomes quite a spiritual leader within European civilization. There's kind of a Tolstoy movement at the time, people who embraced pacifism, vegetarianism, educational reform, the notion of universal human freedom. The writings and the example Tolstoy would go on to inspire some of the major figures of the 20th century, such as Mahatma Gandhi and Martin Luther King Jr.

It is very interesting to see what a writer does at the very, very end of his life. Remember, we expect some final statement, some culminating work coming from the writer. It gives us the sense that his career has a kind of narrative, a story, a trajectory; we like to see that kind of unity and a sense of final statement. This is why we're so glad that Mozart was writing a requiem when he died; that would be exactly the appropriate thing for Mozart to be working on. This is why we don't like that *The Tempest* probably is not Shakespeare's last play. *The Two Noble Kinsman*, coauthored with another writer, is probably the last of the surviving plays, but it's *The Tempest* we like to see in that culminating position because it seems so much like a synthesis of everything that he had done before—refined, condensed, purified, a perfect concluding, a curtain call for the great writer.

Tolstoy is going to give us this surprise at the end of his career. He's in his 70s, and he writes a short historical novel entitled *Hadji*

Murád. It was completed in 1904. (That's right, Tolstoy actually lives into the 20th century.) And so *Hadji Murád* was written in 1904 but was not published until two years after the author's death—another example of a great work of literature didn't come into print until the author himself had passed from the scene.

Hadji Murád is an amazing story. It tells the tale of the Chechen tribal warrior fighting against the Westernized Russian military occupation of his homeland. He's a freedom fighter, and he's scrounging, working with the bare resources available to him, having infighting with other tribal lords, commitment to a family. He's almost like Odysseus; he just wants to get home, and there are so many obstacles in his way to achieving that end. It is an amazing story; it raises a kind of heroism in combat that almost has not been seen in the West since Homer. And who speaks so well of this particular late novel? Harold Bloom. He singles it out in his study of Tolstoy in his volume *The Western Canon*. This is what Professor Bloom says: "My personal touchstone for the sublime of prose fiction, to me the best story in the world, or at least the best that I have ever read."

This is high praise indeed. Harold Bloom has an extraordinary reputation among academics; he is an extraordinarily fast reader, he has a photographic memory, he remembers everything he's read, and he's read just about everything. For him to say that this is the best story in the world, or at least "the best I have ever read," carries a tremendous amount of weight.

Now you notice what he's doing here; he's also revising the canon slightly. He could have written that chapter on *Anna Karenina*; he could have written that chapter on *War and Peace*. He instead shifts his emphasis to this novel that most people haven't even heard of, *Hadji Murád*, and says this is the best one in the world. It reminds us again that in modern times, over the last two or three hundred years, it is the critic, the academic, who will spell out the terms of the Western canon.

In this case, it worked. I went out, bought the book, read it, and I agree with Professor Bloom; this is really one of the best books in the world. It gives us a kind of realism—spare, minimum, sort of grace under fire, looking forward to Hemingway in some of his novels such as *For Whom the Bell Tolls*. In fact, Hemingway was always struggling with a titanic influence of his father figure Tolstoy.

He made the famous statement, "Nobody's going to get me in any ring with Tolstoy unless I'm crazy."

Now remember, he said he'd fought a couple of draws with Stendhal—this idea of male writers going fist to fist with each other—but he's not climbing in the ring with Tolstoy. He can't compete. And that's because he knows the extraordinary achievements of this novel, a novel that will look forward to something very, very modern: the non-Western hero, the hero very often rendered invisible by other writers, very much materializing in a way that challenges Edward Said's stereotypes of Orientalism, because Hadji Murád is an extraordinary, real, intimate character, and one of the things that Tolstoy describes is the warrior dying from his own internal experience, one of the most gripping passages I know in Western literature.

And so what Tolstoy gives us here finally in *Hadji Murád* is a work that will look forward to novels we will talk about at the very end of this course, the postcolonial novels, novels written by the outsider, such as Rushdie's *Midnight's Children*, where the European genre becomes a vehicle for the non-Western writers and their non-Western heroes.

Lecture Twenty-Nine
Joyce's *Ulysses* and the Avant-Garde

Scope:

James Joyce exploits the resources of Tolstoy's "big novel" to explore the intimate lives of common Dublin citizens on June 16, 1904. His "internal monologues" take readers into the minds of the would-be writer Stephen Dedalus, the advertising man Leopold Bloom, and his sexually frustrated wife Molly. Realistic depictions of sex got the book banned in England and the United States, but *succès de scandale* helped its status. Writing during 1914–1921, Joyce looks back at the peaceful, cosmopolitan Europe prior to the massive disruptions of the First World War. Modernity's crisis of values is represented by avant-garde experimental styles, for example Joyce's "stream-of-consciousness" style in Molly Bloom's soliloquy. The book's notorious difficulties conform to the aesthetics of early 20th-century art and music, though *Ulysses* becomes another book more honored as canonic than actually read.

Outline

I. *Ulysses*, reputedly the hardest novel in the Western canon, actually has its roots in children's literature.

    A. Many of the masterpieces of the Western tradition are rooted in juvenile genres—the adventure, the ghost story, even the puppet show.

    B. Joyce admitted that his inspiration for *Ulysses* came from Charles Lamb's children's adaptation, and to this day the plot line of the novel remains incredibly simple.

    C. The difficulty in the novel lies much more in the avant-garde style of writing than in its actual content.

II. *Ulysses* has a reputation for obscenity, but the theme of paternity is much more pervasive in this novel than the theme of sexual love.

    A. Shakespeare was interested in father-daughter relationships, but Joyce focused on father-son relationships, particularly the failure of fathers and the breakdown of patriarchal lineage on familial and cultural levels.

B. Joyce was obsessed with the idea of literary father figures, not as domineering forces but as weak, absentee figures who no longer nourished, challenged, or inspired him.

C. The failure of fathers in the novel fuels its pervasive sense of regret.

    1. Bloom is a figure of middle-aged personal regrets about career, marriage, and family.

    2. Stephen's regrets are more monumental, even global. He has the feeling of belatedness that plagues all artists.

III. In the novel, Stephen says, "History is a nightmare from which I am trying to awake." He means literary history as much as national history, and indeed, Joyce was very much in touch with his literary predecessors.

A. His experimental novel actually returns to the aesthetics of Aristotle as filtered through Aquinas, with the three unities of place, time, and action.

B. Like Saint Augustine in his *Confessions*, Joyce took himself as the subject of exploration; Stephen is the younger Joyce, and Bloom is the middle-aged Joyce.

C. Dante was really Joyce's favorite, hence the complex writing and the intricately crafted texture of the epic.

D. Like Voltaire, Joyce felt that he had been failed by his Catholic father figures; he lost faith in organized religion and in the centrality of Christianity to Western civilization.

E. Shakespeare was the one English-language master against whom Joyce felt he could carry out his Oedipal revolt.

    1. Stephen is a sort of updated version of Hamlet, the intellectual who lives totally inside his own head, forever thinking.

    2. Bloom is a modern version of Falstaff, fully alive to the senses, indulging and enjoying wherever possible.

    3. The problem with Shakespeare is that our lack of information about him makes him a shadow figure, a remote absentee father.

F. Like Tolstoy, Joyce researched his novel for accuracy and was a compulsive reviser.

G. Joyce does not seem to employ the *Aeneid* in his work. This may be because of Virgil's focus on strong paternity and empire, two aspects against which Joyce was revolting.

H. In a sense, *Ulysses* is yet another example of the postcolonial novel before the term itself was invented. Joyce read Chaucer as he was writing, and although there was some influence, Joyce was not part of the mainstream Chaucerian tradition.

IV. James Joyce lived—and wrote *Ulysses*—during a period of huge upheaval in Europe.

A. As the final line of his novel indicates, the book was written in Trieste, Zurich, and Paris during the years of the First World War.

B. This means that *Ulysses* looks back from the war years to the pre-war era in 1904, when Europe was at peace and people like Leopold, Molly, and Stephen moved in a highly cosmopolitan world.

C. In hindsight, World War I emerges as the great event of the early 20th century, casting its shadow across the decades to come as the Napoleonic Wars had done a century earlier.

V. Twentieth-century writers like Joyce had a sense of being failed by European civilization and their cultural father figures, yet they continued to feel the weight of the past upon them. This led to an artistic culture of constant reinvention.

A. At the beginning of his *Confessions*, Saint Augustine makes a great statement about the central human problem: "Our heart is restless."

B. Augustine resolved this by converting to Christianity, but in the 20th century restlessness had become a virtue, not a vice.

C. A great artist in the 20th century is in restless pursuit of reinventing himself, finding new styles for his work.

VI. Joyce's trajectory as a writer was extraordinary, absolutely amazing.

A. His style moved from the straightforward short story to the *Bildungsroman*, then to revolutionary stylistic expressionism, and finally to the outermost limits of linguistic experimentation.

B. Joyce's style represents a fusion of form and content, as can be seen in the stream-of-consciousness subject and style of Molly Bloom's monologue.

C. When *Ulysses* was published, it made Joyce a literary celebrity, but it also became notorious as being obscene and subversive and was banned for many years in America.

D. Even though it was criticized as obscene at the time, Joyce's writing is actually just the realism of Stendhal and Tolstoy applied to people's inner lives.

E. Joyce spent the next 15 years working on the ultimate example of literary experimentation, *Finnegans Wake*.

    1. It is the universal dream of the human race, along the lines of Carl Jung's "universal unconscious."

    2. It absolutely defies the expectations of the Western literary tradition. There is no plot, no protagonist or antagonist, and only one recognizable character.

F. Joyce planned to end his career with a short, simple book but instead drank himself to death at the age of 58.

VII. In Joyce, we have one more example of a canonic author who exhausted the possibilities of his own chosen genre.

A. Shakespeare had the last word on tragedy, Milton the last word on the epic poem, and Joyce the last word on the experimental novel.

B. *Ulysses* would have an immediate impact on the work of Woolf and Faulkner, both writers who worked from the fringes, outside the mainstream.

Suggested Readings:

Joyce, *Ulysses*.

Bloom, "Joyce's Agon with Shakespeare," in *The Western Canon*.

Ellmann, *James Joyce*.

Ladenson, *Dirt for Art's Sake*.

Questions to Consider:

1. Great authors attract great biographers. Since Boswell's *The Life of Samuel Johnson, LL.D.*, the biography itself has helped to create this literary greatness for an author. Why not look at one of the most impressive modern achievements, Richard Ellmann's

James Joyce, to appreciate how much this book boosts the status of *Ulysses* by providing background information about the author?

2. Because of Ireland's bitter history of colonial exploitation, *Ulysses* is an English-language novel with an anti-English political bias. Why not read Joyce's novel with steady attention to the author's antagonism toward English characters, English literary figures, and even "the King's English"?

Lecture Twenty-Nine—Transcript
Joyce's *Ulysses* and the Avant-Garde

The novel in the Western canon that has achieved the reputation as the hardest, James Joyce's *Ulysses*, actually has its roots in children's literature. It's interesting to notice how many of the masterpieces of the Western tradition really are rooted in juvenile fiction. *Huckleberry Finn* is a boys' adventure; *Hamlet*, in a sense, is a ghost story; *Moby-Dick* even, a fishing tale. Goethe is said to have encountered the *Faust* story for the first time as a puppet show. Joyce actually admitted that his inspiration originally came from Charles Lamb's children's adaptation, *The Adventures of Ulysses*, that he read at age 12; hence the novel's title is *Ulysses* and not *Odysseus*.

To this day, the plotline of *Ulysses* remains incredibly simple. It started out actually as a short story that he planned for his collection *The Dubliners*. Here is the basic outline of the story: The 30-something Leopold Bloom, part Jewish, leaves his house in the morning, spends the whole day wandering around Dublin as an advertising canvasser, and returns home late at night. Stephen Dedalus, a recent university graduate and disaffected teacher, is readying himself to leave Ireland to pursue a career as a writer. Bloom's wife, Molly, a semiprofessional singer, commits adultery with her agent, Blazes Boylan. That's it. And so the difficulty that this novel has achieved it shares with other works of the modernist avant-garde: It is much more in the style of the writing than in its actual contents.

Also, *Ulysses* has a reputation for obscenity, but it's really the theme of paternity that is much more pervasive and strong in this novel than sexual love. Shakespeare was very interested in father-daughter relationships in his plays. Notice in *The Tempest* it's the relationship between Prospero and his daughter, Miranda, that is so core to the story. Joyce, however, is mostly interested in father-son relationships, and particularly in the failure of the fathers and the breakdown of this sort of patriarchal lineage that sustains not only families but also cultures. Leopold Bloom's father has committed suicide. Bloom's son Rudy died in infancy. Stephen Dedalus's father is an alcoholic ne'er-do-well, always away from home. Stephen himself is unmarried, has no children, and can't even imagine himself as a family man. But as an artist, Joyce is obsessed with the idea of literary father figures, not so much as those strong, challenging authors against whom to revolt, but much more as a kind of enfeebled or absentee father figure no longer nourishing, challenging, or inspiring to him as a writer.

The failure of fathers in the novel fuels its pervasive sense of regret. Bloom is a figure of middle-aged regrets; he regrets his career, his marriage, his children (or lack of children). Stephen Dedalus's regrets are more monumental, even global. He was born in the wrong country, in the wrong religion, in the wrong century. He has a feeling of belatedness; he's come too late in the great story of the Western literary tradition. In a sense, all artists have felt that they were belated. Even in the story of Gilgamesh, the writer remembers an earlier, grander period, the period of the flood time of Utnapishtim. By the time Homer is writing his first epics, he feels that all the great heroic events were done centuries in the past or in the Trojan War period. But by the 20th century, a writer like James Joyce feels centuries and even millennia of this sort of prior achievement, that he can never really match up, and he feels a great sort of hand, a great weight of the past upon him.

Stephen Dedalus has a famous line in the novel. He says, "History is a nightmare from which I am trying to awake," and he means as much literary history as the whole national history of the conversation. Indeed, Joyce is very much in touch with his historic predecessors. Like Voltaire, Joyce was educated by the Jesuits and very much valued the intellectual rigor of their education. His experimental novel actually returns to the aesthetics of Aristotle as filtered through Saint Thomas Aquinas with the three unities of time, place, and action. In fact, he's very respectful of the unities of time and place. The place is Dublin, Ireland, and the time is a single day, June 16, 1904. In fact, the action is so compact that you can actually walk the streets and follow the path of the characters, as many devotees of Joyce actually do.

Like Saint Augustine in his *Confessions*, James Joyce took himself as the principal subject of exploration; Stephen Dedalus is sort of the younger James Joyce, Leopold Bloom the middle-aged James Joyce. It is probably significant that Augustine was James Joyce's middle name. The Catholic master poet Dante was really Joyce's favorite, hence the incredible complexity of the writing, the intricately crafted texture of the epic. Everything is meaningful, everything is exactly the right place, everything is subject again to layers and layers of interpretation. But also like Voltaire in the 18th century, Joyce felt that he had been failed by his Catholic father figures, so that he'd lost faith in organized religion and also the centrality of Christianity in Western civilization. There's an anecdote that Joyce was once asked, now that he had lost faith in the Catholic Church, had he become a Protestant? Joyce replies something to the effect, "I may have lost my faith, but I haven't lost my reason."

Joyce's great struggle with a father figure involved Shakespeare. Shakespeare was that one English-language master that he really felt that he could do his Oedipal revolt, the son against the father. In fact, there's a whole chapter in *Ulysses*, the Scylla and Charybdis episode, devoted to Stephen Dedalus's theories of the father-son themes in Shakespeare's *Hamlet*. Stephen himself is a sort of updated version of Hamlet, the intellectual who lives totally inside his own head, forever thinking, thinking, thinking. Leopold Bloom, on the other hand, is sort of a modern version of Shakespeare's Falstaff character, a very flesh-and-blood creature, fully alive to the senses, indulging and enjoying wherever possible. The problem with Shakespeare is that he remains this shadow figure, a remote absentee father; we don't have a good biography of Shakespeare, and so we're always sort of looking for that personality in the sonnets and in the plays and always feeling that we come up empty in that search for the real, authentic Shakespeare.

Like his favorite novelist, Tolstoy, Joyce researched his novel for accuracy of detail. He pored over newspapers for June 1904, studied maps, even claimed that, should the City of Dublin be wiped off the map, it could be rebuilt and recreated from his books. Again, like Tolstoy, Joyce was a compulsive reviser, correcting and expanding his book even in the galley proofs. Sometimes he put in as many as 160 changes and additions in a single page. As a result, the text grew a third more than the original submission version that was supposed to be the final version for his publishers.

Missing from this sort of rundown of the greats of the Western canon is Virgil's *Aeneid*, and this is implausible in a sense, because this is a standard school text. Joyce would have read the *Aeneid* like every other good schoolboy. But the point, I think, is that it is the epic with the very strongest sense of fatherhood, emphasizing the bloodline of Aeneas leading down to Julius and Augustus Caesar. The *Aeneid* also, remember, is the epic of empire, and part of the quandary of an

Irishman like Joyce at the beginning of the 20th century is that Ireland was still part of the British Empire at this point, and Joyce felt that it was also subject to the empire of the Catholic Church. So as part of his revolt against the whole idea of empire, he seems to have excluded that one canonic work most successfully from his novel.

In this sense, then, *Ulysses* becomes yet another example of the postcolonial novel before the term itself was invented. Joyce is an Irishman; he's working outside the mainstream of the English tradition, and so he is writing back from the fringes. It's another example of that lovely phrase invented by the critics, "the empire writes back." We've already seen this with *Moby-Dick* writing back from America to the English novel tradition, and we saw it also in Tolstoy in *War and Peace*, writing back from the Eastern fringes of Russia, back to the European heartland, where the novel originated. It is interesting; Joyce said that before he sat down to write *Ulysses*, he also sat down and read father Chaucer. He wanted to revisit Chaucer as he was writing *Ulysses*, and indeed, his character Molly Bloom can be said to have resemblances to Chaucer's earthy, sexy character, the Wife of Bath.

Many of James Joyce's personal books have ended up at the State University of New York at Buffalo. I actually made a pilgrimage when I was a graduate student to look at the books, and lo and behold, there was Joyce's copy of Chaucer. It was Skeet's student edition that Joyce had probably used when he was a student at University College Dublin. I was very anxious to see if he had written anything in his text, and lo and behold, Joyce seems to be the sort of writer who didn't put marginalia in his books like Samuel Taylor Coleridge did, and Joyce didn't even seem to underline. So the entire text of his Chaucer book was blank, no personal notations. In a sense that is significant, because even though he read Chaucer, he really wasn't part of that mainstream Chaucerian tradition, the genealogy of great English writers that look back to Chaucer as the father of English poetry. Again, Joyce's status as a marginal character in Ireland comes out in his sort of blank response to his Chaucer text.

James Joyce lived and worked on *Ulysses* during a period of huge upheaval in Europe. The novel's very last words actually cite the cities and dates of *Ulysses*'s composition. Those last words are

"Trieste-Zurich-Paris, 1914–1921." That is, Joyce wrote entirely through the years of the First World War. When he started off, he was living with his family in Trieste, then a highly cosmopolitan port city for the Austro-Hungarian Empire. And then, for safety, they moved to neutral Switzerland. Zurich at that time was a great polyglot city, crowded with all the refugees, including the Dada artist Tristan Zara, and even Lenin, from Russia, was there. In fact, the great English playwright Tom Stoppard has a play called *Travesties* set in Zurich, bringing all these characters together, and it even has James Joyce as one of the central characters of his play, *Travesties*. Joyce and his family finally arrive in Paris as the fighting of the war is winding down, and that's where he'll finish and complete the publication of *Ulysses*. This means that the action of *Ulysses* looks back from the war years to the prewar era of 1904. Europe was at peace in 1904; people like Leopold and Molly and Stephen moved in a highly cosmopolitan world, all of which would be shattered, along with confidence in national cultures and Western civilization itself, by the Great War.

In hindsight, then, World War I emerges as *the* great event of the early 20th century, casting its shadow across the decades to come, much as the Napoleonic War cast its shadow across those early decades of the 19th century. Look at the writers Ernest Hemingway, Thomas Mann, T. S. Eliot, Virginia Woolf, William Faulkner, Willa Cather, even J. R. R. Tolkien—all were shaped as writers by this massive cultural dislocation, this psychological impact of the First World War.

Now 20th-century writers like Joyce felt that they had, in a sense, been failed by European civilization and their cultural father figures, and yet they continued to feel the crushing weight of the dead past upon them. If they couldn't actually do what their predecessors had done, they could at least experiment with new styles and new artistic languages. In a sense, Joyce resembles some of the Cubist painters like Pablo Picasso and Georges Braque, using their very complicated styles actually to represent rather simple, everyday things—a guitar, a bowl of fruit. Then you look at composers like Igor Stravinsky, who needed to reinvent their musical idiom every time they wrote a new piece of music. So, Stravinsky would start with *The Firebird*, very much rooted in the Russian romanticism of Rimsky-Korsakov, and then go on to the daring *Rite of Spring*, but then also going forward to the *Symphony of Psalms*, written in a very neoclassical mode. An avant-garde artist is constantly reinventing himself; there is a restlessness, a need to do something new, new, new, over and over.

If we go back to the beginning of European tradition, we look at Saint Augustine's *Confessions*. At the very beginning of the *Confessions*, Saint Augustine makes a great statement upon the essential human problem. He talks about *inquietum est cor nostrum*, "our heart is restless." We have the *inquietum cor*, the "unquiet heart." This is the problem for Augustine that he resolves in the course of his conversion to Christianity. In the 19th century, Nietzsche will speak of a transvaluation of values. In the Modernist period, restlessness is being transvalued into a virtue and no longer a vice, as it was for Saint Augustine. Remember what Eric Heller said about Goethe's hero: "What is Faust's sin? Restlessness of spirit. What is Faust's salvation? Restlessness of spirit."

A great artist in the 20th century is even more so—as I've said before—not a single author; he is in restless pursuit of reinventing himself, finding new styles in new works. Joyce's trajectory of a writer is extraordinary, absolutely amazing. He starts off with these rather straightforward, naturalistic short stories in his collection called the *Dubliners*, and then he does this stylistically advanced *Bildungsroman*, a coming-of-age novel, *A Portrait of the Artist as a Young Man*. But then he surprises everyone with the landmark of stylistic expressionism, his *Ulysses* of 1922, and then spent the rest of his career working in the outermost limits of linguistic experimentation in *Finnegans Wake*.

Joyce's style represents a fusion of form and content. There's a lovely story that explains this well. In his Paris apartment, James Joyce had a big picture on the wall; it was of County Cork, his home county back in Ireland. When people would notice the picture and ask what it was, he would say, "It's Cork." They would notice the frame, and they would say, "What's the frame made of?" And Joyce would say, "It's cork." And there is form and content: The picture is of County Cork, the frame is made of cork. So this is very much the sort of style that we find throughout *Ulysses*.

Let's take, for example, the novel's famous last chapter, Molly Bloom's monologue. It is "stream of consciousness," and so if that is the subject, you know the form is going to reflect that. It will be flowing, unpunctuated prose. There's no break in the flow of this stream of consciousness in its 36 closely packed pages. Molly Bloom is the original "desperate housewife" who hasn't enjoyed sex with her own husband for the last 11 years. So as she falls asleep late at night, her memories flow together in this stream of consciousness, and at the very, very end of the novel, she's sort of merging together the streams of thought of her first sexual experience in Gibraltar and the day when she accepted Leopold's marriage proposal. Here are the last words in the novel, Molly Bloom's soliloquy:

> Yes and how he kissed me under the Moorish wall and I thought well as well him as another and then I asked him with my eyes just ask again yes and then he asked me would I yes to say yes my mountain flower and first I put my arms around him yes and drew him down to me so he could feel my breasts all perfume yes and his heart was going like mad and yes I said yes I will Yes.

Ulysses was published finally in Paris in 1922, with subscriptions from Ernest Hemingway, William Butler Yeats, and André Gide. Joyce became an instant literary celebrity throughout Europe and America. There's even a great story about one admirer who came up to him in the street and wanted to kiss the hand that had written *Ulysses*, and Joyce replied, "No, it did a lot of other things." Don't kiss the hand, it did other things, too.

Ulysses also became notorious, ranking high among those books called obscene, blasphemous, and subversive, and enters that long and distinguished list such as *The Decameron*, *Don Quixote*, *Candide*, and *Moby-Dick* that were banned, blacklisted in their own time, and are now masterpieces of the Western canon. That burden of illegality actually persisted for a long time; it wasn't until 1933 in America that a U.S. District Court lifted that ban on *Ulysses* in the United States. Now, of course, you go to any bookstore, and there's *Ulysses* on the shelf, and it's routinely included in college courses. It is so hard for us to remember now what a dangerous book it was at the time.

I actually have a copy of the edition from Paris, 1927, from Shakespeare & Company, the original publisher, given to me by an old family friend. He had actually gone to Paris as a young man in 1922, when the novel first came out. He got a first edition, was bringing it back, but had it confiscated at the Port of New York by customs officials, and it was destroyed. So he went back to Paris in

1927, bought a second copy, and this time he smuggled it in, wrapped it in dirty underwear and socks, as tourists often do, and that way was able to get his copy in, and this is the copy that I myself have now. It is a great treasure for me.

Even though it was criticized as obscene at the time, Joyce's writing is actually just realism. When he talks about the sexual content of his characters' lives and thoughts, he's actually sort of extending the kind of realism that he had already found in Stendhal and Tolstoy, taking them into the inner lives of people, into the realistic fantasies of his characters. If *Ulysses* isn't fit to read, Joyce remarked, life isn't fit to live. When Joyce was asked what he would write after *Ulysses*, he replied, "I think I will write a history of the world."

He spent the next 16 years working on the ultimate example of literary experimentation in a book called *Finnegans Wake*, published toward the end of his life in 1939. *The Wake*, as we call it, is a nighttime book, just as *Ulysses* is a daytime book, in the sense that it descends into Stephen Dedalus's nightmare of history. It is the universal dream of the human race, very much written under the inspiration of Carl Jung's "universal unconscious." The book contains all languages, or at least 60 or 70 languages that we can identify, in a sort of plastic prose style described by one of his contemporaries as a "wholesale safety pun factory." It's a vast encyclopedia of knowledge, language, and everything that will put Melville to shame and, in a sort of sense, the ultimate fulfillment of Goethe's call for a true world literature—all languages, all knowledge, put together in this one single book.

It is hard to find characters in *Finnegans Wake*. That absolutely defies the expectations of the Western literary tradition. There is no plot, there are no single protagonists, antagonists in the story; everything has been dissolved in this great sea, in this great matrix of information and language and music. In fact, Joyce said it wasn't so much literature as a great symphony, a great opera. But one of the archetypal characters who does emerge is a woman. Anna Livia Plurabelle is the name that we have for her, and she is the archetypal woman. She is wife, she is mother, she is Goethe's eternal feminine as she is introduced in the last lines of *Faust*, Part II. She is also the female fluidity principle symbolized by Dublin's River Liffey. Get it? Anna Livia, River Liffey—life returning to its source. Listen, for example, to this description of the woman as the river, the river as the woman. It is very much form and content—one more time, Cork and cork. Here are some lines from *Finnegans Wake*:

> With a beck, with a spring, all her rillringlets shaking, rocks drops in her tachie, tramtokens in her hair, all waived to a point and then all inuendation, little oldfashioned mummy, little wonderful mummy, ducking under bridges, bellhopping the weirs, dodging by a bit of bog, rapid-shooting round the bends, by Tallaght's green hills and the pools of the phooka and a place they call it Blessington and slipping sly by Sallynoggin, as happy as the day is wet, babbling, bubbling, chattering to herself, deloothering the fields on their elbows leaning with the sloothering slide of her, giddgaddy grannyma, gossipaceous Anna Livia.

I said before that the long poem as such dies with Milton; nobody has really tried to do a great long poem after *Paradise Lost*. But what is going to happen is that authors express their ambitions for a massive, artistic, complex, verbally beautiful work no longer in the epic poem but in the novel. And so here you have, in Joyce's *Finnegans Wake*, the ultimate sort of poetic expression written as a novel, but lyrical and inventive in the way we'd expect from the most experimental of poetry.

Like Shakespeare in *The Tempest*, Joyce planned to end his writing career with a short, simple book. He entitled it *On the Sea*. Just as Shakespeare ended up with his sea tale in *The Tempest*, Joyce intended to end his career with a short, economical, condensed book *On the Sea*. Instead, he drank himself to death at age 58.

And so *Finnegans Wake* remained the kind of artistic dead end for literary experimentation with few followers. It was published in 1939, just before the outbreak of World War II, and so it was very much at that end of the period of Modernism, experimentation. After the war was over, people were more practical, sensible. That kind of aesthetic aspiration and stylistic experimentation no longer seemed to be the route that writers wanted to take. It isn't a work that reaches out to much of a posterity. Remember, that's always very important that a work or an artist have his followers later on.

One of the few writers that we can point to would be Anthony Burgess in his novel *A Clockwork Orange*, for example, where Burgess has made up a language for the characters in his novel.

Anthony Burgess was a great fan of Joyce; he wrote a lot about Joyce. He has a very good study of Joyce called *ReJoyce*, or re: Joyce, about Joyce. It's a punning title, as we would expect. And he also wrote (or published) a book called *A Shorter "Finnegans Wake."* It's kind of an abridged version of *Finnegans Wake* with a really excellent introduction by Anthony Burgess himself. So anyone wanting to take the plunge, Anthony Burgess's abridged version with a very, very smart, concise introduction would be the good jumping-off point.

Notice, then, that we have one more example of a canonic author who has very much sort of exhausted the possibilities of his own chosen genre. Shakespeare, for example, had the last word on tragedy. After all, what could ever follow *King Lear*? Milton, again, used *Paradise Lost* to sort of close the book on the classical epic. Nobody can really write a Homeric epic after *Paradise Lost*; they can only do what Lord Byron did in *Don Juan*, write a kind of comical anti-epic. So it is *Ulysses*, really, that remains the inspiration for any writer who would come later with the ambition to write a big, experimental novel rooted very much in a kind of human realism, including the interior experience of a human being confronting a hostile universe.

So in the 1920s, after this immediate impact of Joyce's *Ulysses*, we find Virginia Woolf in *Mrs. Dalloway* and William Faulkner in *The Sound and the Fury* writing very much under the inspiration of Joyce's monumental novel. But notice that these other avant-garde works remain outsider novels by outsider writers. Virginia Woolf, a great writer of the 1920s especially, a woman writer and sometimes-lesbian. And then you have William Faulkner, the Southerner, labeled even as a regional writer when he is being given the Nobel Prize in 1950. And so those who had fallen in the wake of Joyce's achievement also carried that sort of stigma that they, too, write from the fringes, from the outside, not within the mainstream. Because after all, the novel has always been the bad-boy genre of the Western literary canon.

Lecture Thirty
The Magic Mountain and Modern Institutions

Scope:

Completing *The Magic Mountain* in the aftermath of World War I—and profiting from the pioneering psychologies of Freud and Jung—Thomas Mann uses the story of the "ordinary" young man Hans Castorp as a tragic-comic allegory for the intellectual confidence, based on faulty science, that fostered a suicidal trust in national institutions. Going from the institution of the university to a Swiss sanatorium for seven years and finally to the military, Hans forgets his great epiphany, with the implication that those who forget the past—including the great literature of the past—are condemned to repeat its mistakes. Originally conceived as a companion piece for the homoerotic classic *Death in Venice*, this 1,000-page literary monument grapples with Germany's cultural crisis in the wake of the Great War.

Outline

I. It is stunning to realize that Thomas Mann's *The Magic Mountain* started as a novella and grew into this monumental work of the Western canon. I want to talk about what happened in the composition process to create this increase in length and what the novel really contains as a result.

II. It certainly is not the only achievement in Mann's career.

   A. His first novel, *Buddenbrooks*, sold a million copies in its first year and was singled out for reference in the awarding of Mann's Nobel Prize.

   B. In 1912 he wrote his homoerotic classic, *Death in Venice*, about an older writer who falls in love with a young Slavic man at an Italian seaside resort.

III. In 1913 Mann started imagining *The Magic Mountain* as a humorous companion piece to *Death in Venice*.

   A. In it, a young graduate falls in love with an older Slavic woman in the Swiss mountains.

B. In the two works, we have the contrast of an older man's homoerotic obsession with a younger man and a younger man's heterosexual obsession with an older woman.

C. We also see the classic contrast between the Germanic North and the Mediterranean South, as well as an interesting contrast in diseases.

IV. It is worthwhile to examine the function or presence of disease in literature overall.

    A. The motive force behind Sophocles's *Oedipus the King* is the plague that has broken out in Thebes.

    B. Boccaccio's *Decameron* is situated in Florence at the time of the first outbreak of the bubonic plague.

    C. In the 20th century, we have disease-focused works from Camus and Solzhenitsyn, as well as a great outpouring of literature about the AIDS plague.

    D. Why such a tradition of disease literature? Because disease forces men and women to confront their mortality and face the big questions of human existence.

V. What happened to turn Mann's companion-piece novella into a literary monument? The outbreak of World War I in 1914.

    A. Mann was writing the novel during a war that Germany would lose, so this crisis was even more of an assault on his culture's assumptions and optimism than it was for cultures on the winning side.

    B. Mann's reaction to this crisis was to "circle the wagons" of the Western tradition by bringing together the classics of Western civilization.

        1. Dante's *Purgatory* also took place on a mountain, where the poet experienced education, art, and love.

        2. Mann's novel reminds us of the Petrarchan tradition of the idolatry of love.

        3. Mann's use of the sanatorium presents us with a microcosm of European culture. Everyone was there, in a highly cultivated place where art, music, and poetry were used to increase health.

VI. In his attempt to preserve the Western tradition, Mann was able to lean upon the masters of German literature who had emerged in the previous century.

A. The magic mountain had become a traditional element of German art, appearing in the works of Goethe and Wagner. Mann recollects this tradition in the chapter entitled "The Walpurgis Night."

B. In his *The Birth of Tragedy*, Nietzsche had postulated twin forces in the creative process, forces that he associated with the gods Apollo and Dionysus. Mann dramatized this concept in his novel through the characters Settembrini and Naphtha.

C. Mann also put to comical use the Freudian concept of the phallic symbol.

D. Jung was a contemporary of Mann, and his idea of the collective unconscious appears in Hans Castorp's hallucinatory dream.

VII. During his dream, Castorp has a great epiphany in which he realizes that death should not dominate human life. But he lapses into his normal state of unawareness when he returns to the sanatorium. The French cultural historian Michel Foucault examined this impulse toward normalization and ordinariness in his work *The Birth of the Clinic*.

A. In various works, Foucault describes modern institutions that are designed to achieve this normalizing process—prisons, factories, the armed forces, insane asylums, even academic institutions. In Mann's novel, Castorp has been a member of most of these institutions.

B. As Foucault noted, "there is no outside" to these institutional systems of surveillance; in other words, there are no hiding places.

C. According to Foucault, the purpose of these institutions is to "produce bodies that were both docile and capable." Hans Castorp becomes the perfect example of this product.

VIII. In an eerie sense, Mann is anticipating another German institution that would develop within the next two decades: the concentration camp.

A. It is easy to point out the resemblances between the sanatorium and the concentration camp, especially in the diagnosis of the abnormal and the use of medical experimentation.

B. It is extraordinary to see in news footage how quickly and completely the Jews in particular submitted themselves and became "docile, capable bodies" when they reached the Nazi concentration camps.

IX. Thomas Mann was already putting this kind of institutional system under criticism in *The Magic Mountain*.

   A. Hans Castorp emerges from the sanatorium normal and healthy, but he's been reduced to a kind of simpleton.

   B. He joins the army of "docile and capable" men rushing into the trenches of the First World War, and we see him as completely unthinking and dazed, singing as he tramples the bodies of his fallen comrades.

X. *The Magic Mountain* became part of a larger body of literature reflecting the impact of the Great War on both sides of the combat.

   A. The post-war years would see the publication of Joyce's *Ulysses* and Woolf's *Mrs. Dalloway*.

   B. Though on the winning side, the British were especially aware that the progress of European civilization had been disrupted, as can be seen in the works of T. S. Eliot and J. R. R. Tolkien.

XI. Mann, whose wife was of Jewish ancestry, needed to leave Germany during the Nazi period, and they settled for a while in Princeton. While there, he lectured on the European novel and the German tradition, including—of course—Goethe.

Suggested Readings:

Mann, *The Magic Mountain*.

Foucault, *Discipline and Punish*, in *The Norton Anthology of Theory and Criticism*.

Foucault, *The Birth of the Clinic*.

Freud, *Interpretation of Dreams*, in *The Norton Anthology of Theory and Criticism*.

Jung, *On the Relation of Analytical Psychology to Poetry*, in *The Norton Anthology of Theory and Criticism*.

Reed, *Thomas Mann*.

Questions to Consider:

1. Size matters. Though Mann's *The Magic Mountain* was originally intended as a companion piece for the novella *Death in Venice*, the work that achieved greater status within the canon is the novel that grew to far greater length. Are there other cases where sheer bulk becomes a decisive factor in why one literary work, even within a particular author's oeuvre, prevails over others?

2. The number of literary works about diseases raises some interesting questions. For example, does the impact of ancient Greek medical writings upon the earliest historians and philosophers, with their sense of "diagnosis" and "crisis," predispose Western literary texts to the theme of illness, even psychological maladies such as Hamlet's melancholy?

Lecture Thirty—Transcript
The Magic Mountain and Modern Institutions

It is mind boggling to appreciate that James Joyce's *Ulysses* started off as a short story for his collection the *Dubliners*. It is equally stunning to realize that Thomas Mann's *The Magic Mountain* also started out as a novella—or long short story—and grew into this monumental, canonic work of the Western canon. I want to talk about what happened in the composition process to result in this great increase in length and what the resulting novel, this monumental, thousand-page masterpiece, really contains as a result.

It certainly isn't the only literary achievement early in Thomas Mann's career. His very first novel in 1901, *Buddenbrooks*, really struck pay dirt. This novel sold a million copies in its first year. Later on, when Thomas Mann was awarded the Nobel Prize for Literature in 1929, it was this bourgeois novel, *Buddenbrooks*, that was actually singled out for reference in the awarding of the Nobel Prize.

But in 1912, he wrote another work that achieved a certain kind of currency—often taught in the classroom. This is when he published his homoerotic classic *Death in Venice*. This is a novella—long short story—and what is it about? It is about an older, successful writer who, after years of married life, falls in love with a young Slavic man at an Italian seaside resort. This older man dies because his romantic obsession causes him to ignore a cholera outbreak in Venice.

Thomas Mann, a year later in 1913, starts imagining this work *The Magic Mountain* and actually conceives it as a humorous companion piece to *Death in Venice*. So what is *The Magic Mountain* about? It's about a young man who's just graduated from college—university— and he falls in love with an older Slavic woman in the Swiss mountains. Hans Castorp's romantic obsession causes him to linger, too, for seven long years in a tubercular sanatorium despite the fact that he has robust, good health. He even sneaks out to go skiing, and he never dies—at least, not of tuberculosis.

Here we have the contrast of the older man, the younger man; one with the homoerotic obsession, the other with a more normal, so to speak, heterosexual obsession; one in love with a young Polish boy, another in love with an older Russian woman. There is also this classic contrast established by Goethe between the Germanic North and the Mediterranean South: of the Swiss Alps, the Germanic, snowy, cold environment, and of Venice, the warm, sultry climate of the Mediterranean. There is also an interesting contrast in the diseases (i.e., cholera more of a warm-weather disease, tuberculosis more associated with cold climates).

It is worth appreciating the function or the presence of disease in literature overall. If we look back, for example, in Sophocles's *Oedipus the King*, the real motive for the story is a plague that has broken out in the city of Thebes. It is, after all, the reason that Oedipus starts to investigate to find out who murdered the previous king, because the Oracle said that the presence of the murderer in the city of Thebes was the cause of the plague. And again, Boccaccio's *Decameron* is really situated in Florence at the time of the first outbreak of bubonic plague in Italy in 1348. Later, in the 20th century, we'd have Albert Camus's *The Plague*, Solzhenitsyn's *Cancer Ward*, and in the wake of the AIDS epidemic, especially in America, there's been a great outpouring of literature about the AIDS plague. One of the best—I think, anyway—is Edmund White's novel called *The Farewell Symphony*.

Why should there be such a sort of tradition of disease literature in the West? Probably because, like war, disease forces men and women to confront their mortality, the fragility of worldly values, and really to face the big questions of human existence. So you could almost sort of have a canon of works devoted exclusively to the themes of disease throughout Western literary tradition.

Thomas Mann had started out with this sort of small-scale novella meant to be a companion piece with *Death in Venice*, but it grew to this thousand-page literary monument. And what happened? What happened was the outbreak of World War I in 1914. *The Magic Mountain* is going to reflect this crisis in Western culture that was precipitated by the Great War. Mann is writing the novel throughout the years of the war, and it's a war, too, that Germany would lose. So this was even more of an assault on the assumptions and the optimism of the West since the progress and civilization than it would have been for people on the winning side in England and America.

There is a sort of crisis of Western civilization—and "crisis," all the way back to Ancient Greece, is a medical term itself. What is Thomas Mann's reaction, as a literary man, to this crisis? In a sense, he circles the wagons. He brings together the classics of the West. He brings together the great literary masterpieces and predecessors within the tradition as a way of sort of bolstering his sense of the validity of this prior tradition.

For example, *The Magic Mountain* recalls a kind of realistic counterpart to Dante's *Purgatory*. Purgatory itself is a mountain; it is where people get to be cured of their sins. These are purged away in the process. It is also a place of education, even a place of poetry and art. Toward the top of Mount Purgatory, Dante is going to run into the great Italian poet Guido Guinizelli and also the famous troubadour poet of Provence, Arnaut Daniel. Remember, it is also at the top of Mount Purgatory that Dante is finally reunited with Beatrice, and so there's a kind of fulfillment of his love longing also on his own magic mountain of Purgatory.

It also reminds of us the Petrarchan tradition of the idolatry of love. Hans Castorp makes a fool of himself with this kind of overidealized obsession with the Russian married woman, Clavdia. And overall, Thomas Mann, in writing this great novel, is drawing and synthesizing the entire achievement of the 19th-century novel to date throughout Europe. He's thinking of Dickens, Balzac, and of course Tolstoy, who gave everybody permission to write big novels.

The Swiss sanatorium also is a very interesting place to look at European culture; it is very much a microcosm of European civilization. Everybody is there. It's like that scene in Zurich that I mentioned before, at the place where Joyce spent so much of the war and wrote so much of *Ulysses*, a place where everybody was showing up from every end of Europe, all the personalities that Tom Stoppard would take advantage of in his own play, *Travesties*, set in Switzerland during World War I. The sanatorium is also a highly cultivated place; it was believed that art and music and poetry were good for the physical health. So there were constantly concerts and readings and lectures going on at the sanatorium, a perfect place to enter into this sort of cultural conversation. This belief in the hygienic quality of literature, storytelling, music, and so on goes back a very, very long way. It is actually embedded in the whole sense of storytelling in Boccaccio's *Decameron*. It is one reason these young people are maintaining their health during the plague in Florence, because they are keeping their spirits up through telling each other stories.

But in the sense of Thomas Mann circling the wagons during this time of crisis, he is specifically doing something that could not have happened a hundred years earlier. He is able to bring to his kind of sense of security the masters of German literature, the masters who have emerged in the previous hundred years. Starting always with Goethe, because Goethe also has his magic mountains in his work, he recalls the legendary German mountain, the Brocken, the site of *Walpurgisnacht*.

In fact, Thomas Mann has a large and important chapter in *The Magic Mountain* called "The Walpurgis Night." Who else is here? Richard Wagner. Richard Wagner's operas had become a real sort of cultural mainstay within the German tradition, and Wagner has his magic mountains in the opera *Tannhaüser*. There is the Venusberg, the mountain of love. And in *Die Walküre*, from the Ring cycle, there is the fire-encircled mountain where Wotan puts his daughter Brunnhilda the Valkyrie into a sleep, where she will remain in a kind of suspended animation until she is awakened by the greatest hero of the world. In a sense, this is what happens to Hans Castorp: He's put into a suspended animation for seven years on the magic mountain, awaiting for that call to heroic duty that comes in 1914 for him.

Who else is in this great lineup of the German masters now? Friedrich Nietzsche. Now, in his *The Birth of Tragedy*, Nietzsche had postulated a kind of twin force in the creative process. He associated these two forces, these opposite, complementary forces: the god Apollo and the god Dionysus. Mann dramatizes this in his novel. He has the Apollonian spokesman, the reasonable, life-loving Italian Settembrini; but he also has the Dionysian advocate, the voluptuous, destructive Jesuit Naphtha.

Who else has become a classic in the German tradition? Sigmund Freud. In 1900, Freud has published his own masterwork, *The Interpretation of Dreams*, a great, thick, monumental book in its own right. One of the legacies of this—in addition to the Oedipus complex, applying that not only to the character in Sophocles's play, but also to Shakespeare's *Hamlet*—is that this work on the interpretation of dreams has popularized the idea of phallic images. This sort of caught on. It's so easy to spot, and it's so easy to parody and make fun of as well. This is one of the things Thomas Mann does in his novel. Hans Castorp has a kind of erotic fetish associated with pencils. And as Freud said about the fetish, "The fetish is a substitute for the penis." And so, throughout the novel, the pencil has become this sort of penis image, and it's used in a really sort of over-the-top, comical way. Hans Castorp had his first erotic awakening as a schoolboy when a classmate named Hippe loaned him a pencil, and so the pencil is very much associated with that adolescent awakening of sexuality. And in the drama, the romantic inner play at the sanatorium, he will borrow a pencil from the Russian woman Clavdia that he's so much obsessed with, infatuated with—not only a pencil, but a mechanical pencil. As you caress it and turn it, the lead comes out of the tip. As I say, it is very, very sort of broad symbolism, because this kind of Freudian phallic imagery is so easy to sort of make fun of.

I'm reminded of that wonderful scene in the Alfred Hitchcock movie *North by Northwest*. At the very end, Cary Grant has got the girl. They're married, they're going on a honeymoon. They're on a train; they're in a Pullman car. Cary Grant is about to consummate their marriage, and just then, there's a cutaway, and what we see is the train plunging into a tunnel. This is the sort of Freudian sex imagery that became so widespread and recognizable that Thomas Mann is able to incorporate it in a rather comical way in *The Magic Mountain*.

Who else is here among the German greats? Carl Jung: contemporary, even a neighbor in Switzerland at the time. And by 1922, when Mann is still working on *The Magic Mountain*, Carl Jung has already developed his theory of the collective unconscious of the human race. One of the novel's really crucial chapters is called "Snow." Hans Castorp has been sneaking away again to ski. He's actually in very, very good health, a very strong young man, but he gets caught in a blizzard while he's out skiing and almost freezes to death. He has a sort of near-death experience out there in the snow storm, and in these highly stressful situations, he has a hallucinatory dream. In the dream, there's a kind of combination of Goethe's two Walpurgis Nights of the classical and the Germanic. As he is realizing what is going on, Hans Castorp appreciates that his vision, the dream that he has, is a dream that is being shared simultaneously with the rest of mankind. This is what he concludes:

> We don't form our dreams out of just our own souls. We dream anonymously and communally, though each in his own way. The great soul, of which we are just a little piece,

dreams through us so to speak, dreams in our many different ways its own eternal, secret dream.

You can see how very similar this is to Jung's description of the universal unconscious. This is what Jung had said by 1922: "At such moments we are no longer individuals, but the race; the voice of all mankind resounds in us." And it is during this dream, this communal experience of the human soul, that Hans Castorp has this great, life-affirming epiphany—epiphany, originally a religious term, now a literary term. James Joyce talked about epiphanies as that moment when "he suddenly realized." And here is Hans Castorp's mystical, universal epiphany: *"For the sake of goodness and love, man shall grant death no dominion over his thoughts."*

There it is: *"Man shall grant [death] no dominion over his thoughts."* This takes account of the fact that man thinks a lot about death. Man is the only creature that's aware he is going to die and tends to obsess and philosophize about his forthcoming death. And so the epiphany is that death should not dominate human life. But in a sad and tragic sense, the institutional comforts that Hans Castorp lapses back to when he returns, safe and sound, to the sanatorium makes him forget this high revelation that he had seen out on the slope:

> An hour later he was cradled in the highly civilized atmosphere of the Berghof. He did justice to his supper. His dream was already beginning to fade. And by bedtime he was no longer exactly sure what his thoughts had been.

Hans Castorp reenters that state of unawareness that Socrates long ago had described when he talked about the great horse preferring to sleep rather than to be awakened to consciousness by the gadfly. And why is this? Because the 20th century wants men who are not aware; they want unthinking men. Forget about Nietzsche's idea of the superman living beyond good and evil; the modern world wants normal men, men who fit in. One of the things said over and over again about Hans Castorp is that he's ordinary. He is an ordinary man.

The French cultural historian Michel Foucault, in the latter part of the 20th century, is going to talk about this impulse toward normalization and ordinariness. He has a series of works, including one called *The Birth of the Clinic*, in which he describes modern institutions that are very much there for these normalizing processes: prisons, factories, the armed forces, insane asylums, even academic institutions. And Hans Castorp is a perfect example of an institutionalized man. He goes straight from the university to the sanatorium and then to the military. He's been through the German educational system—highly institutionalized—even trained to be a naval engineer—a very rigorous curriculum to be an engineer. And why? Because Germany at just this time is beginning to challenge England's maritime supremacy as a run-up to the war, so it needs naval engineers.

Hans Castorp goes to the sanatorium just to visit his cousin Joaquin, who is there being treated for tuberculosis. And yet Hans gets diagnosed when he arrives there. Foucault makes the great statement, "The judges of normality are present everywhere." And so Hans gets an examination, and the chief physician, Dr. Behrens, and his staff at the International Sanatorium Berghof discover something interesting. Hans is running a temperature. Ninety-eight point six is normal; Hans's temperature isn't normal. So he obviously needs medical treatment to make him normal again, get his temperature down. This means there's a tremendous amount of surveillance, of probing into the patient.

Again, Michel Foucault had a great statement: "There is no outside" to these institutional systems of surveillance. There are no secrets. There are no hiding places. Foucault actually goes back to the 18th century, when Jeremy Bentham came up with a sinister idea for surveillance. Bentham called it "the panopticon." Jeremy Bentham proposed a new way to design prisons and a cell block with all the cells facing inward with just bars, and at the center of the courtyard would be a tower, and atop of the tower in a glassed-in case would be the guards, who could look in every direction and look into each of the cells of each of the prisoners. This was the panopticon, seeing everything. This will develop into modern society as the eye in the sky, where surveillance is all around us. At the medical clinic, it's the X-ray machine that will allow this sort of total surveillance, looking into the secret internal places of the human body. And lo and behold, when the doctors X-ray Hans Castorp, they discover a "moist spot" on the patient's lung that confirms their diagnosis. He's got the beginnings of TB; he'd better be taken care of.

Now, what is the purpose of these institutions? Foucault again summarized it this way: "Their task was to produce bodies that were both docile and capable." These institutions turned out people who are educated, reformed, cured in some way, and then they will be docile, manageable, but also capable, strong to do what society needs them to do.

Hans Castorp is constantly referred to as "life's problem child," and so he needs to have that kind of discipline, what he calls "the horizontal lifestyle." He has to lie and rest a lot. He becomes the perfect example, the docile body; he does what the doctors tell him to do pretty much for seven years.

Now, Foucault comes up with a very sinister view on the way that institutional control extends throughout modern society. He refers to our society as a "carceral society." It is all one big institutional prison, in a way. And we willingly submit to this kind of control, body and soul. "The matrix" was another term used by Foucault to describe this tightly knit grid of material coercions and seductions asserting control over us, rendering us unconscious even to being under the control of all these pervasive powers.

Notice the Russian woman Clavdia; she says she's using the sanatorium as an escape from her married responsibilities. She says, "It is my illness that allows me liberty." But instead of freedom, true freedom, she's really just exchanged the institution of marriage for now the institution of medicine. There is no outside the matrix, as Foucault would say.

In a sort of eerie sense, Thomas Mann, in this novel during World War I, is anticipating another German institution that will develop within the next two decades: the concentration camp. And it is so easy to see the resemblances between the sanatorium and the concentration camp. Again, experts identify the abnormal; they diagnose the abnormal—whether it's sex deviance, whether it's those with physical or mental defects—and the racially abnormal: the non-Aryans, including the Gypsies. Surveillance identifies and locates the abnormal, and then institutions are created to eliminate the infection, or maybe at least where the abnormal can be cordoned off from the rest of healthy society. There's even medical experimentation by German scientists in their white lab coats to cure these people. They tried curing homosexuals, for example, so that these men and women could again be normal.

And so here we have it, this sort of sinister extension and the kind of institutional system that Thomas Mann is already putting under criticism in *The Magic Mountain*. And lo and behold, Hans Castorp is a perfect example. He comes out normal and healthy. He's been reduced to a kind of simpleton, like Voltaire's Candide, Stendhal's Fabrizio, Tolstoy's Pierre, but he is also capable. He's not a fumbling inept like Fabrizio, who forgot to bring a gun to the Battle of Waterloo. What do normal, healthy, capable young men do in Germany in 1914? They join the military. So Hans Castorp, in a kind of mindless frenzy, automatically runs off from the sanatorium and joins the army—again, a "docile and capable" body rushing into the trench warfare of the First World War. Listen to this bleak kind of description toward the end of the novel:

> There is our friend, there is Hans Castorp! ... He runs with feet weighed down by mud, his bayoneted rifle clutched in his hand and hanging at his side. Look, he is stepping on the hand of a fallen comrade—stepping on it with his hobnailed boots, pressing it deep into the soggy, branch-strewn earth. But it is him, all the same. What's this? He's singing? The way a man sings to himself in moments of dazed, thoughtless excitement, without even knowing.

Hans Castorp is singing a Schubert song, "Der Lindenbaum," the height of refinement and culture and sensitivity, even as he runs through the muddy trenches, stepping on the bodies of his fallen comrades. It is a sort of bleak vision that we have at the end. And notice, he is unthinking. He's dazed; he is only following orders.

So *The Magic Mountain* becomes one more work from this period, part of the larger body of literature reflecting the impact of the Great War, what Thomas Mann describes in the last page of the novel as "the worldwide festival of death." So it joins this very distinguished lineup of books emerging at the very end of the war period, coming out of the period. We have James Joyce's *Ulysses* already published in 1922, written throughout the war years, and yet looking back to 1904 almost with a sort of nostalgia for the peaceful, cosmopolitan, still-unified European culture before the breakup. We're going to see in Virginia Woolf's novel *Mrs. Dalloway*, again, the post-war years.

On the winner's side in London in the early 1920s, there's a sense that even the winners have been the losers, because their culture, their sense of optimism, their positive outlook on the progress of

European civilization has been disrupted. For the British, there's a sense that their own empire, 200 years and more in the making, is also beginning to unravel, along with the power and the prestige of the European nation-states. We're also going to see T. S. Eliot coping with the catastrophic collapse of confidence in the European cultural and literary tradition—*The Waste Land*, very much born out of that despair of the war years. And we'll see T. S. Eliot traveling a path that will lead him to a different conclusion, for him more satisfying and a greater consolation—moving toward traditional Christianity in the course of his own literary and spiritual pilgrimage.

Then there is at least one other character, or literary figure, that can't be left out of consideration, and that is J. R. R. Tolkien. He was actually an English soldier; he was at the Battle of the Somme, one of the great, tragic battles of World War I. He was invalided home to recover from the Battle of the Somme, and it was then that he began imagining Middle Earth. And what does he imagine? He imagines back into the past, a primitive Germanic virtue idealized by Nietzsche and embodied now in these warrior kings like Théoden and Aragorn, even in the tenacious little people: the hobbit Frodo and his sidekick, Sam.

But there is that sinister other presence in Middle Earth in his novel *The Lord of the Rings*, and these are the orcs. If you look closely at the orcs, they are much more the infantry of the First World War. They mindlessly obey the all-seeing eye. Sauron's Tower is very much like Jeremy Bentham's panopticon; the eye sees everything, controls everything from its tower. And his soldiers are very much a sort of institutionalized military supported by production-line factories, another institution of the modern world. If you look at the orc army, it is very different from the Riders of Rohan and so on, because they are modern-looking. They have companies, they have commanders, they do drill, they even offer themselves for inspection. As Foucault said, the judges of normality are present everywhere, and in the orc world, there are always people watching their behavior, organizing them in these ways.

Literature itself, it's worth reminding ourselves now, will be institutionalized as well as we come into the 20th century. Literature now is studied at the university—not just engineering but literature, too, is a subject of university study. There are hoops to jump through, there are rules to conform with. Tolkien himself would be part and parcel of this, as would Thomas Mann.

Thomas Mann, his wife with Jewish ancestry, needed to leave Germany in the Nazi period, and one place they settle is Princeton. In the late 1930s, 1938–1940, Thomas Mann is living in Princeton, actually teaching courses at the university. Mann is invited to guest lecture in some of the upper-division courses. What does he lecture on? The European novel. He also gives public lectures in Princeton, and what does Thomas Mann summon together? The same figures that he had visited so powerfully in *The Magic Mountain*. He lectures on Richard Wagner, Sigmund Freud, and of course Goethe.

Lecture Thirty-One
Mrs. Dalloway and Post-War England

Scope:

The British won the First World War and kept their global empire, but at a price. Set on a single day in June 1923, Virginia Woolf's *Mrs. Dalloway* delves into the emotion-laden thoughts of Londoners, mostly the politician's wife, Clarissa Dalloway, and the battlefield veteran, Septimus Smith, the latter still suffering from "shell shock." Woolf learned from Joyce's *Ulysses* how to probe the mental lives of her characters. As Mrs. Dalloway's mind drifts back over a lifetime of memories, ghosts materialize on the day of her party, such as her early love Peter, a failed colonial administrator back from India. Around the time Woolf was writing *Mrs. Dalloway*, Gandhi joined India's independence movement in 1920 and Woolf's friend E. M. Forster wrote *A Passage to India* to dramatize the decline of British rule.

Outline

I. Harold Bloom described Virginia Woolf as the most complete person of letters in England in the 20th century.

   A. Her father edited the *Dictionary of National Biography*, and his first wife was the daughter of William Makepeace Thackeray.

   B. Woolf's girlhood home was visited by George Eliot, Thomas Hardy, and Henry James, among others.

   C. Her own home became a gathering place for the so-called Bloomsbury group, which included novelists, philosophers, poets, and economists.

   D. In addition to her novel masterpieces, she published critical essays on other writers like Chaucer and Jane Austen—once again, genius recognizing genius.

II. Her husband, Leonard Woolf, founded the Hogarth Press to begin printing the experimental works of the Modernist movement, the kind of books that would be shunned by the mainstream press.

A. They were the first to publish T. S. Eliot's *The Waste Land* in book form, and they published the first complete translation of the works of Sigmund Freud.

B. Leonard Woolf had to turn down Joyce's *Ulysses* because it was too big and too complicated, but that does mean that Virginia Woolf got to know Joyce's novel in its prepublication version.

C. Her own experimental novel *Mrs. Dalloway* was printed on her husband's press, and this raises an interesting canonical point: What is the difference between great canonical work and the commercial bestsellers of mainstream presses?

III. Virginia Woolf was born the same year as James Joyce and died by drowning the same year that Joyce died. Like *Ulysses*, her novel *Mrs. Dalloway* telescopes all of its action into one single June day, but almost two decades after Joyce's setting of 1904.

A. Unlike Joyce's characters, Woolf's characters have experienced the Great War and therefore carry a much greater burden of regret.

B. As Joyce had done in the "Wandering Rocks Episode," Woolf shifts the narrative through the minds of minor characters, even passers-by on the street, creating what Erich Auerbach called the "multipersonal representation of consciousness."

C. T. S. Eliot very much admired *Ulysses* when it came out, but Woolf dismissed it as "underbred." Her novel, on the other hand, is of better taste, with upper-class characters in the tradition of Austen, Stendhal, and Tolstoy.

D. Woolf criticized E. M. Forster for depending too much on coincidence in his novels, but her own novel depends on extraordinary coincidences as well.

E. Woolf found in *Ulysses* a kind of pedantry, which she thought was in very bad taste.

IV. Woolf's heroine, Clarissa Dalloway, has a name that recalls one of the classics of the English novel tradition: Samuel Richardson's *Clarissa* of 1748.

A. This was a landmark 18th-century novel, and it prompted Samuel Johnson to give serious consideration to fiction in his criticism.

B. There is an irony in Woolf's reference to Richardson's novel: Richardson recounted "The History of a Young Lady," while Woolf's heroine is no longer young but a woman in her fifties.

V. Another reference we can appreciate recalls Jane Austen's *Pride and Prejudice.*

   A. When Clarissa first met her future husband, she mistook his name to be Mr. Wickham.

   B. Again, the irony is rather lovely, since Richard Dalloway is not a rake but a stable, reliable young man.

VI. The main plotline is paralleled by a secondary plotline involving a World War I veteran named Septimus Warren Smith.

   A. Smith commits suicide during the course of the narrative and therefore is the death figure in the novel.

   B. *Septimus* in Latin means "seventh," and this allusion, combined with Smith's connections to Italy, gives the impression that Woolf is referencing Dante's Seventh Circle of Hell from the *Inferno*—for the suicides.

VII. Though now considered a very experimental novel, *Mrs. Dalloway* is actually deeply rooted in the Greek classics.

   A. She observes the Aristotelian unities of time and place—the action takes place in one day and mostly in one place.

   B. We are reminded of the passing of time within the novel by Big Ben chiming the hours. In fact, the novel's original title was *The Hours*.

   C. The action of the novel begins *in medias res*, much like Homer began his epics, though Woolf's method for recollecting the past differed from Homer's.

   D. Clarissa's party recollects Homer's banquet with the Phaiakians in that it acts as a centripetal force, bringing together characters who might otherwise not have met in the course of the day.

   E. Toward the end of the novel, there is a rather heavy-handed allusion to Greek tragedy in the form of Sir William Bradshaw, the messenger who arrives to reveal the horrible violent events that have taken place offstage.

VIII. Woolf and other writers of the time were bringing together these classical elements to feel a little more secure in a world that seemed different after the war.

    A. Even upper-class men had fought and died in the trenches, so the sense of mortality had hit English society even at its highest level.

    B. Woolf reminds us of the lingering impact of the Great War with the presence of Septimus Smith, who keeps reliving traumatic moments from the trenches.

    C. In the end, Smith disdains the idea of entering a clinic and commits suicide instead. Woolf would later make the same choice herself.

IX. Woolf's *To The Lighthouse* is, again, very much about World War I. But the action is set on two individual days, one before and one after the war.

    A. During the interval between narratives, the Ramsays lose their son, Andrew, in the war.

    B. The before-and-after element of the novel allows it to have a tremendous poignancy, a great degree of *pathos* in its original sense.

X. In addition to exploring the malaise of the individual, Woolf addressed the unraveling of the British Empire itself.

    A. Her character Peter Walsh was a colonial administrator in India, but there is something empty, bureaucratic, and unheroic about his careerism.

    B. It is interesting to note that Woolf was writing at the same time that Forster was publishing *A Passage to India*, his scathing indictment of the corruption of British colonial rule.

XI. Virginia Woolf had a very slow climb up into the Western canon after Modernism fell out of favor in the 1950s.

    A. Woolf started coming back in the 1970s, partly due to the feminist movement.

    B. But gender and politics aside, Woolf was simply a wonderful writer. *Mrs. Dalloway* established the genre of the lyrical novel, and it remains impressive in Woolf's ability to maintain tone and rhythm over 300 pages.

Suggested Readings:

Woolf, *Mrs. Dalloway*.

Auerbach, "The Brown Stocking," in *Mimesis*.

Bell, *Bloomsbury*.

Bloom, "Woolf's *Orlando*: Feminism as the Love of Reading," in *The Western Canon*.

Lee, *Virginia Woolf*.

Levenback, *Virginia Woolf and the Great War*.

Questions to Consider:

1. Virginia Woolf wrote lyrical novels but not lyric poetry—which was thought to be a masculine genre. Why would poetry, whether the epic verse of Milton or the love sonnets of Shakespeare, be considered inappropriate for female writers?

2. When two contemporary authors compete with each other, the newcomer usually becomes more outrageous and shocking than the predecessor. Think of Euripides after Sophocles, Ovid after Virgil, and Boccaccio after Petrarch. But Virginia Woolf "outclasses" James Joyce by becoming more dignified. Can you think of other writers who sought to outdo rivals by becoming more formal and assuming greater gravity?

Lecture Thirty-One—Transcript
Mrs. Dalloway and Post-War England

In his book *The Western Canon*, Harold Bloom has a whole chapter on Virginia Woolf and describes her as the most complete person of letters in England in the 20th century. And I think he's right. Virginia Woolf was another one of those very rare authors who seemed incapable of writing a bad sentence—in her novels, in her essays, in her letters and diaries, even in her suicide note to her husband, Leonard.

She came from a very literary background. Her father, Sir Leslie Stephen, edited the *Dictionary of National Biography*. Stephen's first wife was the eldest daughter of William Makepeace Thackeray, author of *Vanity Fair*—remember, the Napoleonic War novel, the novel without a hero. Virginia Woolf's girlhood home was visited by some of the great literary luminaries of the day: George Eliot, Thomas Hardy, and Henry James, the master. Her own home became a gathering place for the so-called Bloomsbury group, and so she got to know people like the novelists D. H. Lawrence and E. M. Forster, the philosophers Bertrand Russell and Ludwig Wittgenstein, the poet T. S. Eliot, and the economist John Maynard Keynes.

In addition to her novel masterpieces such as *Mrs. Dalloway*, *To the Lighthouse*, and *The Waves*, she published critical essays on other writers like Chaucer and Jane Austen—one more time, genius recognizing genius. These articles were collected into volumes called *The Common Reader*. So one more reason for Harold Bloom proclaiming her the most complete person of letters is that she covered so many bases.

In 1917, her husband, Leonard Woolf, founded the Hogarth Press to begin printing the experimental works of the Modernist movement, the kind of books that would be shunned by the mainstream press. They were the ones who published in book form for the first time T. S. Eliot's *The Waste Land*. They published the first complete translation of the works by Sigmund Freud; this is still what we call the standard edition. When scholars—in English, anyway—cite Freud, they always cite the standard edition, first published by the Woolfs under Hogarth Press. Leonard Woolf had to turn down James Joyce's *Ulysses* because it was just too big and too complicated, but that does mean that Virginia Woolf was on the ground floor, so to speak, getting to know James Joyce's novel even in its prepublication version.

Her own experimental novel *Mrs. Dalloway* would be printed on her husband's Hogarth Press, and it raises a very interesting point. What is the difference between the great canonic work and the sort of commercial bestseller that comes through the commercial presses? There's a sense of elitism that is beginning to show itself very strongly in the Modernist movement; there are only certain people—the very smart people, the educated people—who could understand the books such as *Ulysses* and *Mrs. Dalloway*, and so it's almost better to be privately published, because you're shunning the sort of popular medium for the bestsellers.

Virginia Woolf was born the same year as James Joyce, 1882, and she died by drowning the same year as he did, 1941. Like *Ulysses*, her novel *Mrs. Dalloway* telescopes all of its action into one single day, also in the middle of June, but in the year 1923, almost two decades after the action of Joyce's novel in 1904. Her characters, when you think about it, would have been born about the same time as Leopold and Molly Bloom, but now they are in their 50s, with the Great War in between and, therefore, with a much greater burden of regret than we see in Joyce's characters.

There is the famous opening sentence of her novel: "Mrs. Dalloway said she would buy the flowers herself." And this means that Clarissa Dalloway is going to leave her home first thing in the morning and move around the streets on her errand to buy the flowers. She actually lives in the neighborhood of Westminster, a kind of suburb of London, and it's a very fashionable neighborhood. As she moves about the street in order to go to the florist's shop, the action begins to resemble a great deal one of the chapters in Joyce's novel; we call it the "Wandering Rocks Episode" of *Ulysses* in which, again, characters move in the street and the focus of the narrative actually shifts from one bystander, one person passed, to another. It's extraordinary: In Virginia Woolf's version, every minor person that she passes, the narrative briefly moves into their mind to have a sense of their thoughts, their frustrations, their sadnesses. It is really quite extraordinary how it isn't just the mind, the internal monologue of the main character, but all the characters that Clarissa Dalloway passes in the street.

The great critic Erich Auerbach especially appreciated this, what he called the "multipersonal representation of consciousness," the way that the narrative moves in and out of people's minds, each of these characters with his or her own perspective on the street scene. In a way, you can compare it again to the kind of cubism practiced by Picasso and Georges Braque, showing a subject from several different perspectives, different points of view, as it's seen by several different viewers at the same time.

T. S. Eliot very much admired Joyce's *Ulysses* when it came out, and he was praising it to Virginia Woolf. She immediately dismissed it as what she called the product of a "queasy undergraduate scratching his pimples." She did have a way with words. She also dismissed the novel itself as "underbred." What she's going at here is a sort of snobbery. She was a self-confessed snob, and she was offended by the lower-class vulgarity of Joyce's novel. She was one of those who didn't like the explicit sex fantasies and the foul language that got Joyce's novel in so much trouble with the censors.

Her novel, on the other hand, is a novel of better taste. Her characters are mostly of the upper class, and so she is aligned much more with that tradition of Jane Austen, Stendhal, and Tolstoy, well-bred people speaking in an appropriate and well-bred way. Her friend E. M. Forster admired especially her ability to "combine a humorous appreciation of the muddle of life with a keen sense of its beauty." "Muddle" is a favorite word of E. M. Forster's—things getting mixed up in a kind of social setting. But notice it is only the upper class who can afford and appreciate the luxury of a muddle. For other people, this could be tragedy, where to upper-class people, it is a bit of embarrassment and confusion.

In return, Woolf criticized Forster for depending too much upon coincidence in novels like *Howard's End*. Even in his masterpiece (in my opinion) *A Room with a View*, the whole plot turns upon a very unlikely meeting of people and the consequences of that accidental, improbable meeting. And yet, for criticizing Forster, her own novel *Mrs. Dalloway* depends on extraordinary coincidences of a sort. Clarissa Dalloway's old friends Peter Walsh and Sally Seton just happen to show up in London, just happen to be there on the same day as her party, and just happen to be able to attend that party on the same night. All the characters from her youth are converging at this party by coincidence. These are the "queer elements of the accidental and the arbitrary" that Henry James criticized in Russian novels. But now, into the 20th century, authors are beginning to recognize the way that life actually turns out this way. It isn't, as Aristotle had described, the plausible and logical connections of events, cause and effect in a very coherent way. Accidents happen.

In real life, those events veer characters off in different directions or bring up unexpected recollections of the past. Virginia Woolf is including these accidents and coincidences in her novel. And anyway, it isn't so coincidental. In English upper-class society, people move in very much the same small circles, and they all converge in London. Even in Jane Austen's world, London is one of those places where people from the country will come and run into each other without any kind of planning.

When Virginia Woolf criticized Joyce as a "queasy undergraduate," part of what she meant was a kind of pedantry that she found in his novel *Ulysses*, a kind of show-off quality about his bookishness and what he's read. She thought that that was rather bad taste; it was the sort of thing that a pretentious or queasy undergraduate would do out of a sense of cultural insecurity. For people in her circles, Shakespeare and Keats are simply the cultural ornaments of educated people. It is the baggage that they carried lightly, as did Stendhal, for example, when he could allude rather slyly to Boethius under the name San Severina/San Severino.

Woolf's heroine has a name that actually recalls one of the classics of the English novel tradition, Samuel Richardson's *Clarissa* from 1748. This is really one of the sort of landmark 18th-century novels. It is a novel that partly inspired Dr. Samuel Johnson to give serious consideration to fiction in that *Rambler* essay that we've quoted before. There's an irony to referring back to Richardson's *Clarissa*, and the irony is in the subtitle to the 18th-century novel: *or, The History of a Young Lady*. The irony here—a sad one—is that Clarissa Dalloway is no longer young; she is in her 50s. There is also an interesting reversal that executes here: Her heroine's choices are different than Richardson's, because Richard Dalloway is the man she chooses to run off with, or marry, and he is wealthy and stable. She chooses not to marry the more colorful and impetuous Peter Walsh.

There's another sort of moment that we will appreciate. Back when she was young, Clarissa first met this man who would become her future husband, and she got his name wrong. She thought his name was Wickham, and of course this immediately recalls to us Mr. Wickham from *Pride and Prejudice*. Again, the irony is rather lovely, because Richard Galloway is not a rake; he's not a libertine like Mr. Wickham was in Jane Austen's novel. He is instead a stable, reliable young gentleman who will grow up further to become a stable and colorless politician. This is the man that Clarissa marries.

There's a second plot that moves in parallel (it cuts back and forth to the main narrative line), and this one involves a World War I veteran named Septimus Warren Smith. He is the one who will commit suicide during the course of the novel, the death figure in the novel. It is an odd-sounding first name, Septimus. Septimus, in Latin, means "seventh." I'm pretty sure the rather sly reference here is to Dante's *Inferno*, because it is the Seventh Circle of the Inferno to which Dante consigns the suicides. And indeed, in the course of the novel, Dante's *Inferno* is mentioned in passing the way that educated people do. And moreover, Septimus Smith fought in Italy during the war; Septimus Smith has an Italian wife. So there are all of these sort of inducements to remind us that the Seventh Circle of Hell, Septimus, is where the suicides end up. This sort of literary cross-referencing is carried on rather lightly for her, not the way that Joyce sort of hammers us over the head with literary allusions, and one is supposed to appreciate it and admire it the way one might admire a fine piece of Wedgwood china.

Though now considered a very, very experimental novel, *Mrs. Dalloway* actually is deeply rooted, maybe even more deeply rooted, in the Greek classics than Joyce's *Ulysses* itself. This, again, I think, is one of the reactions of many writers in the wake of World War I. We see it in Picasso: He had his neoclassical period; Stravinsky, also—writing neoclassical music, referencing earlier composers. And so Virginia Woolf also is writing a novel that harkens back to some of the literary standards, all the way back to Ancient Greece. She observes the Aristotelian unities, especially time and place. The place is mostly Westminster, where one could walk around in the course of the day, and it's all in a single day, that day in June.

We're reminded of the passing of time within the novel by Big Ben chiming the hours. In fact, the original title of this novel was *The Hours*. We actually have that original manuscript; it is available in facsimile. One more time we're dealing with the writer who was a compulsive reviser; she wrote and rewrote this novel several times before she was satisfied to publish it. And of course, the title *The Hours* will eventually serve Michael Cunningham in his own sort of lyrical novel, Pulitzer Prize-winning novel about, partly, Virginia Woolf writing *Mrs. Dalloway*.

The action of the novel begins *in medias res*, just as Homer would have begun his epic, and so in the course of the novel we need to backtrack, to go into the past. Now, how she handles this is different from Homer. What she has is individual characters, mostly Clarissa, remembering back 20 and 30 years, remembering spontaneously with a sight or a sound, something that happened in her youth—these characters all when they were young. And then, of course, these characters—her old girlfriend Sally and her old boyfriend Peter—show up at her party, and they, too, bring their own separate recollections of the past. We find out what has happened in the intervening years.

We find out that her old boyfriend Peter Walsh has married unwisely out there in India, where he is a colonial administrator. He divorced, and now he's come to London to seek legal help so that he can marry a younger woman who happens inconveniently now to be married to an army officer. She also finds out that her old girlfriend Sally Seton has been living in Manchester, where she's married—again, against all probability—to a wealthy industrialist and has five big sons, as she announces. Sally was this free spirit. You expected her to go off and do something incredible; instead, she settled down with a wealthy industrialist husband and raised a family of boys. And so the party itself has also a kind of Homeric recollection. It's like the banquet of the Phaiakians that draws all the characters together and then allows the main character to recall the past. It has this centripetal force, spinning things into the center, bringing together characters who might otherwise not have met in the course of the day.

There's even a moment toward the end that is rather heavy-handed allusion to Greek tragedy. Toward the end of the novel, the psychiatrist Sir William Bradshaw arrives at the party. He arrives late, and he announces that one of his patients, Septimus Smith, has committed suicide. It really has a terrible, deep impact on Clarissa to learn this. This is a moment we recognize from Greek tragedy: This is the arrival of the messenger, and it is one of the common traits in

Greek tragedy that violent events take place offstage and that there is this figure, the messenger from Greek tragedy, who comes in to tell us what horrible, violent, deadly events have taken place out of sight.

For example, in Sophocles's *Oedipus the King*, it is the messenger who shows up to tell us that Queen Jocasta has hanged herself from the bedpost, and then King Oedipus has ripped his eyes out with her jeweled brooches. Again, in *Medea* by Euripides, it is the messenger that comes in to tell us that Medea has killed her children and also succeeded in avenging herself by killing her husband Jason's new bride by giving her a poisoned gown, which acts like acid—napalm. And in fact, the king of Corinth has also been killed as kind of collateral damage in *Medea*'s plot. But all of this took place offstage, and the violent events are described and reported by the messenger. So, Sir William arriving at the party is like the messenger from Greek tragedy reporting on the suicide of Septimus Warren Smith. It totally changes the atmosphere of things, especially for Clarissa.

As I say, this is very much what other writers at the time are doing in a time where there is a sense of cultural crisis after the Great War. They are bringing together the classical elements, the great writers, what I call for Thomas Mann "circling the wagons" to feel a little more secure in a world that seems different. This is what Clarissa Dalloway herself says: "The world seems different since the Great War."

The Dalloways didn't have a son; they have only a daughter, part of their own regret. It's like Molly Bloom and Leopold; they have a daughter, also, who would be about the same age by now. And because the Dalloways didn't have a son, they did not lose anyone in the trench warfare, but everybody else did. This was a war where the upper class fought and died in the trenches. If you go to Oxford and Cambridge colleges, there are these long inscriptions of all the students who went off to fight and died in the trenches. Remember, Tolkien went off with his three best friends, and of the four who went off to the war, only two came back. So this was the kind of mortality that had hit English society at the very upper reaches of society, as well. And everybody, as a result, including Mrs. Dalloway, feels this. This is what she says: "This late age of the world's experience had bred in them all, all men and women, a well of tears. Tears and sorrows; courage and endurance; a perfectly upright and stoical bearing." And so here we have those imperial virtues of courage and endurance left over in faded form from Virgil's *Aeneid*.

Woolf reminds us of the sort of lingering impact of the Great War with that presence of Septimus Smith. He fought in Italy, that lesser-known battlefront described also in Hemingway's *A Farewell to Arms*. But now he is suffering from post-traumatic stress syndrome, as we'd call it, but they called it shell shock. He is hallucinating over his dead friend Evans, who he keeps seeing killed, and he's beginning to hear voices from the walls ordering him to kill himself. And yet he resists and ultimately refuses the help of modern psychiatry. They want to take him off to a clinic so they can cure him and make him normal again—like Hans Castorp perhaps, normal after a stay in a clinic.

And indeed, T. S. Eliot allowed himself to check into a Swiss clinic when he was finishing up *The Waste Land* for nervous problems and mental collapse. There's something almost heroic in Virginia Woolf's account of it, that Septimus Smith should decide to throw himself out the window, impale himself on the spikes of the fence below, rather than allow himself to be taken off, institutionalized, and subjected to the cruelties of modern psychiatry. It looks forward, in a very tragic sense, to Virginia Woolf's own decision in 1941, when she felt her own mental breakdown, her depression coming back, to put stones in her pocket and walk into the river and drown herself rather than again submit herself to the doctors.

Erich Auerbach singles out Virginia Woolf for a privileged final placement in his survey of Western literature in his classic study *Mimesis*. And the novel that he really prefers is *To the Lighthouse* from 1927. It is, again, a book very much about World War I. The action is set on two individual days 10 years apart—one before the war, and the other after the war. So there's a movement over the decade of this family, the Ramseys, and in the course of things, they have lost a son—their son Andrew was killed in the war. And so the before and after has tremendous kind of poignancy built into it, far more sort of pathetic in its way—in the original sense of *pathos* that we find in *Mrs. Dalloway*.

It is another example of this kind of lyrical sense of elegy. It reminds us that the elegiac strand in English literature runs straight through from the Anglo-Saxon poetry of *Beowulf* up to the present. One feels in *To the Lighthouse* that old English sense of *ubi sunt*—where are they now, where are the children, where are the optimistic adults, where, where, where? In fact, a strain of sadness that runs through English literature seems so contrary with the Chaucerian tradition of humor and mirth. *Hamlet* is melancholy. Lord Byron writes endlessly about his sorrows. In fact, melancholy was sometimes called "the English disease," and Virginia Woolf, herself, very much a victim of depression that eventually led to her own suicide.

World War I also spelled a malaise for individuals, but a kind of unraveling for the British Empire itself. All the imperial powers were beginning to feel strain after this European conflict, and things are beginning to go badly in the colonies. Clarissa's old boyfriend Peter Walsh tells us that he has administered a district in India twice the size of Ireland. And yet there is something empty, nearly bureaucratic, definitely unheroic about the heroism, or the careerism, of Peter. Gone are the days of Tennyson's *Charge of the Light Brigade*, Thomas Hardy's *Drummer Hodge*, and Rudyard Kipling's *Gunga Din*. Those heroic days of empire are definitely over after the First World War.

It is interesting to note that exactly when Virginia Woolf was writing *Mrs. Dalloway*, her friend E. M. Forster published his novel *A Passage to India*—1924. That was a scathing indictment of the corruption, racism, and overall decline of the British colonial rule in India; 1920 was also the date in which Mahatma Gandhi joined India's independence movement. At the end of this lecture series, we're going to look at Salman Rushdie's novel *Midnight's Children*, which is telling the same story of this unraveling from the Indian perspective itself. In an interesting way, Rushdie's story starts at exactly that point where Forster's *A Passage to India* had left off.

After her success in the 1920s, Virginia Woolf had a very slow climb up into the Western canon. Even though Auerbach had put her in that privileged last position in his *Mimesis: The Representation of Reality in Western Literature*, her reputation went into decline after World War II. Modernism, with its experimentation, seemed rather decadent and effete in the 1950s. Virginia Woolf started coming back in the 1970s partly because of the feminist movement. She had her wonderful lecture series, *A Room of One's Own* from 1929, very much a landmark declaration on the challenges of women writers.

Also, her novel *Orlando* opened up questions of gender and sexuality, very much related to her own lesbian relationship with

Vita Sackville-West. Interestingly, it was published the same year, 1928, as the classic lesbian novel *The Well of Loneliness*, by Radclyffe Hall. It reminds us that the literary experimentation of the 1920s was sort of paralleled by a lot of social and sexual experimentation of the 1920s, even experimentation with drugs like cocaine. We can see that the 1970s would be exactly the right time—a time of liberation, of sex, drugs, and rock 'n' roll, when Virginia Woolf would get back in again within the sort of culture and readership that emerged in the 1970s.

But gender and politics aside, Virginia Woolf is simply a wonderful, wonderful writer. Her friend E. M. Forster said that her prose "pushed the light of the English language a little further against the darkness." Virginia Woolf, with *Mrs. Dalloway* and her other novels, establishes almost a new genre; we call it the lyrical novel, a great prose poem sustaining a distinct rhythm over the length of almost 300 pages. And this is an achievement even greater than Joyce's, because Joyce has a different style in each of his chapters.

There is always a kind of break, sometimes quite a radical disjunction, in the style, the rhythm, the content, the language between one chapter and another in Joyce's *Ulysses*. It's a much greater challenge to keep that rhythm, that tone, even a kind of coloration, sustained throughout 300 pages. It is quite an extraordinary achievement of hers, and it is one of her legacies.

Remember, you need to reach out to your posterity, and so now, in the late 20th century and the early 21st century, we have some of our masterpieces very clearly within the tradition of Woolf's lyrical novel. Ian McEwan's novel *Saturday*, again, takes place on one single day and also with a sense of kind of post-traumatic stress—in this case, for Ian McEwan's novel, the aftermath of 9/11. Michael Ondaatje's *The English Patient* that we'll see at the end of this series: again, a very lyrical novel that doesn't tell a straightforward story, shifts of time and place. Michael Ondaatje actually is a poet who happens also to write novels.

And then, of course, Michael Cunningham's novel *The Hours* that fictionalizes Woolf's struggles as she tried to write *Mrs. Dalloway*: This, too, is a lyrical novel that has learned the lessons of how to be successful by studying the original *Mrs. Dalloway* itself. And of course, good novels, successful novels, very often make that leap to the silver screen, and Michael Cunningham's novel *The Hours* made into a very successful, star-studded film version. Nicole Kidman won an Oscar for playing Virginia Woolf in that film. It reminds us again that there is a sort of symbiosis between the novel and the film, that the bad-boy genre is the one also that is more likely to sort of make that leap into Hollywood fame. There is, in fact, a pretty decent film version of *Mrs. Dalloway* starring Vanessa Redgrave as Clarissa.

You wonder whether the Modernist writers would have approved of this relationship between novel and film. After all, Virginia Woolf aimed at a rather elite audience; she had her work published privately. It is almost as if she aimed at that sort of elite audience that Milton described as a "fit audience, though few." And it raises also that suspicion that anything that is too popular, that can make the leap into the popular medium of film, might not really be that good. It is a question that we'll come back to toward the end of this course when we look at Tolkien's *Lord of the Rings*, because there is the book that has a huge popular readership and also made into hugely successful Hollywood adaptations by Peter Jackson. And so, again, where is that standard of judgment that we can say a work has the kind of literary merit to move upward into that very, very elite membership of the Western canon?

Lecture Thirty-Two
T. S. Eliot's Divine Comedy

Scope:

Lyric poetry occupies a marginal position in the Western canon dominated by narrative works from Homer onward. Like Dante, T. S. Eliot created a narrative outline for his overall career. After Harvard, he studied at Oxford during the First World War and remained in London to become a poet. A friend's wartime death contributed to Eliot's mental breakdown—coinciding with the cultural breakdown of post-war Europe—out of which came *The Waste Land*. Eliot's personal solution included a return to traditional Christianity. His *Ash Wednesday* records this leap of faith, while his *Four Quartets*, completed during World War II, describe a deeper plunge into the realm of the spirit. Awarded the Nobel Prize for Literature in 1948, the *Four Quartets* completed Eliot's 20th-century "divine comedy."

Outline

I. T. S. Eliot was the product of university education. He received his undergraduate education at Harvard and pursued further study in philosophy at Merton College, Oxford.

   A. What we begin to see as we enter the 20th century is university-educated writers producing books that are ready-made for a university curriculum.

   B. Eliot provided footnotes for *The Waste Land*, making it look like an academic text.

II. Eliot had already been introduced to the Bloomsbury group in London by the time he wrote *The Waste Land*, and Virginia Woolf herself helped hand-set the type when the poem was printed by her husband's Hogarth Press.

III. In his essay "The Metaphysical Poets," Eliot claimed that the "poets in our civilization … must be *difficult*."

   A. Over the course of the essay, Eliot attempted a bit of canon formation, arguing to insert the poet John Donne into the English tradition because he saw Donne as a predecessor for the kind of difficult poetry that he himself wanted to write.

B. His attempt was successful—Donne is now in the canon.

IV. Eliot became friendly with James Joyce while in Paris and greatly admired the parts of *Ulysses* that were being published serially in literary magazines.

A. In some sense, *The Waste Land* is Eliot's attempt to achieve in a 433-line poem what Joyce had achieved with his massive novel.

B. Both *Ulysses* and *The Waste Land*, along with many other influential works, were published in the landmark year of 1922.

V. *The Waste Land* became yet one more reflection of the Great War and the crisis that followed in Western civilization.

A. The opening line of the poem is one of the most famous in English literature and is reminiscent of both Chaucer and Whitman.

B. In his allusions to Chaucer and Whitman, Eliot was connecting himself to the beginnings of both the English and American traditions.

C. Eliot cancels his predecessors' sense of optimism and life's renewal, focusing instead on "dead land" and "dull roots."

VI. Another fallout of World War I for Eliot was the death of his close friend Jean Verdenal in 1915.

A. Eliot had dedicated his collection of poems that included "The Love Song of J. Alfred Prufrock" to Verdenal.

B. Some interpret *The Waste Land* as a sort of guilt-ridden confession of homosexual longing rendered very cryptically and obscurely.

VII. Eliot defended his overall evasiveness in his poetry in terms similar to Oscar Wilde: "To be intelligible is to be found out."

A. One wonders whether Eliot was really worried about being "found out"; homosexuality was still a crime in England and America.

B. In Forster's novel *Maurice*, we have a case of how very careful writers were if they approached the subject of homosexuality in literature during this part of the 20th century.

VIII. The ending of *The Waste Land* continues to have a cryptic quality; it disintegrates into snippets of poetry in Italian, Latin, French, and even Sanskrit.

  A. The quoted authors in these snippets really give us a sense of Eliot's take on the Western canon.

  B. Writers such as Homer, Augustine, and Milton are assembled, then deconstructed and disassembled in the fragmentary telling of the poem.

IX. Like other Modernists, Eliot was very conscious of the weight and intimidation of the past.

  A. In his essay "Tradition and the Individual Talent," Eliot expressed this obligation to prior writers, claiming that no artist "has his complete meaning alone."

  B. Instead of having a sense of positive reciprocal interaction between the living and the dead, Eliot saw his predecessors as a kind of dead weight pressing from the past upon the present.

X. Eliot opened up the Western canon of European literature to include a whole branch of language and literature that had not been acknowledged before: the Sanskrit classics of India.

  A. *The Waste Land* and the *Four Quartets* allude to sacred words and episodes from Eastern religious texts.

  B. Eliot took the trouble to study Sanskrit while he was at Harvard, and his transcripts reveal that he did very well in this study.

  C. Why did Eliot make such an effort to learn Sanskrit?

   1. In the 18th century, Sir William Jones had discovered that the language used in ancient Indian texts resembled the classical languages in which he had been trained.

   2. This discovery led to a breakthrough in recognizing that several hundred languages were related and were originally part of some single family group called the Indo-European languages.

   3. The Indo-Europeans spread not only their language but also their technology and their religion, as evidenced by the similarity in mythic symbols among Greek-, Scandinavian-, and Sanskrit-speaking civilizations.

4. For T. S. Eliot and others, this linguistic and cultural connection meant that the Indian literary tradition could be annexed to the English tradition.

XI. One genre has been missing so far in our course on the Western canon: the lyric poem.

   A. The lyric poem is problematic on many fronts; it tends to be easy to lose and can be very hard to date.

   B. There is also difficulty in translation, since its structure and wording is far more delicate than the narrative form.

XII. T. S. Eliot had an idea of shaping his career so that it would fit a kind of narrative form that had become the norm within the Western literary tradition.

   A. In 1927, he became a British citizen and converted to the Anglican Church, which connected him to one of the great narrative models of the Western tradition.

   B. He began clearly and successfully to pattern his career on the template of Dante's *Divine Comedy*.

   C. Just as Dante had set up a canon of Christian poets in the *Divine Comedy*, Eliot created a preferred "spiritual canon" in his work, including Saint Augustine, Saint John of the Cross, Dame Julian of Norwich, John Milton, and the author of the Hindu *Bhagavad Gita*.

XIII. In the final section of "Little Gidding," Eliot tells of a mystical experience in which he encounters a "familiar compound ghost" of all the dead father figures of the literary tradition.

   A. This encounter is reminiscent of Aeneas meeting his dead father, Dante meeting his dead teacher, and Hamlet encountering the ghost of his dead father.

   B. This final encounter shows a change in Eliot's attitude toward his literary forefathers: They now provide a nourishing, uplifting, even consoling moment.

   C. These final lines are constructed in imitation of Dante's own verse form, *terza rima*.

XIV. Eliot spent the last two decades of his life watching himself transform into a canonic author. His style is now immediately recognizable.

Suggested Readings:

Eliot, *Collected Poems*.

Eliot, *The Waste Land*.

Ackroyd, *T. S. Eliot: A Life*.

Eliot, *Selected Essays*.

Questions to Consider:

1. Unlike the Chinese tradition that begins with the *Odes*, the European tradition has been relentlessly narrative. Dante organized his early lyrics into a personal narrative in his *New Life*, and critics extract a personal love drama from Shakespeare's sonnets. In the whole Western canon, is there a major poet whose lyrics have not been arranged and read as the "story" of the author's life?

2. There are two ways great writers attract recognition: either publishing so much that they are always in the public view—like Voltaire and Goethe—or publishing so little that each new work becomes a major event. Eliot clearly chose the second option. Can you think of other canonic authors who published so little that each of their works is treasured?

Lecture Thirty-Two—Transcript
T. S. Elliot's Divine Comedy

When T. S. Eliot praised Joyce's *Ulysses* and Virginia Woolf dismissed it as the product of a "queasy undergraduate scratching his pimples," Eliot himself must have winced, because he, too, was the product of a university education, and his literature also would have show-offy references that would have seemed to someone like Virginia Woolf as pedantic and pretentious. Eliot actually learned many, many languages—Latin, Greek, French, German, and even Sanskrit—when he was an undergraduate at Harvard. In 1914, he went to study philosophy at Merton College, Oxford—later Tolkien's college—and became even more of a university-educated intellectual.

What we are beginning to see as we come into the 20th century is university-educated writers producing books that are ready-made for the university curriculum. T. S. Eliot even supplied footnotes for *The Waste Land*, making it look like an academic text, the sort of thing that other professors would welcome into their classroom. Eliot remained in London during World War I, married an Englishwoman mostly so that he could stay in England. The marriage turned out to be pretty much of a disaster, however, dramatized in the film *Tom and Viv*. Eliot himself admitted, "To her the marriage brought no happiness … to me, it brought the state of mind out of which came *The Waste Land*."

In 1921, Thomas Mann was writing *The Magic Mountain* about a young man undergoing treatment in a Swiss sanatorium. In the very same year, 1921, T. S. Eliot actually checked himself into a Swiss sanatorium after a nervous breakdown, and there he completed *The Waste Land*. Eliot had already been introduced to the Bloomsbury group in London. Leonard Woolf, Virginia Woolf's husband, would later print *The Waste Land* in book form on his Hogarth Press. In fact, Virginia Woolf herself would help hand-set the type for *The Waste Land*. She also heard T. S. Eliot recite his poem, and in her diary she made this notation: "It has great beauty & force of phrase. … What connects it together, I'm not so sure."

Eliot had predicted this challenge of difficulty in his 1921 essay "The Metaphysical Poets." This is what he had said there:

> Poets in our civilization … must be *difficult*. Our civilization comprehends great variety and complexity. … The poet must become more and more comprehensive, more allusive, more indirect, in order to force, to dislocate if necessary … language into his meaning.

In the course of this essay, T. S. Eliot is also doing a little bit of canon formation. He wants to elevate and insert into the English tradition the poet John Donne. For one reason, he saw John Donne as a predecessor for the sort of hard, difficult poetry that he himself wanted to write. It was successful, by the way: John Donne is now in the canon, in the Norton Anthology and everywhere else. Here is one more example of the way that the Western canon almost always generates itself backwards, from the future to the past.

In 1920, Eliot even became friendly with James Joyce while in Paris and greatly admired the episodes of *Ulysses* that were then being published serially in literary magazines. In some sense, his *The Waste Land* will attempt to achieve in a 433-line poem what Joyce had achieved in his massive novel. Both works, *Ulysses* and *The Waste Land*, would be published in the landmark year of 1922. It was an amazing, watershed year in 20th-century literature; it was the same year as F. Scott Fitzgerald's *The Beautiful and the Damned*, Sinclair Lewis's *Babbitt*, Hermann Hesse's *Siddhartha*, Ludwig Wittgenstein's *Tractatus*, and Willa Cather's *One of Ours*, her World War I novel for which she won the Pulitzer Prize.

And so in this sense *The Waste Land* becomes yet one more reflection of the Great War and the crisis in Western civilization that followed it. The opening lines remain some of the very most famous in English literature, in English poetry, and when I read Eliot, you may notice I have sort of an affected British accent and sound a bit pompous, and this is for a very good reason. T. S. Eliot is one of these 20th-century writers who has actually been recorded; we know what his voice sounded like when he read his own poetry, and so it is a tremendous temptation to imitate Eliot himself when we read his poetry. Here again is the beginning of *The Waste Land*:

> April is the cruellest month, breeding
> Lilacs out of the dead land, mixing
> Memory and desire, stirring
> Dull roots with spring rain.

In this opening, he refers to April, and this automatically reminds us of the beginning of Chaucer's *Canterbury Tales*: "Whan that Aprill with his shoures soote." The lilacs in these opening lines remind us of Walt Whitman's famous Lincoln elegy, "When Lilacs Last in the Dooryard Bloom'd." And so he is connecting the very beginning of his poem with the beginnings of both the English literary tradition with Chaucer and the American poetic tradition that he sees beginning with Walt Whitman. The difference, however, is really clear; he cancels their sense of optimism and life's renewal. Now we have dead land, and now we have dull roots.

Another part of the sort of despairing fallout of World War I for T. S. Eliot was the death of his very close friend Jean Verdenal in 1915. Jean was a good friend; Eliot had dedicated his collection of poems that included "The Love Song of J. Alfred Prufrock" to his friend, and some see his emotional reaction to his friend's death as evidence that they can interpret *The Waste Land* as a sort of guilt-ridden confession of a kind of homosexual longing rendered very cryptic and obscure in Eliot's telling.

Eliot would defend overall his evasiveness in his poetry against Wordsworth's sort of Romantic aesthetic. This is what Eliot said: "Poetry is not a turning loose of emotion, but an escape from emotion; it is not the expression of personality, but an escape from personality."

But in saying that, one is also reminded of Oscar Wilde's famous line, "Nowadays to be intelligible is to be found out." So one wonders whether Eliot was really worried about being found out. Because, after all, the Oscar Wilde's scandal itself was still part of living memory at this time; homosexuality was a crime in England and in America. In 1913, E. M. Forster wrote his famous homosexual novel, *Maurice*. He continued working on it until putting the final touches on it in 1960, and yet *Maurice* was not published until after Forster's death in 1971. So here we have a case of how very closeted, how very careful writers were if they approached the subject of homosexuality in literature during that part of the 20th century.

The ending of *The Waste Land* continues to have this kind of cryptic quality, as in fact it sort of disintegrates into snippets of poetry in Italian, Latin, French, and even Sanskrit. As Eliot says, "These fragments I have shored against my ruins." The quoted authors, though, that you can see labeled as such in the footnotes really give us, though, his take on the Western canon. Who is here? Homer, Herodotus, Sophocles, Virgil, Ovid, Saint Augustine, Dante, Chaucer, Shakespeare, and Milton. There's the lineup of the great writers, all of them sort of assembled, and then deconstructed and disassembled in the course of the fragmentary telling of *The Waste Land*.

Like other Modernists, then, T. S. Eliot is very self-conscious about the weight and intimidation of the past, especially those other Modernists like Joyce and Ezra Pound, who were on the receiving end of a university education. Eliot's famous 1919 essay "Tradition and the Individual Talent" expresses this crushing weight of the past, this obligation to prior writers. Here is what he said:

> No poet, no artist of any art, has his complete meaning alone. His significance, his appreciation is the appreciation of his relation to the dead poets and artists. You cannot value him alone; you must set him, for contrast and comparison, among the dead.

So here we have it: We have the famous DWEMs, the Dead, White, European Males, and as much as that is a problem for women and other writers, it is also a problem for Eliot. And what is the problem? DWEMs are dead. As far back as Homer, there's been a sense of a kind of positive reciprocal interaction between the living and the dead. Remember, Odysseus goes to the land of the dead. He wants advice, he wants wisdom, and he wants direction, and he gets it. But for Eliot, now there is a sense that the dead are kind of dead weight pressing from the past upon the present.

Eliot opens up the Western canon of European literature to include a whole branch of language and literature that just wasn't there before: the Sanskrit classics of India. *The Waste Land* uses the sacred words from one of the *Upanishads*—*datta*, meaning "give," and *damyata,* meaning "control." And he ends with the repetition *shantih, shantih, shantih*, which means "the peace that passeth all understanding," at least according to the footnote that Eliot himself provided for those lines. Later, in the *Four Quartets*, he is going to allude to the Hindu classic *Bhagavad Gita*: "I sometimes wonder if that is what Krishna meant." Here he is talking about the conversation between the incarnate god Krishna and the human warrior Arjuna on the eve of a great, great battle. This is the same sacred Hindu text that Robert

Oppenheimer would quote when watching the first atomic bomb blast in New Mexico: "I am become death, destroyer of worlds." The *Bhagavad Gita* will encourage us in English to begin absorbing words that are actually fairly commonplace now—karma, dharma, and even the word yoga—an important concept of discipline and unity of effort in the *Bhagavad Gita*.

T. S. Eliot, as I mentioned before, actually took the trouble to study Sanskrit while he was at Harvard. A funny story from my own education: I attended the Eliot lectures while at Oxford, delivered by Dame Helen Gardner. And Professor Gardner was a great expert on Eliot; she had known Eliot personally, and she told the story about how an American professor was very curious about Eliot's education at Harvard. He wrote the registrar's office and actually was sent back a transcript of Eliot's undergraduate record. This, of course, is highly illegal now, but it was also highly illuminating at the time, because we learned that Eliot got an "A" in Sanskrit. He really did know the language and could read the literature. But why was he taking such effort to learn Sanskrit, and what exactly is Sanskrit?

Let me provide a little backstory here. Back in the 18th century, there was a man named Sir William Jones who was a colonial administrator serving as judge of the supreme court of Bangui in India. He was the sort of colonial administrator and civil servant that the British specialize in, and his training for this career was actually studying the classics at Oxford. It is sort of an oddity that to be a great politician or civil servant, they thought that studying the classics was the appropriate background.

And so Jones is in India, and he decides to look at these ancient texts in India dating back to about 1500 B.C.—very, very ancient texts. What he discovered was a resemblance between the language of these texts—the Sanskrit language—and the classical languages that he had been trained at back in England. In 1786, he delivered a famous lecture detailing the resemblances among Sanskrit and Greek and Latin, and even English. Look at some very simple words. The Sanskrit word *mata* gives us the Latin word *mater*, leads to the English word *mother*. Mother, *mater*, *mata*. They are related in some way. This discovery led to a great breakthrough in recognizing that several hundred languages, including the far-flung Celtic languages of Britain and the Persian groups of modern-day Iran, were related and originally part of some single, family group that we call the Indo-European languages.

Scholars and scientists are still studying the origins and the dating of the Indo-European parent language. They think it's pretty much somewhere in the area of the Black Sea that the original language family originated, maybe as far back as 5,000 B.C. In fact, the latest theory is not only somewhere around the Black Sea, but maybe actually in the Black Sea. This is called the "inundation theory"; there is a belief that the Black Sea area was actually dry land, that at the end of the last Ice Age, as the sea level rose, the land bridge at the Bosporus was breached, and the ocean came in and flooded this entire area of the Black Sea. This is a very plausible theory, and it also explains why these people were actually forced out of their homeland and began the migrations that would spread their language into western Europe and as far east as India.

Not only the language went with the Indo-Europeans but their technology, their pastoral developments (they had domesticated cattle), and also their religion, their gods, and their myths. For example, the Greeks and the Romans share a myth that the Sun is a great chariot driven across the sky by the god Apollo. But lo and behold, way up in Scandinavia, 1400 B.C., we have evidence from the Viking Bronze Age that they too had this myth. There is a wonderful artifact in Denmark; we call it the Trundholm sun chariot. And what does it show? It shows a chariot drawn by a horse, and in the chariot is a great gold disk of the Sun. So 1400 B.C., in the Viking Bronze Age, they too have the myth of the Sun in a chariot. Then, lo and behold, we go to India and look at the ancient text of the *Rig Veda*, and there is the sun god Sarya. And how is the sun god Sarya described? With "seven bay mares carry you in the chariot." So the Sanskrit god Sarya also is in the chariot taking the Sun across the sky.

To show you how this has sort of come back into our own society, people who practice yoga in America today and elsewhere (and yoga is very popular), they go through a series of moves called "sun salutation," and using the Sanskrit in the yoga studio, this would be called *surya namaskar*. There it is: *surya*, again: the Sun. Salutation, Sarya, the Sanskrit god of the Sun.

For T. S. Eliot and others, this linguistic and cultural connection that can be recreated among the Indo-European peoples meant that the

Indian literary tradition of very, very ancient times was part of the family, that it could annexed to the English tradition. It wasn't entirely separate from Latin, Greek, German, French, and the other Indo-European languages. Now, in a sort of political and imperial sense, it also somehow further justified the English in annexing India into the British Empire. It was almost like welcoming a family member back into the circle. As an interesting kind of side note, I am told that in India today there is still a tremendous amount of interest in T. S. Eliot. It is a hotbed of Eliot studies. Why? Because the Indian scholars even today are very much appreciative that he included them and their language traditions in his poetry.

An interesting thing in the course of the lectures that I've offered on the Western canon is a sort of missing genre: the lyric poem. It is almost like the lyric is an embarrassing stepchild within the Western literary tradition. The lyric is problematic on many, many fronts. For one thing, the lyric poem tends to be ephemeral, easy to lose, easily scattered. Remember, the poems of Sappho are mostly lost to us now, but also the lyric poems of the Latin poet Catullus are fragmentary in their survival—very, very incomplete. We know, for example, that Chaucer wrote lyric poems, the so-called roundels and Vera lays that are mentioned by him and his contemporaries. None of Chaucer's lyric poems have come down to us. So lyric poems are slippery; they tend to move away. It's very hard to date them.

There is also a problem with translation of lyric poems. The Western tradition tends to be narrative, beginning with Homer, Herodotus, the Greek tragic playwrights, very much enforced by Aristotle's *Poetics*. Narrative storytelling is the consistent way of managing literature in the Western tradition. The good thing about narrative is that it translates pretty well. You can make a mess of some of the phrasing, but still the story itself is likely to survive even a fairly poor translation. Lyric poetry is much more vulnerable; it is much more delicate; it doesn't tend to survive this kind of translation process.

For example, there is a very good translation, to my mind, the translation of the Persian-language poet Rumi. It is in the Norton Anthology; it is a bestseller in its own right. I even wrote a fan letter to the translator, I thought it was so very good. Then, not too many years ago, I was teaching Rumi in a survey course and talking about how wonderful this translation was, and there in the class, a very bright Iranian student raised his hand and announced, "I have read

Rumi in the original Persian. Compared to Rumi in Persian, these translations are mere laundry lists." And so there it is. What I thought of a good translation is so far away from the original that a native reader would consider it a laundry list.

Eliot felt this in his own career—not so much the problem of translation, but the problem of having a kind of shape, having a kind of coherence to his poetic output. He had a mentor, a predecessor, in managing this problem, and as usual for him, it was Dante. Dante had the same problem; he had written these wonderful lyric poems early in his career, and Dante's solution was to create a narrative frame of his own devising that would make sense out of his own lyrics. This is that work called the *Vita nuova*, the "*New Life*," in which he provides a narrative description of the occasion for these poems, what he meant by them, how it fit into his larger love story with Beatrice. And so T. S. Eliot has an idea of shaping his career so that it will fit a kind of narrative form, which has become certainly the norm within the Western literary tradition.

The tip-off as to how he is going to approach this challenge comes in 1927. It is a major year for T. S. Eliot; he became a British citizen in 1927, and he converted to the Anglican Church in 1927. Thereafter, he defined himself as "classicist in literature, royalist in politics, and Anglo-Catholic in religion." Once he has made that commitment to Catholicism, or Anglo-Catholicism—traditional Christianity—then he has recourse to one of the great sort of narrative models in our tradition. And what he begins to do very clearly and successfully is to pattern his career on the template of Dante's *Divine Comedy*. In this self-generated narrative of his career, his *The Waste Land* becomes his hellish nightmare equivalent to Dante's *Inferno*; the *Ash Wednesday* poems that he's been writing in the 1920s become his *Purgatorio*, describing his conversion, his cleansing, his getting rid of the emotional barrenness and sterility and moving toward a sense of redemption; and then, at the end of his career in the 1940s, he is writing his *Four Quartets*, which for him will become his spiritual arriving point, his *Paradiso*.

So just as Dante in his *Divine Comedy* is setting up a canon of Christian poets, by the time he is writing his *Four Quartets*, T. S. Eliot is also creating, or shifting, his own sort of preferred canon. You can call it a spiritual canon, much more wide ranging. And so in the *Four Quartets*, who do we find? Saint Augustine, of course;

Saint John of the Cross, a great mystic poet from Spain; Dame Julian of Norwich, a wonderful late 14th-century spiritual writer from England; John Milton, of course; and the Hindu *Bhagavad Gita*. So a very, very wide scope, but lining up for him his new spiritual canon.

The final section of "Little Gidding," the most-often-anthologized section of the *Four Quartets*, recalls Eliot's work as an air-raid warden during the Blitz in London. He imagines himself out on the sidewalks late at night, looking for the bombers, and he has this sort of mystical experience. He meets what he calls the "familiar compound ghost" after a night of bombing in London. And in this figure are combined and telescoped all the dead father figures of the literary tradition, all of the sort of DWEMs, the dead weight of the past, come together in this sort of mystical encounter. Here is a sort of recollection of Aeneas meeting the ghost of his dead father Anchises in the underworld in Virgil's *Aeneid*. Here is Dante meeting his old teacher Brunetto Letini among the Sodomites in the *Inferno*. Here is even Hamlet having his encounter with the ghost of his dead father in Shakespeare's play.

But there is something better now that we begin to have a sense of in this particular encounter. It's not so much that dead weight of the past anymore; it is a much more sort of nourishing, uplifting, even consoling moment. It takes us back almost to Homer's *Odyssey*, where Odysseus has that encounter with Tiresius and learns and profits and has wisdom to go forward in his life. Remember, Tiresius was a very important character in *The Waste Land*, but in *The Waste Land* he was a pathetic figure, a blind prophet who could see past and future but, because of his blindness, couldn't even see the present moment. He was a character out of Ovid who had shifted between man and woman, woman and man. And so he was this sort of sad, pathetic, barren character, deformed. But now there is a sense that the dead available in the past have a kind of positive message to bring forth. The "dead master" here gives a kind of grave advice, or series of advice, to Eliot, and one more time we have a sense that the DNA has passed down from Boethius's *Consolation of Philosophy*. There is a sense that the past is there to offer that kind of broader view, a providential outlook, almost a kind of stoic commitment to go forward with the kind of resolve into the future.

One of the beautiful things about this passage is that it not only recalls the encounter that Dante had with his dead master, Brunetto

Latini, but Eliot even translates into English that moment of meeting. Dante had said "*Siete voi qui?*"—"Are you here?"—and that is exactly what Eliot says in this poem. He says, "What, are you here?" actually translating verbatim. But the other beautiful thing is that these lines are written in imitation of Dante's own verse form, *terza rima*. It is a very complicated verse form in Italian. English writers almost never get it right. Probably the best example of *terza rima* was done by the poet Shelley in a poem of his called *The Triumph of Life*. It is unfinished, because Shelley actually drowned before he finished it.

So here is Eliot trying to bring *terza rima* into the English language in homage to his master, Dante. Dante would have given him, as I say, a sort of template for his own career. He cheats a little; it is unrhymed, it is blank verse, but it's still set up with the rhythms and the stanzaic quality of the *terza rima*. Here is the end of the compound ghost's advice to Eliot on the sidewalk during the blitz:

> "And last, the rending pain of re-enactment
>> Of all that you have done, and been; the shame
>> Of motives late revealed, and the awareness
> Of things ill done and done to others' harm
>> Which once you took for exercise of virtue.
>> Then fools' approval stings, and honour stains.
> From wrong to wrong the exasperated spirit
>> Proceeds, unless restored by that refining fire
>> Where you must move in measure, like a dancer."
> The day was breaking. In the disfigured street
>> He left me, with a kind of valediction,
>> And faded on the blowing of the horn.

Eliot wrote almost no new poetry after the *Four Quartets*, for which he would be awarded the Nobel Prize for literature in 1948. He spent the last two decades of his life watching himself transformed into a canonic author. Poems like "The Hollow Men" were routinely printed in textbooks, his first play—*Murder in the Cathedral*—regularly performed, especially in churches. Recordings were made to preserve Eliot's own voice reading his poems; these are now available on CD releases. Even his whimsical group of poems, the *[Old Possum's] Book of Practical Cats*, had a following and eventually was used by Andrew Lloyd Weber for his long-running

Broadway musical, *Cats*, for which, incidentally, T. S. Eliot himself was posthumously awarded a Tony in 1983.

One of the great things that we can say about any artist in any medium is that they have a style so recognizable that you can spot it from afar. If you hear a few bars of Brahms or Debussy, you recognize it. You can spot a van Gogh or Georgia O'Keefe across a gallery. And this is one of the great things about T. S. Eliot; he has a style immediately recognizable and therefore also subject to parody. Let us remember that parody is one of the greatest compliments that any writer can pay to any other.

I want to end this talk about T. S. Eliot with a 1941 parody done by Henry Reed. It is called "Chard Whitlow," a takeoff on "Burnt Norton" from the *Four Quartets*. And you'll notice that it's written and published very shortly after the original poem. So I end with this homage to Eliot called "Chard Whitlow":

> As we get older we do not get any younger.
> Seasons return, and today I am fifty-five,
> And this time last year I was fifty-four,
> And this time next year I shall be sixty-two.
> And I cannot say I should care (to speak for myself)
> To see my time over again—if you can call it time,
> Fidgeting uneasily under a draughty stair,
> Or counting sleepless nights in the crowded Tube.
>
> . . . .
>
> Oh, listeners,
> And you especially who have switched off the wireless,
> And sit in Stoke or Basingstoke, listening appreciatively to
>   the silence
>
> (Which is also the silence of hell), pray not for yourselves
>   but your souls.
>
> And pray for me also under the draughty stair.
> As we get older we do not get any younger.

Lecture Thirty-Three
Faulkner and the Great American Novel

Scope:

There is no Great American Novel, because the United States is really a mosaic of regional cultures that frustrates any unified literary tradition. If Hawthorne and Melville represent the New England tradition, William Faulkner typifies Southern writers haunted by their own separate history, particularly the Civil War. *The Sound and the Fury* opens with "a tale told by an idiot" as the autistic Benjy Compson remembers 30 years of Mississippi family history, fragmented and disjointed, like the shattered consciousness of Eliot's *The Waste Land*. The strong presence of the Negro servants contributes to the picture of a multiracial culture, as well as one marked by regional differences, even a different dialect of English. Faulkner's ongoing legacy includes the emergence of African American literature.

Outline

I.   American literature is a mosaic of regional literatures. No region is quite as distinct as the South, and no Southern novel is quite as distinctive as Faulkner's *The Sound and the Fury*.

    A. Literary history belongs to the winners; after the Civil War, the North proceeded to privilege the Puritan tradition of New England at the expense of the Southern tradition.

    B. When Southern writers did emerge in the 19th century, their Southernness was generally camouflaged or somehow denied, as we can see in the case of Edgar Allen Poe.

II. William Faulkner was from Mississippi and was essentially a Southerner, though he did get away from home when he joined the Royal Air Force during World War I.

    A. He is another writer who was deeply affected by the Great War; both his first novel, *Soldier's Pay*, and his Pulitzer Prize-winning novel, *A Fable*, address issues from World War I.

    B. In Faulkner's mind, the First World War tended to blend very much with the Civil War. In both cases, a state of bewilderment and dislocation of culture occurred, a sense of the failure of ideals and chivalry.

    C. The Faulkner family tree embodies another dual sense of failure; Faulkner's grandfather was a Confederate colonel and a novelist who had both lost the war and been marginalized as a writer.

III. Faulkner worked very hard at joining himself and his works with the mainstream of the Western literary tradition.

    A. Because he was not university trained, he was able to encounter the literary classics on his own and avoid the fatal inferiority complex that had plagued Joyce and Eliot.

    B. He famously neglected his duties as a postmaster to read the classics of the Greek tradition.

IV. The fingerprints of Aeschylus and Sophocles are especially clear in *The Sound and the Fury.*

    A. Like Greek tragedy, the story is haunted by essential taboos—in this case, fratricide and incest.

    B. The Compson family resembles Agamemnon's family in the *Oresteia*, a family suffering the long-term effects of a devastating war.

    C. Quentin emerges as the suicidal Orestes, Caddy resembles headstrong Antigone, and Jason is very much a modern version of Creon.

V. Shakespeareian tragedy also forms a core constituent within Faulkner's thinking.

    A. The title of the novel is taken from *Macbeth*, where the tragic hero describes his life as "a tale told by an idiot, full of sound and fury, signifying nothing."

    B. This title plays out in the form of Benjy, the family idiot who provides the substance of the first chapter.

    C. Quentin Compson becomes another Hamlet, thinking constantly as he spirals toward insanity.

VI. Despite his Southern roots, Faulkner had an amazing knack for connecting himself with the Modernist avant-garde in France.

A. He was such an admirer of Joyce that, while in France, he haunted the same café in Paris but was too shy to introduce himself.

B. Faulkner was given *Ulysses* as a gift just two years after its publication, and it is easy to see its impact on the writing of *The Sound and the Fury*. Faulkner's Quentin has an internal monologue much along the lines of Stephen Dedalus in the "Proteus Episode."

C. Faulkner also came to know Eliot's *The Waste Land* while in Paris; his use of Benjy as a type of central consciousness mimics Eliot's use of the blind prophet Tiresius.

    1. We now know that Benjy was most likely autistic, and his narrative gives the sense of time jumping throughout several periods.

    2. There is a beginning, middle, and end to the narrative, but not necessarily in that order.

VII. Faulkner was creating a Southern tradition by hooking it firmly with the mainstream tradition of Europe.

A. In his own works, he relied on the traditions of the Greek classics; the novel form of Flaubert, Balzac, and Dostoevsky; and the influence of the Modernist avant-garde in Paris.

B. In the process of creating a Southern literary tradition, he had to find his literary ancestors. He identified Mark Twain as "the father of American literature," but notice that he chose a Southern writer as this ancestral figure.

VIII. Faulkner also identified and zeroed in on a specific genre that belonged to the South: the "plantation novel."

A. This was a subgenre of the novel and had been written over and over again since the 19th century, most famously in Margaret Mitchell's *Gone with the Wind*.

B. Faulkner was following the trajectory of this tradition, recounting the decline of Southern culture into a kind of decadence in the 20th century. This type of literature would be known as "Southern Gothic."

IX. In terms of establishing a literary culture, there also has to be a reach forward into the future, and Faulkner was remarkably successful at this.

A. Faulkner was followed by an extraordinary array of distinguished authors: Tennessee Williams, Truman Capote, Flannery O'Connor, and Eudora Welty, to name just a few.

B. These writers not only established themselves in the classroom but continue to make their separate appeals to individual readers.

X. *The Sound and the Fury* raises an interesting question about when a masterpiece is done.

A. The story as originally published ends with Benjy being driven out of town on the way to the insane asylum.

B. Faulkner wrote a supplemental family history for a later edition. He intended this supplement to appear as an introduction, but the publishers printed it as a conclusion, where it remains to this day.

C. Once again, we are reminded of the role that the editor or publisher plays in manufacturing a canonic text.

XI. It is also important to recognize the importance of prizes in the establishment of a canonic author. Faulkner was awarded the Nobel Prize, the National Book Award, and two Pulitzers and has often appeared on the Oprah Book Club list.

XII. The problem of race in America became the driving force throughout nearly all of Faulkner's fiction.

A. Quentin Compson's thoughts on race remind us of Herodotus: one is defined by comparison to a racial "other."

B. By his forthright treatment of race, Faulkner encouraged several future generations of African American writers.

XIII. As I said earlier, America comprises a mosaic of regionalisms, based not just on geography but on race, ethnicity, gender, and sexuality as well. The portrayal of this mosaic would become more and more the norm in American literature, as we will see in Willa Cather's *Death Comes for the Archbishop*.

Suggested Readings:

Faulkner, *The Sound and the Fury*.

Nobel Prize Library: William Faulkner.

Williamson, *William Faulkner and Southern History*.

Questions to Consider:

1. Like *Huckleberry Finn*, Faulkner's novel disturbs today's readers because its characters use the word "nigger" over and over. What should be done? Stop reading *The Sound and the Fury*? Change the word to "Negro" or even "African American" in future editions? Or accept the book's historical identity and look instead at the author's message beyond this offensive word?

2. Faulkner intended the first chapter of *The Sound and the Fury* to be printed in different colors of ink, keyed to the different time periods, to help the reader follow the jumps in chronology. His first publisher could not manage this, but modern printing technology would have no problem. Should contemporary editors "manufacture" the masterpiece by printing Benjy's "internal monologue"—as the author intended—in different colors of inks?

Lecture Thirty-Three—Transcript
Faulkner and the Great American Novel

In 1950, William Faulkner was accepting the Nobel Prize for Literature. The presentation address began, "William Faulkner is essentially a regional writer." Now this sounds a bit dismissive, but in fact it points to an extraordinary and important truth about American literature generally: American literature is a regional literature, or many regional literatures—or, as I like to say, a mosaic of regional literature. This is one reason probably why there is no Great American Novel, because of the essential regionalism of the American culture. And no region is quite so distinct as the South, and no Southern novel quite so distinctive as *The Sound and the Fury*.

I say over and over again that literary history, like other history, is written by the winners. After the Civil War, the North proceeded to privilege the Puritan tradition of New England very much at the expense of the Southern tradition that was belonging to the losers in that great national struggle. Therefore, Hawthorne, Melville, Emerson, Thoreau, Whitman—these became the fraternal pantheon of authors belonging to this Northeast/New England tradition. And there are famous critical studies, like Ethel Matheson's *American Renaissance: Art and Expression in the Age of Emerson and Whitman*, that very much solidify this idea within the 20th century that there is a sort of core group of writers, all concentrated in the Northeast, all joined within a kind of Puritan tradition that formed the American tradition to the expense of any other regional literature in America.

Because the South lost the culture war during the Civil War, there is a whole lot of sort of falsification that needs to be done in terms of American history, because a lot of the early episodes in our national history belonged to the South. Englishmen first arrived in Jamestown in 1607, an event that also connects the Jamestown Colony with the mainstream of English literature, because Shakespeare's *The Tempest* is so deeply rooted in these early accounts of the Virginia colony. Englishmen in Virginia were actually celebrating the first Thanksgiving at Berkley Plantation in 1619, a year before the Pilgrims even landed on Plymouth Rock. Captain John Smith wrote a great deal about the Virginia colony, began publishing these books back in England, culminating with his general history of Virginia in

1624. You can call that a starting point for American literature, published by someone deeply connected with the Virginia colony in the South.

And later on, when Southern writers would emerge within the 19th-century tradition, they would tend to have their Southernness camouflaged or somehow denied. Edgar Allen Poe is a very good example. He was actually born in Virginia (there is a Poe House in Richmond), and he attended the University of Virginia. To this day, there is a room set aside on the old grounds of the University of Virginia as a kind of museum of what a student's room looked like in the 19th century; it is called the Poe Room, because it very much resembles the kind of dorm student's room that he would have lived in. And yet most histories of American literature tend to associate Edgar Allen Poe with Baltimore or even New York City, so that his Southern backgrounds have tended to be effaced within the general telling of American literary history.

William Faulkner is an interesting character. He is from Mississippi. He is an essential Southerner, but he did get away from home, so to speak. He joined the Royal Air Force during World War I. He did get to France, though he did tend to spend the rest of his life much as a fiction writer ought to, enhancing and even lying outright about his heroic exploits during World War I. He is another one of these writers who is deeply affected by the Great War. His very first novel, *Soldier's Pay*, was about a wounded aviator who comes back to a small Southern town after the war. Later on, his Pulitzer Prize-winning novel, *A Fable*, was actually set in France during World War I. And so the First World War, in his own mind, tends to blend very much with the other Great War, the Civil War—in both cases, wars that led to a sort of dislocation of culture, a disaffectation of the people, a disillusion, a kind of sense of bewilderment with the failure of their ideals and their chivalry. If there is a lost generation after World War I, there had been two generations of the lost generation, so to speak, in the wake of the South's loss in the Civil War.

Faulkner himself is a kind of interesting character in this way, because his own grandfather was very much a kind of representative of this loss. He had been a colonel in the Confederate Army, but he'd also written novels. And so in the Faulkner family tree itself there is a kind of combination of this sort of dual sense of defeat on the one hand—a loser within the Civil War. And as a literary figure,

Faulkner's grandfather had been marginalized as a novelist who could not be admitted into that mainstream of American literature so much dominated by the winners in the Northeast.

Faulkner himself would work very, very hard at joining himself and his works with the mainstream of the Western literary tradition. It is almost that he bypassed the Northeast tradition of America to go straight to Europe and the classics. Later on in his life, he would say in *The Paris Review* in 1956, "No matter how much [an author] admires the old writer, he wants to beat him." Notice that this is a kind of self-assurance that he can get in competition with the great writers of the Western canon. Here is a sense of the ability to compete with the old writers that you don't much find in James Joyce, T. S. Eliot, and Ezra Pound, because they were university-trained, and they felt a kind of burden, a sort of dead hand of the past. Faulkner's advantage is that he wasn't university-educated. He barely graduated from high school. This means that Faulkner read the European masters—Flaubert, Balzac, Dostoevsky, Joseph Conrad, Henry James—on his own, not within that kind of institutional setting, where he would have felt a kind of fatal inferiority complex. Ironically, later on in his career he would find himself within that institutional context. He would find himself as writer-in-residence at the University of Virginia in the late 1950s onward—Edgar Allen Poe's university before him. And so he found himself in that position that he himself had never sort of occupied as a student: a university man.

He also had spent a lot of time early in his career reading the classics of Greek tradition, as well. There is a famous story that he was appointed postmaster of the university post office in Oxford, Mississippi in 1921. But instead of attending to the business of sorting the mail, he sat around reading Greek tragedy. And the effects of this literary encounter, his own kind of self-education with the masters of Athenian plays, very much sort of reflected in the kind of literature he himself would write, and nowhere clearer than in *The Sound and the Fury*. The fingerprints, the influence, so to speak, of Aeschylus and Sophocles are especially clear within this great novel of the 1920s.

Like Greek tragedy, the story is haunted by these essential taboos—in this case, fratricide, sort of killing the brother or wanting to eliminate the brother, and also brother-sister incest: the kinds of stories of essential cultural taboos that have always been part of the mechanism of the tragic plays of the Greeks. And in this version, Quentin very much lusts after his sister Caddy, and Jason is out to kill, so to speak, his younger brother Benjy, really planning to send him off to the state mental asylum. And so, in a sense, the family looks almost like Agamemnon's family in the *Oresteia*, a family suffering the long-term effects of the devastating war. And in the Greek tragic tradition, that would have been the Trojan War, but for Faulkner, in his cast of characters, that war that cast a long shadow would be the American Civil War.

Quentin also emerges as a kind of character out of the *Oresteia*; he is Orestes himself, the mad brother driven mad and moving toward suicide. Also stepping out of Sophocles's Theban tragedies you have Caddy, very much the headstrong sister like Antigone in ancient Greece, and Jason as the mean-spirited brother, very much a kind of modern do-over of Creon from the Theban tragedies.

Not only Greek tragedy but Shakespearean tragedy, as well, forms a core constituent within Faulkner's thinking and his imagining of his characters. The title of the novel itself is taken from Shakespeare's play *Macbeth*, where the tragic hero of the Scottish king describes his life as "a tale told by an idiot, full of sound and fury, signifying nothing." In the very first chapter, we begin to see how this Shakespearean title begins to work out—the "tale told by an idiot". The family idiot is the youngest brother, Benjy, whose sort of deranged, time-skipping mind actually provides the substance of the first chapter of the novel. Quentin Compson, the other brother, also becomes another obvious Shakespearean character; he is Hamlet. He is the character who thinks, thinks, thinks constantly as he himself spirals downward into insanity and not only the temptation to suicide that Hamlet had, but the actual killing himself in the course of the story.

Despite his southern roots in Mississippi, Faulkner had an amazing knack for connecting himself with the real cutting edge of the Modernist avant-garde in France. He had gone overseas during the war and then used this as the opportunity to get to know what was going on in France. He got to know about James Joyce. In fact, he was such an admirer of James Joyce that he haunted the same café in Paris but turned out to be too shy to actually go over and introduce himself to the great author of *Ulysses*. One is reminded of that famous statement from Ovid that he only saw Virgil. You imagine a similar sense of intimidation, shyness—the young writer in the presence of the older writer, but not really able to go over and make that direct, personal contact.

Faulkner made literary contact; he received, as a gift, a copy of *Ulysses* itself in 1924, just two years after the original first printing of *Ulysses* in Paris. And it is so obvious to see the impact of *Ulysses* on the writing of *The Sound and the Fury*. For example, there is a chapter in *Ulysses* where the young university student, recent university graduate Stephen Dedalus, is walking around the city. It's called the "Proteus Episode," and in it, Stephen gets deeper and deeper into his own mind, again a kind of Hamlet figure, completely enclosed in his own sort of intellectual ruminations and self-pity. Quentin Compson has a chapter just like this, very similar to this in the way the narrative style works out. It is all his internal monologue on the day that he wanders around a different city, Boston, also thinking obsessively about his family past, his regrets, his sense of being entrapped in this Irish culture of imperial colonial subjugation, also a sense of being entrapped within the confines of the Catholic Church. And so here you have Quentin Compson at the end of his freshman year at Harvard, very much done in the style, the internal monologue style, that Joyce had used in that episode from *Ulysses* to describe his young university man, Stephen Dedalus.

Another work that William Faulkner came to know through this Paris connection with the avant-garde of Modernism was T. S. Eliot's *The Waste Land*. In fact, the way that Eliot sets up the telling of his epic in miniature, sort of an epic in 433 lines, is to have the whole story told through the consciousness of the character Tiresius, with the kind of time jump allowed, because Tiresius, the blind prophet, can see all periods of human history all at the same time. Now what Faulkner is going to do with this is to use his character Benjy as a kind of central consciousness for the first chapter of his novel, with a sense of time jumping throughout the periods of his own life. This is the tale told by an idiot, and some current researchers have pointed out that Benjy probably was a person with what we would now call autism. And when you begin to realize that autism is the correct diagnosis, then you see the entire kind of closed-in nature of Benjy, his inability to cope with reality, but also a sort of rigid sense of needing to organize his world in one specific way in order to feel comfortable with it. He has his routines, his habits of the places he sits, the places he stands, and that becomes the world of Benjy.

And so we have the first chapter told through the mind of this autistic man, age 33 at the time, skipping back and forth through his own personal history. The French filmmaker Jean-Luc Godard was once told that a movie needs to have a beginning, middle, and an end, and his response was, "but not necessarily in that order." And that is a lovely little anecdote, because that exactly explains and describes how the first chapter of *The Sound and the Fury* is set up. There really is a beginning, middle, and end, but not necessarily in that order. The beginning is the death of the family's grandfather way back in 1898, when Benjy himself was just three years old—beginning. The middle would be the date of the sister Caddy's marriage, her wedding day in 1910. And then the end of the story would be the current moment, in 1928, when Benjy is having his 33rd birthday celebrated, and his brother Jason is getting ready to pack him off to the loony bin.

Faulkner is creating a kind of Southern tradition by hooking it very firmly with the mainstream tradition of Europe. He's gone back to the Greek classics; he's gone back to the 19th-century novel tradition of Flaubert, Balzac, Dostoevsky; and now he has also reached into the Modernist, avant-garde of Paris with James Joyce and T. S. Eliot as his contemporary masters in the 1920s. What he is in the process of doing, and doing magnificently well and successfully, is creating a Southern literary tradition. It is almost as if he were doing what Goethe had done in the late 18th and early 19th century in creating a German literary tradition within Europe. And as a result, he needs to sort of find his ancestors, so to speak. Faulkner used to say that Mark Twain was "the father of American literature," but notice this is very special pleading on the part of a Southern writer to find a great ancestor figure within the Southern tradition, and Mark Twain would be the obvious choice for that.

Faulkner is also identifying and zeroing in on a specific genre that belongs to the South. And the genre that he will fasten on is called the "plantation novel." It is a sort of subgenre of the novel, and it's actually being written over and over again from the 19th century onward. The most famous example probably is Margaret Mitchell's *Gone with the Wind*, but *Gone with the Wind* itself had already built upon many generations of writers who had been doing the Southern plantation novel. In a sense, what Faulkner is doing in advance is following the trajectory, the decline of the generations after Rhett Butler and Scarlet O'Hara into a kind of decadence of the 20th century, with a sense of loss, of financial difficulty, of cultural marginalization and political weakness, and even a kind of decline of the whole dynasty itself as it comes into the 20th century. This is what is going to be known as "Southern Gothic," literature of the sort of decadent, impoverished South. Maybe this is one reason that William Faulkner always said that *The Sound and the Fury* was his favorite novel, because it had so successfully linked into the longstanding Southern genre of the plantation novel and fit so much within that kind of cultural mainstay within his native tradition.

In the terms of establishing your own separate literary culture, there also has to be that reach forward into the future, that appeal to a posterity, that welcoming of successors within this tradition, and Faulkner, again, was remarkably successful at that. The South has produced so many distinguished writers that once you begin naming them, it is very, very clear that there is a kind of regional culture with extraordinary literary output. So it would be Robert Penn Warren, Tennessee Williams, Truman Capote, Flannery O'Connor, Carson McCullers, Peter Taylor, Eudora Welty, Harper Lee. These are the writers that not only established themselves in the classroom and so on but continue to make their separate appeal to readers. Even though academics may pooh-pooh a novel like *To Kill a Mockingbird*, teenagers are still reading about Scout and Atticus Finch.

The Sound and the Fury also raises an interesting question about when is a masterpiece done. When is it actually in its definitive form? The novel was published in 1929, and in the version that came out, the first authorized printed version of *The Sound and the Fury*, there were three chapters, and it ended as a story on the day of his 33rd birthday, when Benjy is being driven out of town on his way to the insane asylum. And they make the mistake of trying to drive the wrong way around the town square; this upsets the autistic man, and he makes a big to-do until they reverse and go the proper way. This, then, was the conclusion of the 1929 version of *The Sound and the Fury*:

> The broken flower drooped over Ben's fist and his eyes were empty and blue and serene again as cornice and façade

flowed smoothly once more from left to right, post and tree, window and doorway and signboard each in its ordered place.

End of story. But it isn't really the end of the story, and if you've read the novel, you know that that is not the ending that we now have in the current published versions of *The Sound and the Fury*.

This is what happened. In 1945 Faulkner was asked to write a supplemental family history entitled "Compson, 1699–1945." This was going to be published in the new *Portable Faulkner* being published by the Viking Press. And when he did this, Faulkner immediately realized the advantage of explaining the whole family history, the dynasty, giving an objective look at the scene to which his more experimental storytelling made reference. He actually said, "I should have done this when I wrote the book" and then concluded: "Then the whole thing would have fallen into pattern like a jigsaw puzzle when the magician's wand touched it."

Faulkner wrote this supplemental section on the Compson dynasty as a kind of lead-in. He wanted it printed first, as an introduction, when the novel was reprinted by Random House in their Modern Library edition. But instead of having it printed first, it was printed last. And that is where it remains to this day. It is the fourth and final chapter of *The Sound and the Fury*. But notice, this is not what the author, Faulkner himself, ever intended. Number one, he didn't have it in the first edition in 1929, and when he did write it in 1945, he wanted it as an introduction, not as a conclusion.

So here we have, right in the 20th century, a reminder one more time that it is the editor, the publisher, who very much manufactures the canonic text as we have it. Remember again, it was the Athenian and the Alexandrian scholars in the libraries who gave us Homer in the version we have. They were the editors that divided the *Iliad* and the *Odyssey* into 24 books. The Bible remains this sort of paradigm of a central literary text very much the creation of its early editors. It was Eusebius of Caesarea, remember, who made this crucial decision to combine the New Testament with the Old Testament in one single volume. Chaucer's *Canterbury Tales*, as we have it now, is very much the product of a scribe. We now know his name, Adam Pinkhurst, and he put the fragments of the unfinished work into an order in the Ellesmere manuscript that now becomes our received text. There's no indication that that was Chaucer's arrangement, but that's what we have. Shakespeare's plays were divided into five acts by his editors. Interestingly, Ezra Pound gives us the version of Eliot's *Waste Land* that we read. Eliot had given him the typescript; Pound went through with a blue pencil, and then Eliot accepted every cut that Ezra Pound had suggested, giving us the published poem that we still deal with.

Also important to realize is the importance of prizes, all the way back to the Dionysian competition, and Faulkner begins to make his way into the canon because of the prizes he won. He started at the top of the ladder, winning the Nobel Prize for Literature, and then later on the National Book Award for his collected stories. His novel *A Fable* won the National Book Award again and a Pulitzer Prize, and his last novel, *The Reivers*, won a second Pulitzer Prize posthumously in 1963. Faulkner appreciated the importance of prizes like this for new and up-and-coming writers, and so part of his Nobel Prize money actually went to contribute to a fund to support and encourage new fiction writers. This is still around—we call it the PEN/Faulkner Award—and very important for launching the career of a young novelist.

In our day and time, one of the big prizes is to end up on the Oprah Book Club list. And lo and behold, Faulkner is very ably represented there with *As I Lay Dying*, *Light in August*, and of course *The Sound and the Fury*. And why such prominence on Oprah's list? Because Faulkner tackled the big question of the African American experience in the old South.

Back in 1903, W. E. B. Du Bois had predicted in his book *The Souls of Black Folk* that "the problem of the 20th century is the problem of the color line." And this is the problem, then, that becomes the driving force throughout nearly all of Faulkner's fiction. Listen to the suicidal Quentin Compson as he reflects on race issues, walking the streets of Boston:

> When I first came East I kept thinking You've got to remember to think of them as colored people not niggers, and if it hadn't happened that I wasn't thrown with many of them, I'd have wasted a lot of time and trouble before I learned that the best way to take all people, black or white, is to take them for what they think they are, then leave them alone. That was when I realised that a nigger is not a person

so much as a form of behavior; a sort of obverse reflection of the white people he lives among.

Faulkner sounds almost like Herodotus way back in *The Histories*, defining one's own self by a kind of racial otherness. So what is white? It is everything that is not Negro. What is Negro? It is everything that is not white, despite, or disregarding, the actual racial identity of that individual. The truest word at the end of the novel really has to do with the Negro characters, the house family, and especially Dilsey, the matriarch, who has been that stability within a family otherwise deteriorating. The last words in the novel as we have it now: "They endured."

This is the strain within Faulkner's fiction that reaches into the future to encourage a whole second posterity for him and his Southern literature. What he has encouraged, by his very forthright address of racial issues in the old South, is a whole generation, several generations, of African American writers, writers like Zora Neal Hurston and Alex Haley, famous for his bestselling family history, *Roots*. And beyond that, there will be African American women writers like Alice Walker and Toni Morrison. And beyond that, there will be African American gay women writers, like Audre Lorde and Ann Allen Shockley.

So here you have it: As I said at the beginning of the lecture, American literature is a mosaic of regions. Some of these regions are geographic; you have the North, especially the Northeast; the South, the traditional South, the loser in the Civil War; eventually there will be the Plains states; there will be the Southwest with its Hispanic heritage, as well. But there are other kinds of regionalisms by which Americans create the mosaic of a national identity, and these regionalisms will be based not on place but on race, on ethnicity, gender, and sexuality. It is, as I say, one good explanation of why we don't have that one, single book that we can point to and say, "It is the Great American Novel," because that would presume a single, homogenous culture, a national culture that would give rise to that one book, and instead we have this mosaic of identities within our culture.

And it isn't new. Probably one of the reasons why *Moby-Dick* continues to stand there in the first half of the 19th century as a kind of prototype for the sort of fictions that will evolve in the future of the American tradition is because the crew of the whaling ship is that original, multiracial mix of people. The three harpoonists are a very clear microcosm of that mix: one of them, the American Indian; another, the African; and the third, the Pacific Islander. As we move forward, this is going to become more and more the norm within our literature, and one reason that I want to move next to Willa Cather's *Death Comes for the Archbishop* is because she focuses on a wholly different region, New Mexico, where there's a wholly different mix of ethnic and racial and language cultures, so that there is going to be a moving together of the old American Indian culture, the longstanding Hispanic culture, and English-speaking Yankee culture. They're meeting in 19th-century New Mexico, along with the most unlikely of outsiders: two French priests sent by the Roman Church.

Lecture Thirty-Four
Willa Cather and Mosaics of Identity

Scope:

Cather wrote *Death Comes for the Archbishop* about New Mexico as a region with a completely different history going back to Spanish conquistadors and Franciscan missionaries, including a different literary history starting with De Villagrá's epic *History of New Mexico* (1610). As a pioneer and rugged individualist, the French Bishop Latour arrives as the complete outsider in a multicultural society of Native Americans, old Hispanic settlers, and new Yankee soldiers and merchants. By the end of the 20th century, English literature is no longer strictly English, or even mainstream American, but a mosaic of writings based on the minority identities of African American, Native American, Latino American, and Asian American voices, as well as the other minority voices defining themselves through gender and sexuality.

Outline

I. We can hardly overestimate the role played by librarians in the creation of a canonic literary tradition.

   A. In ancient times, the librarians at Alexandria and Caesarea picked out which texts to edit and preserve.

   B. I read Willa Cather's *Death Comes for the Archbishop* because my high school librarian put it on a list of recommended readings.

   C. *Death Comes for the Archbishop* has also appeared on lists of great books compiled by *The American Oxonian* magazine and Modern Library.

II. Cather was born in Virginia and might well have become a well-known Southern writer a generation before Faulkner if her family hadn't moved to Nebraska when she was a child.

   A. She, too, wrote a World War I novel, *One of Ours*, about a veteran returning from the war and suffering disillusionment, unhappiness, and the restlessness of a lost generation.

   B. In reaction to the war, Cather reached back into the pioneering era of the 19th-century American West, when gallant deeds and old-fashioned virtues could still be described without cynicism.

III. Cather's New Mexico novel opens up a whole alternative history for the United States and also suggests other traditions within American literary history.

    A. This region has a very different history from the one taught on the East Coast, where people trace their national and state histories back to the arrival of the Puritans.

    B. The area was first crossed by Franciscan missionaries in 1539, well before the English began settling in the New World. In 1610, Pedro de Peralta established the Spanish colonial outpost at Santa Fe, which remains the oldest capitol of any U.S. state.

    C. In that same year, Gaspar Pérez de Villagrá published his epic poem *History of New Mexico*, modeled very much after Virgil's *Aeneid*.

IV. In this way, political and literary history in New Mexico can claim priority over New England and Virginia, but it is a different history with different major events.

    A. After decades of unrest and revolt, the region was fully pacified after the reconquest of 1692 and finally became a part of Mexico during its war of independence.

    B. The region of New Mexico was ceded to the United States in 1846, but it did not become a full-fledged state until 1912. It is this "territorial period" on which I want to focus, because it was in this Wild West atmosphere that Cather set her novel.

    C. This region had distinctive literary milestones as well, including *Ben-Hur: A Tale of the Christ* by the territorial governor of Mexico, Lew Wallace.

V. Novels like Cooper's *The Last of the Mohicans* laid the foundation for the frontier novel of the 19th century.

    A. There was a real heyday for these cowboy novels in the 1870s and 1880s.

    B. The tradition continues in contemporary American literature, with works like E. Annie Proulx's *Close Range: Wyoming Stories*.

C. Proulx's achievement underscores the unlikelihood of a woman writing these cowboy stories of the Old West. Willa Cather was already feeling this challenge long before she wrote *Death Comes for the Archbishop*.

VI. The main character in Cather's novel is Jean-Marie Latour, who was based on the real-life Archbishop Jean Baptiste Lamy.

A. Lamy had arrived in Sante Fe in 1851 and lived to see the region transformed and its own cathedral rising.

B. Cather's protagonist of the archbishop conforms to type, in a sense: He is a pioneer but is even more of an outsider than this term suggests.

C. He has been sent from Rome, and what we have here is a parallel history of colonialism: the religious colonialism embodied earlier by Saint Augustine.

D. Latour manifests the kind of paternalism that accompanies imperialism—what Kipling called "the white man's burden."

E. Latour had come to New Mexico to tame the wilderness and to shape up a corrupt priesthood, and after many struggles he does accomplish this. Part of the power of this novel is this sense of one world giving way to another.

VII. Cather's novel does not seem experimental, but it is very much a part of the Modernist experimentation with form and structure.

A. Its narrative constantly digresses into local history and vignettes of the New Mexico past.

B. The loosely connected episodes consciously, I think, recall the "land sagas" of Iceland, which were enjoying a vogue in European and American readership at the time the novel was written.

VIII. It is said that Cather was inspired to write her novel after visiting the Cross of the Martyrs in Santa Fe. This initial inspiration influenced the subject of the novel itself.

A. It reads like a Christian martyrology or saint's life. There are trials and tribulations and spiritual doubts along the way, yet with perseverance and divine intervention, Latour succeeds.

B. Like a good saint's life, the story even contains a miracle.

C. This reminds us that the novel itself has a special debt to the saint's life, which was one of the early types of European prose biographies that underlie the novel form.

IX. Fiedler's idea of "innocent homosexuality" is easy to see in *Death Comes for the Archbishop*, despite all of the landscape and local history.

A. The central storyline of the novel involves the archbishop's lifelong friendship with his fellow priest, Father Vaillent.

B. When the archbishop is dying, he does not think of Christ and Mary; he thinks about his boyhood friend.

C. In this way, the story joins the tradition of heroic, manly yarns going all the way back to *Beowulf* and *Gilgamesh*.

X. This innocent homosexuality is not at all unexpected, because of Cather's own same-sex values.

A. As a young woman, Cather conscientiously took on many male attributes, and she had several relationships with women over her lifetime.

B. She was very secretive about these matters for the same reason that Forster was discreet: because homosexuality continued to be illegal, and such a scandal could wreck a writer's life.

XI. In her critical writing, Cather tended to focus on writers from what could be called a "gay canon."

A. In terms of canon formation, Cather's lesbianism actually worked in her favor in the 1970s, when there was a renewed interest in staking out one's own claims for a particular sexuality.

B. It is now rather routine in literary academics to take specific interest in gay or possibly gay writers, as it points to a unique sexual identity that fits into the larger picture of America as a mosaic of identities.

C. Cather's novel gives us an extraordinary coming together of this mosaic, and it bespeaks a new direction in American literature, where the ethnic minority peoples begin to write their own literature.

Suggested Readings:

Cather, *Death Comes for the Archbishop*.

Lee, *Willa Cather*.

Swift, *Willa Cather and the American Southwest*.

Questions to Consider:

1. How well has Willa Cather produced her "story of adventure, … a manly battle yarn, anything without wine, women, and love," to show that a woman writer does not need to restrict herself to the romance-driven fiction of Jane Austen?

2. Does *Death Comes for the Archbishop* make a surprisingly strong claim as the Great American Novel because it taps into the core narrative of the national experience—immigrants taming the wilderness—while bringing together so many different ethnic participants in this epic adventure?

Lecture Thirty-Four—Transcript
Willa Cather and the Mosaics of Identity

We could hardly overestimate the role played by librarians in the creation of a canonic tradition in literature. All the way back to ancient times, it was the librarians at Alexandria and Caesarea who were picking out which texts to edit, to copy, and to preserve in their collections. Even before that, in ancient Mesopotamia, it was the caretakers of the royal libraries who were determining which clay tablets to preserve and which ones to catalog in their list-making enterprises. Remember, as a teenager, I myself read Willa Cather's New Mexico novel *Death Comes for the Archbishop* specifically because my high school librarian, Ms. Cunningham, had put it on that one-page list of books that she recommended for high school students to read.

Imagine my surprise, then, when not too many years ago the editor of *The American Oxonian Magazine* asked a number of distinguished former Rhodes Scholars to list their favorite books and novels. One of the individuals asked to submit a list was Daniel Boorstin, who was Librarian of Congress. When all of these lists were put together in *The American Oxonian*, it was interesting to see how often *Death Comes for the Archbishop* appeared on those lists. Then again, in 1998, Daniel Boorstin again was asked to join a distinguished group of literary men—Gore Vidal, Shelby Foote, and William Styron—on a committee to compile a list for the Modern Library of the hundred best novels in the English language. Not too surprisingly, topping the list was James Joyce's *Ulysses*, followed by novels from the pens of Virginia Woolf, William Faulkner, and Salman Rushdie. And on this list, Willa Cather's *Death Comes for the Archbishop* ranks in at number 61.

Here you have it: The list-making enterprise will come up with certain titles over and over again, and one of the winners on the list drawn up by librarians, including the Librarian of Congress, will be Willa Cather's famous New Mexico novel. Cather herself was born in Virginia and might well have become yet one more Southern writer a generation before Faulkner. But even when she was a child, her family relocated and moved to Nebraska, and this Plains state, then, would become the setting for her best-known novels such as *O Pioneers!* and *A Lost Lady*.

But she also wrote her own World War I novel, *One of Ours*, and it actually won the Pulitzer Prize for 1922. It was a novel about a veteran coming back after the war and suffering a sort of disillusionment, unhappiness, and restlessness of the lost generation. There's more than one way to react to the sort of fallout of the First World War. One was to describe the current disillusionment; another was to retreat back into the past. This is going to be the route that J. R. R. Tolkien takes, retracing man's history back to the dawn of recorded history, where heroism was still imaginable. This is also what Willa Cather is going to do, going back only to the pioneering era of the 19th century in the American West, when these gallant deeds were still possible and old fashioned virtues like courage, tenacity, and rugged individualism were still describable without cynicism.

Willa Cather's New Mexico novel opens up a whole sort of alternative history for United States and also suggests other traditions within the American literary history itself. In terms of history, this region has a very, very different one from the one I was taught in Virginia as a schoolboy, very different from the history taught in New England states, where people would of course trace their national and state histories back to the arrival of the Puritans. In New Mexico, the area was first crossed by Franciscan missionaries from Spain in 1539. 1539! This is long before the English are beginning to explore with Sir Walter Raleigh and Sir Francis Drake. In 1598, there is a full-scale military invasion of the area led by Juan de Oñate; it's a campaign specifically against the Pueblo Indians in this part of the Southwest and very clearly an effort to extend the power of the Spanish Empire into this large region in what is now the southwest part of the United States.

In 1610, a full decade before the Pilgrims landed on Plymouth Rock, Pedro de Peralta establishes his colonial outpost at Santa Fe, Santa Fe remaining even to this day the oldest capital of any U.S. state. In that same year of 1610, there was a literary event, as well. Gaspar Pérez de Villagrá published his epic poem the *History of New Mexico*, describing Oñate's campaign and modeling that campaign and the literary work itself very much after Virgil's *Aeneid*. This is signaled in the opening line of his epic history, where he says, "I sing of arms and the heroic man," a very clear echo, especially in Spanish, of the first line of the *Aeneid*, "*Arma virumque cano*."

Like the Roman epic, his story is about conquering and taking possession and bringing civilization to what they perceived as a savage and heathen land. It also contains accounts that continue to echo over the centuries of brutal treatment of some of the native Indians of the territory, especially the famous episode at the Acoma Pueblo, where they cut feet off the Indians to punish them for what the Spanish saw as disobedience and resistance to their campaign.

And so American History and literary history in New Mexico can actually claim priority over Massachusetts and even Virginia. It is a different history, with different major events unfolding over the generations. For example, in the mid-17th century in Santa Fe, the Spanish Inquisition had arrived, and they were burning heretics and Jews in the plaza of Santa Fe. This would be the historical equivalent to the Salem witch trials in New England, though not nearly as well known today. In 1680, there was what we call the Pueblo Revolt. The Indians organized and rose up against the Spanish missionaries, mostly Franciscans, in their churches at the various pueblos. It actually forced the Spanish to retreat from their capital at Santa Fe. They came back a dozen years later, and there was what we call the reconquest of 1692, led by Diego de Vargas. This region, then, was fully pacified after the reconquest of the 18th century and then finally became part of Mexico during its own war of independence in the earlier 19th century. In fact, the Mexican War of Independence can almost be seen as an extension of the Napoleonic Wars into the Americas.

The region of New Mexico was ceded to the United States in 1846, following the U.S.-Mexican War, and yet it didn't actually become a member of the United States, a full-fledged state, until 1912. This is a long story in itself, partly explained by this xenophobia of the mainstream Americans on the East Coast, because most of the population in Mexico was nonwhite, non-English-speaking, and in fact mostly Catholic. It is important to sort of remember that there was tremendous anti-Catholic bias in the United States until fairly recent decades. This gives an even more interesting spin to the story in which the hero is a Catholic archbishop.

But it is this period I want to focus on, between the New Mexico territory coming into U.S. possession and statehood in 1912. This is what we call the "territorial period," very much a period of the Wild West in New Mexico. This is a time of Kit Carson and Billy the Kid, and this is the period in which Willa Cather will set the action of her novel *Death Comes for the Archbishop.* In terms of regional literature, this part of the country is going to have its distinctive milestones as well, and one of the most curious ones is the writing of *Ben-Hur: A Tale of the Christ.* This book by Lew Wallace is going to become the bestselling American novel of the 19th century. It outsold *Uncle Tom's Cabin*, and it would hold the record as the bestselling American novel until Margaret Mitchell's *Gone with the Wind* came along. And the interesting thing is that Lew Wallace wrote *Ben-Hur* while he was serving as territorial governor of New Mexico in the late 1870s. Though there seems to be no relationship between this story set in biblical times and the place where Lew Wallace happened to find himself as territorial governor, you can certainly understand how the very, very ancient Christian culture of that part of the country, also with its very ingrained Catholic practices, could have encouraged him (as, indeed, it later encouraged Willa Cather) to think of a story with a very strong Christian message and content to it.

In the course of her novel *Death Comes for the Archbishop*, Willa Cather actually mentions the "romances of Fenimore Cooper," and these are books not much read. They were certainly on my high school recommended list from the librarian—these would include *The Last of the Mohicans* and so on—but these are the novels that, in a sense, laid the foundation for the frontier novel that would eventually become the cowboy fiction of the 19th century. These are the famous dime novels, which sometimes rose to literary status as well. Mark Twain wrote his *Roughing It* as an example of the kind of cowboy fiction from the period. It is interesting to remember that at the end of *Huckleberry Finn*, the hero is said to, "he lights out for the territory." Clearly, Huck Finn himself is going West to join that kind of cowboy culture in the Wild, Wild West.

So there is a real heyday in these cowboy novels in the 1870s, 1880s. Some of them became classics that are still with us—at least as titles now: Owen Wister's *The Virginian* and Zane Grey's *Riders of the Purple Sage*. There continues to be a kind of cowboy fiction being written even in contemporary American literature—Cormac McCarthy's *All the Pretty Horses* and other novels of his from the West; Larry McMurtry's *Lonesome Dove* series; even Annie Proulx's Wyoming stories and, most famously, "Brokeback

Mountain," made into an Oscar-winning screenplay coauthored by Larry McMurtry.

The interesting thing about Annie Proulx's achievement is that it underscores how unlikely it would be for a woman to be writing these cowboy stories of the Old West. The challenge was already felt by Willa Cather herself. Back in 1895, long before she came to think about a New Mexico novel, Willa Cather reflected on previous women novelists, including Jane Austen, whom she called "the greatest of them all." But then she felt a special challenge breaking beyond the limits that were usually imposed upon women to write the so-called social novel. This is what Willa Cather was already thinking in 1895:

> When a woman writes a story of adventure, a stout sea tale, a manly battle yarn, anything without wine, women and love, then I will begin to hope for something great from them, not before.

And so, in a sense, years and years later, *Death Comes for the Archbishop* will become exactly that for her: a story of adventure written by a woman, but without the wine, women, and love in the story.

Willa Cather first came to New Mexico in 1912, the year of statehood, and started a fascination with this very sort of strange and alien region within the United States. In the 1920s, she was back vacationing in Santa Fe, staying at the famous La Fonda Hotel, still to this day called The Inn at the End of the Trail. While she was vacationing in Santa Fe, she came upon a book that she spent evenings reading. It was by William Howlett and called *Life of the Right Reverend Joseph P. Machebeuf.* It really focused her interest on local history and would, in fact, provide a tremendous amount of background information for her forthcoming novel and especially the secondary character, Father Vaillent, in *Death Comes for the Archbishop.*

Her main character in this New Mexico novel is called Jean-Marie Latour, but based on the real-life and sort of bigger-than-life character of Archbishop John Baptiste Lamy. Lamy had arrived in Santa Fe in 1851 and then lived long enough to see the region transformed and its own cathedral rising. It is interesting: He came personally from the South of France, so when he built this new cathedral in Santa Fe for his diocese, he decided not to use the local mission style but to build it after the design of Provence in the South of France. If you go there today, here is this Romanesque cathedral in the French model in the middle of the adobe town of Santa Fe, very much the legacy of the French archbishop.

Willa Cather's protagonist of the archbishop really conforms to type, in a sense; he is a pioneer, he is a rugged individualist, and yet he is even more of an alien outsider than most of these drifters and these loners tend to be. He has been sent directly by the authorities in Rome; the first chapter in the novel actually takes place in Rome. And what we have then is a sort of parallel history of colonialism. It is a sort of history we've seen from the late Roman period, when Saint Augustine served as a governor and a bishop in his own region. It is a sense of sort of religious invasion in colonialism that the Venerable Bede was describing in his *Ecclesiastical History of the English People*. But now we don't have Roman legions anymore; we have Roman priests coming as missionaries. They also bring that sort of imperial notion summed up in Rudyard Kipling's phrase, "the white man's burden." Archbishop Latour very much embodies that kind of paternalism toward his flock. He's dealing with the nonwhite peoples, the American Indians and the Hispanics, and he has that sense of being a father to them in that sort of colonial, paternalistic manner.

What is his goal when he reaches his new diocese in New Mexico? It is to tame the wilderness and specifically to shape up a corrupt and negligent priesthood. And he does this—many battles, many confrontations, long struggle, eventually to bring the practices of the local churches into conformity with the modern Roman practices of the Catholic Church. As he lies dying, the archbishop himself thinks about what a kind of heroic survey of achievement he has. He thinks, "He had come with the buffalo, and he had lived to see railway trains running into Santa Fe. He had accomplished an historic period." This is part of the power of this novel, the sense of generations passing, one world giving way to another.

In a sense, Willa Cather's novel doesn't seem particularly experimental, and yet, in an interesting way, it's very much part of the kind of Modernist experiment with its form and structure. It seems to have not much form at all. It is a narrative constantly digressing into local history and vignettes of the New Mexico past.

In a sense, it's a novel about New Mexico, the same way that Tolstoy's *War and Peace* is "about Russia." And these loosely connected episodes also meant, I think consciously, to recall another popular genre at the time: the land sagas of Iceland. These were mostly 13th-century sagas, long prose works like the famous *Laxdaela Saga*, and also stories much like her own about people coming to a wild land and taming the wilderness. The Icelandic sagas had been enjoying a vogue in European and American readership. William Morris had translated these in the late 19th century, and they had some important readers, including J. R. R. Tolkien, very much influenced by the Icelandic sagas in his own writings.

It is said that Willa Cather was inspired for writing her novel after visiting the Cross of the Martyrs, above Santa Fe. This is a monument commemorating the mission priests who had been massacred during the Pueblo Revolt of 1680. It is interesting how that initial inspiration really influences the nature of the novel itself. It reads like a great Christian martyrology. Not only does the archbishop die in the end, but along the way there is a body count of 96 other people who die in the course of this single novel. In this sense, the archbishop's story starts reading a lot like a modern saint's life. There are trials and tribulations and setbacks and spiritual doubts along the way, and yet with perseverance and a bit of divine intervention, he succeeds.

Like a good saint's life, the story even contains a miracle. Early on, the bishop is lost in the New Mexico desert. He's thirsty; he's out of food and afraid of his life. And he comes upon a juniper tree in the shape of a cross. He kneels down, he prays, and very soon after that he comes upon a ranch in the middle of nowhere. He's given food and water and also an opportunity to be of Christian service. He can sanctify marriages and baptize children. So there it is—a little miracle at the very beginning of the archbishop's story.

This reminds us that the novel itself has a special debt to the saint's life. It is one of those earlier European prose biographies that very much sort of underlies the genre of the novel itself, so that so many of these novels really become secularized versions in which the heroes (or more often, heroines) have their virtues tested along the way. They suffer, but at the end they are rewarded. There is one Jane Austen novel, *Mansfield Park*, that probably causes modern readers the most difficulty, because the heroine of *Mansfield Park*, Fanny Price, probably comes closest to the original suffering saint of this particular tradition, and modern readers find it hard to sympathize with that kind of moral rigor and inflexibility in a character.

Remember, in the 1960s Leslie Fiedler published a book, *Love and Death in the American Novel*, that really shocked readers of the period by suggesting that so many of the classics of American literature involve what he described as "innocent homosexuality." He had detected it in Melville's *Moby-Dick* and in Mark Twain's *Huckleberry Finn*, also in Fitzgerald's *The Great Gatsby*, and even Jack Kerouac's *On the Road*. It is so much easier to see this particular theme in *Death Comes for the Archbishop* despite all of the kind of landscape and local history, because, if we follow Aristotle's principles, the real central storyline has to do with the archbishop and his lifelong friendship with his fellow priest, Father Vaillent. It is these two men in a friendship that goes back to their school days and follows them from Europe to America, and then to the end of their lives. This is the central backbone of the narrative that otherwise has the kind of scattered quality of an Icelandic land saga. This particular story even carries over to the very end of the plot when, finally, death comes for the archbishop, as the title reminds us. And here he is, the venerable archbishop, dying, but he doesn't think about Christ and Mary; he thinks about his boyhood friend even at the very last moments of his life:

> But in reality the Bishop was not there at all; he was standing in a tip-tilted green field among his native mountains, and he was trying to give consolation to a young man who was being torn in two before his eyes by the desire to go and the necessity to stay.

In a sense, when Willa Cather tells this story of the archbishop and his vicar, she's finally getting around to telling that manly battle yarn that she had predicted in her 1895 essay on women writers, because it may not have been exactly the sort of battle yarn that Tolstoy had given us in *War and Peace* or Hemingway would give us in his novels like *A Farewell to Arms*, but it is still manly in the sense of two men. It is a battle in their struggle to tame the wilderness and bring the Church and its recalcitrant priests into the fold. It is a yarn; it tells the story over their whole lifetime. And in this sense, it's perfect for a kind of frontier literature—not only American frontier, but a whole sort of literary tradition—heroic, manly yarns that go back to *Beowulf*, all the way back further to the foundational narrative in our current tradition of *Gilgamesh*. Because it is in *Gilgamesh* that this kind of buddy story, if you want, with Gilgamesh and his partner Enkidu, this establishes a kind of prototype that will reach throughout the tradition and even into Willa Cather's novel.

The sort of innocent homosexuality (to use Leslie Fiedler's term) that we find in Willa Cather's novel is not at all unexpected because of her own particular and personal same-sex values. As a college student, Willa Cather was cutting her hair short, she wore men's clothes, she sometimes took the male roles in college plays, and she even sometimes signed herself as William Cather. Over the course of her lifetime, she had several relationships with other women, and one of these women would become the trustee of her estate after she died.

She was very private, very secretive about these personal matters for the same reason that E. M. Forster was quite discreet—and presumably also T. S. Eliot—because homosexuality continued to be illegal, and any scandal of this sort could wreck a writer's life, even as it had wrecked Oscar Wilde's in the 1890s, when Willa Cather came of age as a woman and as a writer. And yet Cather was not entirely closeted. Remember, the 1920s were a period of great social and personal experimentation, and this was the era that gave us this particular novel. In her critical writing, also, she tended to focus on writers who form what you might call a kind of gay canon. She wrote about Sappho, Lord Byron, Oscar Wilde of course, Walt Whitman, and Henry James.

Rather than being a stumbling block to her reputation, here in the modern world, her own sort of sexual orientation, her lesbianism, has actually worked in her favor since the 1970s, when there has been a kind of renewed interest and curiosity, and even a kind of championing, of any kind of independence in staking out one's own claims for a particular sexuality. Remember, this also very much assisted the reputation of Virginia Woolf. Virginia Woolf's reputation as a novelist had gone into much decline after World War II, after her death. So in the '50s and '60s, she was not much favored even in the college classroom, but then Virginia Woolf comes back very, very strongly in the 1970s with the women's movement, with the sort of sexual liberation period in American culture, and this sort of renewed interest in earlier lesbian writers or bisexual writers very much has benefited Willa Cather's career as well.

And so now it is rather routine in the literary world, in the college classroom, to take specific interest in gay writers. We're reading Walt Whitman in a much more interesting, maybe more authentic way than he was read before. Oscar Wilde has become a major cultural figure and interesting as a moralist, interesting even as a figure of early postcolonial writers—the Irishman writing back to the heart of English literary tradition in London. There is also interest in what we call "possibly gay" writers, or bisexual writers, people very interested in what Shakespeare says about himself in his sonnets. Thomas Mann is the author of the homoerotic classic *Death in Venice*, and even Ernest Hemingway in a variety of writings, including his posthumously published novel *The Garden of Eden*.

But what's really interesting here is that a kind of unique sexual identity fits into this larger picture of America as fundamentally a mosaic of identities—regional identities such as Willa Cather herself is exploring in New Mexico, also identities of gender, male and female; identities of ethnicities; and linguistic roots. Because, in a sense, the United States, as it is developing into the 20th century, is very much like earlier successful, imperial enterprises like the Persians, in the sense that it will combine and embrace and tolerate and allow to live harmoniously many different ethnic groups within its borders.

Here you have Willa Cather's novel giving us that extraordinary coming together of very, very different cultures within the Southwest. There's the Native American culture—and she's sensitive to the Navajo culture versus the Apache culture versus the Pueblo cultures of the Rio Grande valley—the old Hispanic communities, and the newly arrived Yankees, as well. This also bespeaks a sort of new direction in American literature, where the ethnic minority peoples begin to write their own literature.

During recent decades, the Hispanic culture from California to Texas has, on the one hand, engaged in a reclamation project, finding its earlier literatures. For example, there was a thriving literary culture in California in the 19th century producing what is called "hacienda novels," almost equivalent of a plantation novel in the Southern tradition. In our own time, modern masters emerge like Rudolfo Anaya in his wonderful World War II coming-of-age novel *Bless*

Me, Ultima. And there are also crossover writers like John Nichols in his New Mexico trilogy, most famously *The Milagro Beanfield War*, made into a really good movie by Robert Redford. So this fracturing of American literature along these identity lines—American Jewish writers, American Asian writers, and Native American writers—continues to sort of fill out the full mosaic of American literature so that the Puritan tradition itself, already an outsider tradition, had provided a kind of template for respecting and dignifying these minority groups with their own literary productions. We'll actually look forward into the 20th century and beyond to literatures written by non-English people in non-English places about non-English cultures. This is what we'll look forward to in the final lecture on the postcolonial novel.

Lecture Thirty-Five
Tolkien's *The Lord of the Rings*—Literature?

Scope:

J. R. R. Tolkien was educated at Oxford, where he later became a professor of Anglo-Saxon. Invalided home from the Somme in 1917, Tolkien began devising mythologies for some lost antiquity of enchantment and heroic causes, as an antidote to the cynicism and industrial ugliness of 20th-century England. Half-forgotten lore survived, he thought, in Old English classics like *Beowulf* that were taught at Oxford. He became a campus writer, assimilating the contents of the required syllabus. Continuing through the darkest days of World War II, his literary fantasy grew into *The Lord of the Rings*. Though his top-selling trilogy continues to inspire the genre of fantasy literature—as well as blockbuster movies and video games—what justifies *The Lord of the Rings* as a literary masterpiece? How solid is the Western canon if there is room for Frodo and Gandalf?

Outline

I. Tolkien's *The Lord of the Rings* had a slow takeoff when it was first published in the 1950s, but over the years it has become a publishing phenomenon beyond anything imaginable by *The Da Vinci Code*.

    A. On average, almost 4 million copies of Tolkien's books are sold each year.

    B. *The Lord of the Rings* has also passed the translation test: It has been translated into nearly 40 languages.

    C. In the course of things, Tolkien essentially invented the genre of fantasy literature, or at least popularized it to a degree that never existed before.

    D. Tolkien's writing has even encouraged a whole proliferation of video games.

    E. In 2000, Amazon.com pronounced *The Lord of the Rings* not only the book of the century but the book of the millennium.

II. We really need to put this marketing and sales phenomenon into a larger context of criticism and other benchmarks for determining a literary canonic work.

A. One benchmark is to have critical appreciation accounting for the popularity. One critic who comes to mind in Tolkien's case is Carl Jung, whose idea of "a thousand voices" can be seen in Tolkien's echoing of traditional literatures.

B. Another is that genius must recognize genius; in this case, W. H. Auden hailed Tolkien's work as a supreme literary achievement.

C. It is always important for scholars and teachers to give their approval to a work; Tolkien is now taught in universities and is the subject of academic conferences.

D. A great writer must constantly renew himself with the current critical modes; Tolkien has easily plugged into modern eco-critical discourse.

III. Tolkien is another author whose canon was established after his death. Like Chaucer's son, Tolkien's son took charge of editing and publishing posthumously many of his father's works.

IV. To understand Tolkien's position in literary history, we need to appreciate that he, too, belonged to that lost generation after World War I.

A. He had firsthand experience training for the cavalry before the war, but he ended up as a signaling officer in the Lancaster Fusiliers.

B. He became extremely frustrated with the breakdown of communication in the field of battle, and he fantasized in his writing about systems of communication that can work effectively over great distances.

C. Tolkien was sent home with trench fever after the Battle of the Somme, and while he was recuperating, he started inventing languages and mythologies of England's lost prehistoric past.

D. *The Lord of the Rings* is filled with images of trench warfare—lifeless faces in the water, corpses stacked up like cordwood, and Aragorn's sympathetic reaction to shell-shocked warriors.

V. There is a sad strain in the story; Frodo's great achievements are forgotten almost as soon as he returns home.

A. A counterpart can be seen in the works of Faulkner and Cather, where war veterans encounter an unappreciative reception when they return to their small towns in the South or the Plains states.

B. Frodo himself seems to experience a kind of post-traumatic stress, eventually withdrawing psychologically, and ultimately physically, into the company of the elves.

VI. J. R. R. Tolkien had a real professional stake in the Western literary canon.

A. In 1912, he had taken a first-class degree in English, which was not a very reputable degree at the time.

B. He knew many languages and made his scholarly reputation with the Oxford edition of *Sir Gawain and the Green Knight.*

C. In 1925, he was appointed professor of Anglo-Saxon at Oxford, and he later delivered a famous lecture about *Beowulf* that catapulted the epic into the canon.

D. After becoming Merton Professor of English Language and Literature, Tolkien remained in that position until his retirement; in essence, he spent his entire professional life at Oxford.

E. Oxford's influence can be seen in Tolkien's fictional city of Minas Tirith, a place of knowledge and ancient heritage.

F. He spent most of his career dignifying English as an academic field and put great effort into organizing the syllabus with major authors and major works.

G. He also became the prototype of the campus author, a figure that we now find often on college campuses.

VII. Tolkien had an interesting sense that *The Lord of the Rings* was really history.

A. He liked to make believe, in a sense, that the stories he was telling were true stories passed along in the oral traditions and surfacing later in the earliest written works of England.

B. Tolkien's premise for his fiction was that these stories had a sense of heroism and adventure that fixed them in people's minds.

C. He looked carefully at the archaeology in the region around Oxford and used the Neolithic sites there as inspiration for episodes in his work.

VIII. T. S. Eliot, another man of Merton College in the early 20th century, gave us a way to appreciate the greatness and durability of Tolkien's achievement.

   A. In his essay "Tradition and the Individual Talent," Eliot proposed that truly new pieces of art could reorganize the existing tradition of great works.

   B. Tolkien did this in all of his writing—introducing the new in a way that reconfigured not only the shape but the membership within the literary canon.

   C. He faced a real problem with Chaucer, who had done such an effective job of establishing himself as the starting point of English literature.

   1. In doing this, Chaucer had essentially erased prior writers, especially the Old English writers.

   2. Because of his direct influence on Shakespeare, Milton, Joyce, and others, Chaucer's claim as the father of the tradition was almost insurmountably strong.

   D. Tolkien bridged the canonic gap between Old English writers and Chaucer by presuming a continuous arc of tradition that sailed past Chaucer to the earliest surviving Old English text. In doing so, he redefined the length and inclusiveness of the English literary canon.

IX. This means that readers of Tolkien have an incentive to go back and read *Beowulf* and *The Wanderer* to know the texts that influenced Tolkien himself. This new talent that Eliot had predicted actually encourages readers, not just academics, to engage with original works.

Suggested Readings:

Tolkien, *The Lord of the Rings*.

Carpenter, *J. R. R. Tolkien: A Biography*.

Garth, *Tolkien and the Great War*.

Shippey, *J. R. R. Tolkien: Author of the Century*.

Questions to Consider:

1. Professor Tolkien represents the class of academics—including Harold Bloom—who have taken charge of the Western canon. Can you think of an author or a literary work that enjoys a large number of readers but is *not* included on the classroom syllabus at colleges and universities?

2. There are authors whose appeal shrinks over time—for example, the prolific Voltaire is now represented only by *Candide*—and authors whose audiences are eager for any scrap of new writing, however mediocre. Does the Western canon's harsh processes of exclusion and extinction sometimes save us from marginal works such as *The Children of Húrin* and *Farmer Giles of Ham*?

Lecture Thirty-Five—Transcript
Tolkien's *The Lord of the Rings*—Literature?

The guardians of the Western literary canon demand books with long shelf life. Therefore, they are very suspicious of instant bestsellers like Dan Brown's *The Da Vinci Code*. But remember, the Spanish literary establishment of the early 17th century also was very suspicious of *Don Quixote*, because it was way too popular way too quickly. Tolkien's *The Lord of the Rings* actually had a slow takeoff when it was first published in the 1950s, but over the years it has become a publishing phenomenon beyond anything imaginable by *The Da Vinci Code*.

These are just the current statistics: more than 20 million copies of *The Lord of the Rings* sold worldwide, more than 50,000 copies of *The Lord of the Rings* sold each month. *The Hobbit* itself has sold more than 35 million copies. Even *The Silmarillion* sells 100,000 copies a year. That means that there's a total of almost 4 million copies of Tolkien's books sold each year. It has also passed the test of translation; *Lord of the Rings* has been translated into nearly 40 languages, including some pretty obscure ones like Basque, Hebrew, Korean, Turkish—really unlikely ones—and even Icelandic, a language that would have pleased Tolkien a great deal, because one of his sources was the *Völsunga Saga* from Iceland.

In the course of things, Tolkien has pretty much invented a new genre, or at least popularized it to a degree that never existed before, and that is fantasy literature. One of the tests here is that there is posterity of fantasy writers active even today. I would single out one: Diana Wynne Jones, the author of *Howl's Moving Castle*. I single her out because I know that she actually attended Tolkien's lectures as an undergraduate at Oxford, and I know this because she attended with her future husband John Burrow, who became a medievalist and my tutor when I was at Oxford as an undergraduate.

Tolkien's Middle Earth has also encouraged a whole sort of proliferation of video games. To see something like the "World of Warcraft" is really to appreciate the long reach of Tolkien into a technology that he couldn't have imagined. Peter Jackson's blockbuster films merely have boosted the marketing and sales of the books, so much so that by the millennial year of 2000, Amazon.com did its survey and pronounced *The Lord of the Rings* not only the book of the century but the book of the millennium.

Now we really need to sort of put this marketing and sales phenomenon into a larger context of criticism and the other sort of benchmarks for determining a literary canonic work. And one of them is to have a kind of critical appreciation, some authority figure who will account for this kind of popularity. The one who immediately comes to mind is Carl Jung, who is writing immediately after World War I. This is what Jung says is about an archetypal appeal of some great literary work:

> Whoever speaks in primordial images speaks with a thousand voices. … Therein lies the social significance of art: it is constantly at work educating the spirit of the age, conjuring up the forms in which the age is most lacking.

And here you have it in a nutshell: Tolkien's books speak with those many, many voices. He is an echo chamber of English and European literatures, and he goes at what the age most lacks, that sort of disillusionment following the Great War. It fills that particular cultural vacuum, harkening back to a heroism and chivalry that existed before the collapse of European confidence in the Great War.

Also, it is necessary for greatness to appreciate greatness, genius to recognize genius. And lo and behold, one of the first reviewers of *Lord of the Rings* was the great poet W. H. Auden. Auden is arguably the major English-language poet from the middle decades of the 20th century. He undertook to do a review of Volume III, *Return of the King*, in *The New York Times* when the volume was published in 1956. He really hailed it as a supreme literary achievement, connecting it with the classic English genre of the quest-romance and specifically discussing quest-romance in view of Erich Auerbach's chapter on the genre in *Mimesis: The Representation of Reality in Western Literature*.

Here you have a really sort of strong group of champions—W. H. Auden summoning the authority of Auerbach to proclaim the extraordinary achievement of Tolkien's *Lord of the Rings*. Academics eventually caught on—always important for scholars and teachers to give their approval to a work. Tolkien is now taught at the universities. There are conferences about Tolkien. There are books galore by academics about Tolkien. One of my favorites is by Tom Shippey (a professional medievalist himself), not too modestly entitled *J. R. R. Tolkien: Author of the Century*.

One of the other tasks of a great writer is constantly to renew himself or herself with whatever the current critical modes are, and Tolkien is a wonderful nature writer. He is one of the great painterly authors in our tradition. Lo and behold, he is now discussed very much in terms of eco-criticism—that is, a kind of environmental criticism of literature. He is perfect to plug into that particular mode of critical discussion.

Tolkien is another author whose canon, whose total output in corpus, was established after his death. Just as Geoffrey Chaucer's son Thomas Chaucer apparently was quite responsible for producing and getting his father's works out after the poet had died, Tolkien's son Christopher, also trained as a medievalist, took charge of editing and publishing posthumously many of his father's previously unpublished works—*The Silmarillion*, for example; various translations that Tolkien had done, like his rendering of *Sir Gawain and the Green Knight* into modern English; also, those 12 volumes of *The History of Middle Earth*; and, as recently as 2007, another Tolkien book has appeared: *The Children of Húrin*. But the question persists for us as students of the Western canon: Shouldn't these works be more like *Moby-Dick* or *War and Peace*? Shouldn't they have an elite readership, a specialty readership, a classier readership, and not sort of the favorite pastime of high school stoner dudes, who just can't get enough of their Tolkien?

To really understand Tolkien's position in literary history, we need to appreciate that he, too, belonged to that lost generation after World War I. He was a soldier; he fought in World War I. He had originally trained in a cavalry regiment—interesting, because he would take such interest in the cavalry exploits of the Riders of the Mark. So he actually had firsthand experience in training for the military cavalry before the war, but he ended up as a signaling officer in the Lancaster Fusiliers. And if you think about this, he was a signaling officer who became extremely frustrated with the breakdown of communication in the field of battle. So he fantasizes in his work "the seeing globes" in which people can communicate over great distances, and even the lighting of the beacons of Gondor to summon help during the siege of Minas Tirith. This is the kind of signaling that Tolkien as a signaling officer would have very much appreciated.

In 1917, Tolkien was actually invalided home with trench fever from one of the great and tragic encounters in the First World War, the Battle of the Somme. As he was recuperating, he started inventing languages, and as he invented languages, he began to invent mythologies about England's lost, prehistoric past. His wartime experience was a sad and tragic one. He went off to war with his three closest friends. There were four of them total, very much like the four hobbits who go off on their great enterprise in Middle Earth. He actually says in the foreword of the second edition of *Lord of the Rings* that he lost two of his four closest friends in the impact of the war.

It is easy enough to see again another autobiographical strain, that Tolkien and his friend Wiseman were the survivors, like Frodo and Sam, and his other two friends died. But remember, there's this long sequence in *Lord of the Rings* where everybody thinks that Merry and Pippin have died. They've been kidnapped by the Orcs, they are thought to have been massacred, and it is almost a wish-fulfilling fantasy that you can read in Tolkien's ultimate story that Merry and Pippin are found alive, almost as if he could kind of wish his two dead friends back to life again, as well.

The Lord of the Rings is filled with images of trench warfare in the hideous scenes of the First World War—the lifeless faces up in the water in the Dead Marshes, the corpses piled up like cordwood at the siege of Helmsdeep. There is even a moment on the march to the Black Gates where Aragorn reacts very sympathetically to some of the warriors who show what we now call shell shock, or battle fatigue, and he allows them to go the rear guard or even to return home—a much more sympathetic treatment of shell-shock victims than many of the returning veterans had when they came back from the trenches.

There is also a kind of sad strain in *Lord of the Rings*; Frodo's great achievements are forgotten almost as soon as he returns home to Hobbiton. You can almost see a kind of counterpart to those novels, such as those by Faulkner and Willa Cather, about the sort of unappreciative reception, difficult re-entry that these war veterans had when they came back to their small hometowns in the South or in the Plains states. This is what is said about Frodo:

> Frodo dropped quietly out of all the doings of the Shire, and
> Sam was pained to notice how little honour he had in his

own country. Few people knew or wanted to know about his deeds and adventures.

In fact, Frodo himself seems to experience a kind of post-traumatic stress, as he explains to Sam, "I have been too deeply hurt." And at the very end, he withdraws psychologically, and ultimately physically, into the realm, from the realm of Middle Earth, into the company of elves. It is almost like retreating from reality into a kind of fantasy space. One is reminded of the character Septimus Smith in Virginia Woolf's *Mrs. Dalloway*, who begins to hallucinate. He sees his dead friend Evans, who had been blown up in battle, and begins hearing voices from the walls eventually telling him to kill himself. Now Frodo doesn't kill himself; instead he leaves, but only after he has written down all of his adventures in the Red Book under the title *The Downfall of the Lord of the Rings and Return of the King*. There is a sense that the writing process has been part of a kind of life-saving therapy for Frodo, as in fact probably—possibly, at least—it was for J. R. R. Tolkien, too.

J. R. R. Tolkien had a real professional stake in the Western literary canon. He had taken a first-class degree in English in 1912, after switching from the classics. English, by the way, was not a very respectable degree at that time, and you can always see a little chip on the shoulder of the scholar as he goes forward in his career. Now Tolkien had an early job at the *Oxford English Dictionary*, specialist on the history of the language (he knew words in many, many languages), and then made his scholarly reputation with the Oxford edition of *Sir Gawain and the Green Knight*. In 1925, he was appointed professor of Anglo-Saxon at Oxford and later delivered the famous lecture "*Beowulf*: The Monsters and the Critics" that did so much to catapult that Old English epic into the canon, into the syllabus, as literature and not just a kind of archive for historical linguistics.

Tolkien later became the Merton Professor of English Language and Literature in 1945 and remained in that post until his retirement in 1959. So what I'm saying is that he spent his entire professional life in Oxford. It is very interesting to read this into *The Lord of the Rings*, because the great city of Minas Tirith, with its libraries and towers and ancient halls, has an extraordinary resemblance to Oxford, even to this day. Remember, when Gandalf wants to find out about the ancient War of the Ring and what happened with the loss of the ring, he goes to the ancient manuscript archives of Minas Tirith. He does scholarly research in the libraries of the capital. There was actually a legend that Oxford was founded by King Alfred the Great, so it would have a kind of Anglo-Saxon heritage. There was even a statue of King Alfred in the High Street at Oxford through the 19th century.

But indeed, Oxford actually was a capital in a sense. Twice in English history it had served as a provisional capital. The first time, during the Civil War, King Charles I and his Royal Court had their capital in exile at Oxford; Oxford is the capital city of England at that time. In fact, Merton College hosted Charles's queen, Queen Henrietta, and the room in which the faculty, the dons, of Merton College take their sherry before dinner is still called the Queen's Room, because that is where Queen Henrietta lived. The second time that Oxford became a provisional capital was during World War II, when Tolkien is working hard at *The Lord of the Rings*. London was being bombed during the Blitz, and many of the offices of government had been removed to a safer location at Oxford. And so around Tolkien, while he is working on *Lord of the Rings*, Oxford feels like a capital city besieged during wartime as a kind of reflection that he puts into the story itself.

In fact, there is a sort of lovely experience to stand in Tolkien's old rooms at Merton College, because you look out the window and you look over the old medieval walls of the City of Oxford, and beyond the walls are the playing fields of Christ Church School, and then you look way down toward the river. And it occurs to you that this is the view from Minas Tirith, "Over the wall, across the fields of Helenor and finally to the river beyond." What Tolkien would have seen looking out his windows were the schoolboys playing rugby and English football, but what he translates this into his imagination is the great battle scene that will take place on those fields outside the city wall. In fact, it almost harkens back to that famous statement by the Duke of Wellington that the Battle of Waterloo was won on the playing fields of Eton, a kind of equation between the playing fields where the boys play their sports and the great battlefield of Waterloo.

I said before that Tolkien's English degree that he took a first-class status in was recent at Oxford. So, in a sense, he spent his whole career dignifying this particular academic field. He edited, he translated, he lectured on medieval literature, very much to sort of "up" the status of his discipline. He worked very hard at getting the syllabus organized with major authors and major works. Because he had to grade the exams a lot, some of these works, like *Paradise Lost*, will have a great influence on other works, like *The Silmarillion*.

He was also very keen on getting works like *Beowulf* and *Sir Gawain and the Green Knight* on the syllabus, very much as kind of ancient classics almost in parallel to the ancient masterpieces of Greece and Rome. In a sense, he also became a figure much more familiar in modern times; he becomes a campus author in the course of his lifetime. In fact, there was a predecessor at Oxford who became a great famous author. Lewis Carroll wrote *Alice in Wonderland*, and he had a contemporary and friend, C. S. Lewis, who becomes another Oxford author, and then, later on, the Oxford novelist Iris Murdoch. So here you have a kind of prototype that something has become quite commonplace on campuses, especially in America.

Tolkien has an interesting sense that *The Lord of the Rings* is really history. He says at the opening of the foreword:

> This tale grew in the telling, until it became a history of the Great War of the Ring and included many glimpses of the yet more ancient history that preceded it.

He liked to make believe, in a sense, that the stories he was telling were true stories that had passed along in the oral tradition, in the folklore, to surface later in the earliest literature. There is precedent for this: the idea that the Trojan War and the heroes of that great conflict had also entered an oral tradition and then surfaced only many centuries later in Homer's *Iliad* and the *Odyssey*. In the Germanic countries, the work of Jacob Grimm, and the folklorists also believed that there were early actual events that entered the oral folklore and then were retrievable by modern scholars in the world. This is Tolkien's premise for his fiction; he wants to ponder about how these stories have sort of an adventure quality, a heroism that fixes themselves in people's minds. Sam actually makes a speech to this effect to his friend Frodo. This is what Sam says:

> The brave things in the old tales and songs, Mr. Frodo: adventures as I used to call them. ... The tales that really mattered, or the ones that stay in the mind. I expect they had

lots of chances, like us, of turning back, only they didn't. And if they had, we shouldn't know, because they'd have been forgotten.

And so Tolkien is imagining that he is writing that lost prehistory of the English people out of the evidence that is passed along in oral tradition, surfacing in the earliest literary accounts, so that when he reads *Beowulf* and sees the character Grendel, he imagines that this character is based ultimately on Gollum. So his Gollum, he imagines, is the original type, the source for the literary Grendel. The Anglo-Saxon kingdom of Mercia was one of the four kingdoms—Tolkien's mother was from that region—and yet Mercia produced no important literature. And so Tolkien has to imagine the lost prehistory of the Mercian people. Anglo-Saxon word was *Mearc*, and so these are the Riders of the Mark. And so this whole area of Rohan is a kingdom that he has imagined as the lost, prehistoric forerunner of Mercia, his mother's own homeland.

He also looked at archaeology in the region around Oxford and then would use the Neolithic sites, these Stone Age sites, as a sort of inspiration. For example, the statues of the Púkel-men at Dunharrow would have been imagined by him as surviving into his own day as the stone ring at Avebury and Rollright Stones at Long Compton, Oxfordshire. One of the great sort of prehistoric monuments of this whole region is the White Horse at Uffington, this great sort of chalk-white horse in the side of a hill. He actually sort of imagines two inspirations for this in his own fiction. There's a point where King Théoden's great white horse Snowmane is honored with a monument, and in a sense, this explains the great White Horse at Uffington. There is also a sense that Tolkien is inspired by this monument to think up Gandalf's great white horse Shadowfax, and so that prehistoric hill monument at Uffington has a kind of dual function in inspiring what he thought of as the lost examples that led to what survive.

Tolkien died September 2, 1973, at age 81, still in residence at Merton College, Oxford. He had moved back into college housing after his beloved wife died and so continued to live the scholar's life, the life of the college, very much, and still not as famous as he would eventually be. I had a classmate who lived on the upper floor of the house where Tolkien lived on the lower floor, and every day he would pass what he still describes as a "rum old man," and they would exchange hellos as they went in and out. It was only much later that he realized that he had been exchanging hellos on a daily basis with the author of *The Lord of the Rings*.

There was another man of Merton College at the beginning of the 20th century, T. S. Eliot, who would very much sort of give us a way to appreciate the greatness and the durability of Tolkien's achievement. Eliot wrote an essay in 1919 entitled "Tradition and the Individual Talent," and he looks forward to special kinds of achievement, what a really great newcomer on the scene of literature can do because, remember, we said over and over again that the literary canon configures itself backwards, so that it's people in the modern period who will select from what is available and configure it in a way most appropriate to themselves. And this is what Eliot himself had said very pointedly in this 1919 essay:

> The existing monuments form an ideal order among themselves, which is modified by the introduction of the new (the really new) work of art among them.

Of course, Eliot was sort of paving the way for his own new, really new work of art, *The Waste Land*, that would reconfigure the Western canon, would put in his favorite canonic writers and also introduce something that hadn't been there before, the Sanskrit literature of ancient India. But he also sort of lays the groundwork for what Tolkien himself is going to be doing in all of his writings— *The Hobbit, The Lord of the Rings*, and eventually *The Silmarillion*—to introduce the new, the really new work of art that will reconfigure, redefine, not only the shape but the membership within the literary canon.

Here is a problem for the English literary tradition, and the problem is Chaucer. Chaucer did an incredibly effective job of establishing himself as the starting point; he is the father of English literature. Remember, to establish himself there in the late 14th century as the starting point of a national literature, Chaucer had to do several things, and one of them was to erase his predecessors. Chaucer not only elbows away his contemporaries, like William Langland, author of *Piers Plowman*, and the anonymous *Gawain* Poet, but he also has to render invisible, pretend like they never existed at all, any prior English writers, and especially Old English writers. Remember, there were a lot of these Anglo-Saxon manuscripts still around in Chaucer's time. The dissolution of the monastery hadn't resulted in so many destructions of these ancient manuscripts, and just the wear and tear of history had itself meant that more of these Old English texts were available for Chaucer. But he absolutely refused to acknowledge them as he established himself as the father of English poetry.

In the later configuration of the English tradition, the syllabus—if you were—continued to accept the paternity of Chaucer as an absolute starting point that you really couldn't get past, because you have Shakespeare using Chaucer's works for the sources of his plays; you have Milton still thinking about Chaucer, Wordsworth still thinking about Chaucer, James Joyce sitting down to read old father Chaucer when he is writing *Ulysses*. And so Chaucer is a starting point very, very hard to get beyond.

Now they discovered the Old English poetry. *Beowulf* has come to light; there is a 19th-century edition followed by many other later editions. They are discovering these wonderful treasures that popped up in various places, like the Vercelli Manuscript way off in Italy. These are being edited now. There is a body of Old English literature that a scholar such as Tolkien has dedicated his life to study. The problem is bridging this gap that has opened up between the Old English literature, *Beowulf*, and the official starting point of Chaucer. This is Tolkien's great achievement, because *The Lord of the Rings* presumes a continuous arc of tradition that actually sails over Chaucer as it traces the beginnings back to the earliest surviving Old English text. Tolkien has introduced that new, really new work that has redefined the length and the inclusiveness of the English literary tradition, making it a continuous tradition in which Chaucer is no longer the starting point; Chaucer is a midpoint in a tradition that starts perhaps as early as the 9th century with works like *Beowulf*.

The work that Tolkien does in his fiction enforces this at every turn. For example, there is a lovely moment where Aragorn is looking over the barrows—the burial places of 16 kings of the Riddermark, spanning five centuries—and there is a chant, a dirge, going on in the ancient language of the Mark. The hobbits don't understand the language; it is too foreign for them—it's Anglo-Saxon. And so Aragorn translates it into the common tongue, and this is part of Aragorn's translation of the ancient dirge of Riders of the Mark:

> Where now the horse and the rider? Where is the horn that was blowing?
>
> Where is the helm and hauberk, and the bright hair flowing? ...
>
> They have passed like rain on the mountain, like a wind in the meadow;
>
> The days have gone down in the West behind the hills into shadow.

What we have here, then—"where [now] the horse and the rider"— this is the classic *ubi sunt* theme of Anglo-Saxon literature. Where are they now? Where are thee now? What Tolkien is offering as a kind of premise is that this is the original version of these poems, this sentiment expressed and preserved here in his recreation of that history in *The Two Towers*. It is this original version that will then pass into the oral tradition and then only surface centuries later in the literary text of *Beowulf* and the Old English poem *The Wanderer*.

This means that readers of Tolkien have an incentive to go back to the beginning and read *Beowulf* and read *The Wanderer* in order to know those texts that then influenced Tolkien himself. Here it is: The really new talent that Eliot had predicted has enforced a reconfiguration that now encourages readers—and not just the people who put together anthologies and college syllabuses—to go back and read the originals. There was a success in this enterprise on Tolkien's part so that even my students in Las Vegas, Nevada are willing to take courses in history of the English language and then go on to take a course in introductory Old English. And there's just a few that go on to read *Beowulf* in the original Anglo-Saxon language. Almost always, you can tell who are the students who will persevere to read *Beowulf* in the original; they are the stoner dudes from high school who started off by reading *The Lord of the Rings*.

Lecture Thirty-Six
Postcolonialism—The Empire Writes Back

Scope:

The literary culture of England became the property of the non-Western nations wherever the colonial language had been imposed. Rushdie's *Midnight's Children* traces Saleem Sinai's life from midnight of August 15, 1947, when both he and the new nation of India were born. Rushdie assimilates the tradition of Lawrence Sterne, Charles Dickens, and E. M. Forster to write a completely un-English novel, reaching into native mythologies, the Sanskrit *Ramayana*, and the Muslim *Arabian Nights*. Ayatollah Khomeini's death threat against Rushdie only elevated his status. Michael Ondaatje's *The English Patient* tells how the Hungarian archeologist corrects and expands Herodotus's *The Histories*, indicating how European history—including literary history—can be rewritten by the outsider. The film *The English Patient* won nine Academy Awards, as a reminder of how movies, with global audiences, actually bolster the status of books in the 21st century. The Western canon remains a "survivors' list," a work-in-progress always generated backward, expanding to welcome new members and dropping authors who no longer speak to the needs of current readers.

Outline

I. The postcolonial novel in English has become an unexpected fulfillment of the prediction made in 1848 by Marx and Engels about the globalization of literature.

    A. They foresaw that Western books would become a kind of export to non-Western countries.

    B. Something happened in world trade in the second half of the 20th century that Marx and Engels had not expected: The cultural forms of the West provided models for domestic manufacture in non-Western nations.

    C. The English language, especially in the genre of the novel, became the chief means for non-Western writers to appropriate the cultural heritage of both the English and American traditions.

II. Postcolonial novels have come especially from the subcontinent of South Asia, and it is easy to see why historically.

   A. India had come under English influence very early, with the arrival of the East India Company licensed by Elizabeth I.

   B. Even after India's independence from British colonial administration, English itself would continue as the official language of India.

III. I want to consider two cases of outstanding postcolonial novelists, both with family roots in South Asia: Salman Rushdie and Michael Ondaatje.

IV. Rushdie was born into a secular Muslim family in Bombay in 1947, the same year that India achieved its independence.

   A. He was educated at Rugby School in England and went on to King's College, Cambridge, where the writer-in-residence was the elderly E. M. Forster, author of the famous Anglo-Indian novel *A Passage to India*.

   B. Rushdie recognized himself as the Indian half of this Anglo-Indian equation, writing in the English language but as a transnational with a very different point of view.

   C. The title of Rushdie's *Midnight's Children* comes from a famous pronouncement by India's first Prime Minister: "At the stroke of the midnight hour … India will awake to life and freedom."

   D. Rushdie's novel gives utterance to a nation torn and divided across the split represented by midnight itself, looking back at the past and forward into the unfolding future.

V. Rushdie did the work of any writer who aspires to join the canon by making *Midnight's Children* assimilate prior canonic works, specifically in the English novel tradition.

   A. Rushdie also appropriated the native, non-Western techniques of storytelling from his homeland, namely the oral tradition of circular narrative.

   B. Despite these gestures toward the native Indian tradition, Rushdie otherwise made all the right moves to insert himself into the Western canon, including the accumulation of important prizes and the creation of a prolific body of work across genres.

C. Rushdie also achieved the dubious type of celebrity associated with scandal; his fourth novel, *The Satanic Verses*, garnered him a *fatwa*, or death sentence, from the Ayatollah Khomeini of Iran, and he came close to joining the long list of literary martyrs.

D. Another important move for Rushdie was his acceptance by academics and scholars. *Midnight's Children* almost always ends up now on the syllabus of the modern British novel or postcolonial literature course.

E. As a critic, Rushdie summoned up the authority of T. S. Eliot, reiterating the idea of a new work reshaping the tradition.

VI. I move now to the work of a second postcolonial novelist, and we will ponder again whether he, too, has made the right moves to join the Western canon. The author is Michael Ondaatje, and the work is *The English Patient*.

A. Ondaatje was born in Sri Lanka of mixed heritage, including Dutch and Portuguese.

B. Because of his travels to England, his education in Canada, and his teaching career at York University, Ondaatje knew the Western canon from the inside. It was almost second nature for him to connect his own work with the prior masterpieces of the canon.

C. *The English Patient* is a wartime love story set in Italy, and in this way it connects itself to both Hemingway and Stendhal.

D. It is also a lyrical novel very much in the tradition of Virginia Woolf. Ondaatje was known as a poet before he became a novelist, so the lyrical novel came naturally to him.

E. As a Canadian, Ondaatje also aligns himself with the American tradition. Like *Moby-Dick*, *The English Patient* is brimming with encyclopedic, technical, how-to information.

F. The eventual playing out of a scenario from Herodotus among the characters in the novel reminds us of the Platonic process of mimesis that has functioned in the Western canon for thousands of years.

G. The Hungarian archaeologist, one of the main characters of the novel, has a real passion for Herodotus and uses *The Histories* as a guidebook to the Egyptian desert, correcting and supplementing as he goes along.

VII. Like Rushdie, Ondaatje operates as a transnational author schooled in a tradition not originally his own.

    A. This turns out to be a great boost for a writer aspiring to enter the global marketplace, as people once colonized by English-speaking cultures assimilate and domesticate the language.

    B. The English language has a huge, flexible vocabulary and a plasticity that makes it a superb vehicle for writers from other traditions.

    C. But writing in English does not make an author English, and this points to an irony in Ondaatje's novel—most of the main characters are not actually English.

VIII. If you look at the continuing reception of *The English Patient*, you'll see that Ondaatje, like Rushdie, has made all the right moves for entering the canon.

    A. He has won the prestigious Booker Prize and has himself been the subject of a long biography.

    B. *The English Patient* has been translated into multiple languages and was adapted as a prize-winning movie.

    C. Ondaatje continues to write and publish and has paid special attention to the ruthlessness of the literary tradition when it comes to eliminating authors and works.

IX. There is good news in the relentless process of canon formation: Inclusion is also a constantly operating principle.

    A. Professor Harold Bloom worries that we have, in fact, gained too many masterpieces.

    B. I am more optimistic; we continue to be a culture that respects the classics, if only sometimes in the naming and the citing.

X. We remain "the people of the book."

    A. The old book bazaar in Istanbul continues to function in the same way that it has for a thousand years, trading everything from economic texts to works by Rumi. One can see here the whole story of the Western canon in one place.

B. Our culture remains one organized around the marketing and consumption of books, as we can see in our ubiquitous bookstores, libraries, and online resources.

C. I have tremendous confidence that the Western canon is alive and well in the 21st century.

Suggested Readings:

Ondaatje, *The English Patient.*

Rushdie, *Midnight's Children.*

Ashcroft, Griffiths, and Tiffin, eds., *The Empire Writes Back.*

Ondaatje et al., eds., *Lost Classics.*

Questions to Consider:

1. In addition to women writers, the great English novelists have frequently been outsiders. As precursors of the postcolonial, American novelists have continued this trend by writing their novels in English, but not as Englishmen. Does the novel as a genre basically belong to "marginal" writers? Can you think of a single canonic English novelist who is 100 percent mainstream English?

2. Think of a favorite book of your own that did not "make it" into the canon. What went wrong? What factors might have changed the outcome?

Lecture Thirty-Six—Transcript
Postcolonialism—The Empire Writes Back

The postcolonial novel in English has become an unexpected fulfillment of prediction made in 1848 by Marx and Engels about the globalization of literature. This is what they said:

> The intellectual creations of individual nations become common property. ... And from the numerous national and local literatures, there arises a world literature.

What they foresaw was that Western books would become other kinds of exports to non-Western consumers. This is very much like Sir Thomas More imagining that those wonderful little Aldine editions of the Greek classics would be exported to Utopia. But also remember that More pointed out that the Utopians also were importing paper and the printing press. So this suggests at a very early point that these non-Westerners would be in a position to start producing their own books.

Something happened in terms of world trade in the second half of the 20th century that Marx and Engels would not have imagined. Detroit exported American automobiles to Japan, and then the Japanese learned how to make cars and started exporting their Nissans and Toyotas and Hondas back to the United States. Just so with the literary productions. The cultural models of the West, especially the novel, provided models themselves for domestic manufacture in these non-Western nations. The English language, especially in the premier English genre of the novel, became the chief means for non-Western writers to appropriate and adopt the cultural heritage of both the European and the American traditions. Hence that really terrific descriptive phrase, "the empire writes back."

Postcolonial novels have come especially from the subcontinent of South Asia, and it is pretty clear to see why, historically. India had come under English influence very early, with the arrival of the East India Company, licensed by Queen Elizabeth I. Remember that first recorded performance of *Hamlet* in 1607 on board a ship off the coast of West Africa? That ship was an Indian ship heading for the Indies as part of this commercial gesture. So already at the beginning of the 17th century, the English are on their way to India. This commercial relationship would persist over the centuries until England itself took over colonial administration of India, which lasted almost a century, until independence in 1947. Even after independence, English itself would continue as the official language of India; it would be taught in the schools and would be used in government and business. And to this day, people answering the telephones in Bangalore and Mumbai not only speak English, but their current ambition is to learn "unaccented" English. (In this day and age, that would be unaccented American English.)

I want to consider two cases, then, of outstanding postcolonial novelists, both with family roots in South Asia. The first would be Salman Rushdie, and the second, Michael Ondaatje. Rushdie was actually born into a secular Muslim family in Bombay in 1947, the same year as India's independence and the same birth date as the hero of his novel *Midnight's Children*, the hero named Saleem Sinai. But Rushdie moved on; he was educated in England at Rugby school—very prestigious—and then he went on to King's College in Cambridge. It's kind of an interesting fact that when he was an undergraduate at King's College, the writer in residence was the elderly novelist E. M. Forster, author of the most famous Anglo-Indian novel to date, *A Passage to India*.

Rushdie would recognize himself as the Indian half of this Anglo-Indian equation, writing in the English language but as a transnational immigrant with a very, very different viewpoint. He works this into his own novel *Midnight's Children* in an interesting way. Before he can actually get his hero born, he needs to do what other English novelists did, like Laurence Sterne in *Tristam Shandy*; he has to back up—a long ways in this case, two generations—to describe the courtship of the hero's grandfather in 1915.

It's interesting: The hero's grandfather is called Dr. Aziz, living in the north of India. And what we'll recognize immediately is, wait a minute, that's the same name as the native character in Forster's *A Passage to India*. Now, Forster's character Dr. Aziz at the end of the novel moves up to the north of India to practice medicine and get on with his life. And so this is the exact same name and the exact same time period, 1915, where Rushdie begins his story. It is almost that his Dr. Aziz links up with Forster's character, almost as if *Midnight's Children* becomes a sequel to *A Passage to India*.

The title of Rushdie's novel comes from a famous pronouncement by India's first prime minister, Nehru. This was this sort of historic moment that the prime minister was looking forward to: "At the stroke of the midnight hour, [while] the world sleeps, India will awake to life and freedom." Rushdie's novel about the children born at that stroke of midnight gives utterance to a nation so torn and divided as it will still become in the sprawling allegory of the split represented by midnight itself: looking back at India's past, looking forward to the unfolding of India's future.

Rushdie does the work of any writer who aspires to enter into the Western canon by making his novel *Midnight's Children* assimilate a great deal of the prior canonic works, and specifically the English novel tradition. I want to take just one example, and this comes from the very opening of Charles Dickens's classic novel *David Copperfield*, as it turns out that Dickens sets up the same premise for his narrator, his hero. David Copperfield is actually born also on the stroke of midnight. This is how the hero himself describes this in first-person narrative:

> I record that I was born (as I have been informed and believe) on a Friday, at twelve o'clock at night. It was remarked that the clock began to strike, and I began to cry, simultaneously.

And what is the significance that David Copperfield should be born at midnight? "I was destined to be unlucky in life," the old wives tell him, "and I was privileged to see ghosts and spirits." This is a fate also shared by Rushdie's hero: that he will be very, very unlucky at life, and we see exactly how tumultuous and traumatic his life is in the course of the novel. And he will have supernatural experiences. In this case, he is psychically linked with all the other children in India born at the stroke of midnight, when their nation achieved independence from England.

In the course of writing back to the English tradition, one of Rushdie's techniques is also to appropriate the native, non-Western techniques of storytelling. He tells us, for example, that *Midnight's Children* reproduces the traditional oral storytelling of India—for example, in the Sanskrit classic the *Ramayana* and in the Muslim literary masterpiece the *Arabian Nights*. And so this retreat took an oral tradition much more circular, becomes a very important assault on that primary Aristotelian principle of storytelling with a clean, character-driven narrative. This is how Rushdie describes it in an essay:

It is not linear. An oral narrative does not go from the beginning to the middle to the end of the story. It goes in great swoops, it goes in spirals or in loops, it every so often reiterates something that happened earlier to remind you, and then takes you off again.

And so despite these gestures toward the native Indian tradition, Rushdie is otherwise making all the right moves to insert himself and his novel into the mainstream of the English literary tradition and thereby into the Western canon itself. *Midnight's Children* won the prestigious Booker Prize as the best English novel. In 1993, it won the extraordinary honor of being the Booker of Bookers, the best British novel of a previous quarter century. In the year 2005, *Time Magazine* included it on their list of the best English-language novels ever, which would include also *The Sound and the Fury*, *Mrs. Dalloway*, *Death Comes for the Archbishop*, and *The Lord of the Rings*.

Ever since the time of Voltaire and Goethe, size matters in determining one's position in the canon, and again Rushdie has made all the right moves. He's extremely prolific, with a steady stream of novels, short stories, essays, reviews, and journalism.

We also know that, since ancient times, one way to gain much greater celebrity status is success by scandal. This was a kind of dubious form of success achieved by Ovid rather accidentally and actually courted by some controversial writers like Voltaire. Rushdie's fourth novel, *The Satanic Verses*, won for him a *fatwa*—a death sentence—from Iran's Ayatollah Khomeini for what was alleged to be a blasphemous depiction of the Prophet, Mohammed. This really put Rushdie's life in some jeopardy. He was very close to joining that rather honorable list of literary martyrs—Socrates, Boethius, Sir Thomas More, the *Gawain* Poet maybe, John Milton (almost, if he hadn't gone blind), and Thomas Mann (almost, again, if he hadn't fled Nazi Germany).

Another important move for Rushdie's status is inclusion within the university; he's been accepted by academics and scholars. There are many, many studies of his novel. *Midnight's Children* almost invariably now ends up in the syllabus with the modern British novel, and if there is a course on the postcolonial novel, Rushdie's *Midnight's Children* is always the centerpiece of any reading list that is going to be involved in that very fashionable course these days on campuses. In fact, I myself first read *Midnight's Children* when I was directing a dissertation, now a book, on Rushdie, Ian McEwen, and A. S. Byatt, all of them winners of the Booker Prize.

Rushdie, in his essay "'Commonwealth Literature' Does Not Exist," actually summons up the authority of T. S. Eliot—this concept, this paradigm within canon formation that Eliot described as when some new, the really new work of art emerges that then reshapes the whole prior tradition. Again, this is what Rushdie has to reflect:

> I think that if *all* English literatures could be studied together, a shape would emerge which would truly reflect the new shape of the language in the world, and we could see that Eng. Lit. has never been in better shape, because the world language now also possesses a world literature, which is proliferating in every conceivable direction.

So here we have that notion of the new shape very much fostered by the descendents of the Sanskrit authors that Eliot himself had begun drawing into the Western tradition when he began quoting the *Upanishads* and the *Bhagavad Gita*. Here also we have the idea of a world literature much more truly global than Goethe would have imagined when he coined the phrase *Weltliteratur*, but not the products of the industrial West shipped to non-Western countries and markets, as Marx and Engels would have predicted in 1848.

I want to begin concluding by consideration of a second postcolonial novelist and sort of pondering whether he, too, has made the right moves to move into the Western canon. The novelist I'm thinking about is Michael Ondaatje, and the work I want to focus on is *The English Patient*. Ondaatje was born in Sri Lanka with mixed parentage, including Dutch and Portuguese. He traveled first to England and then to Canada to complete his education at the University of Toronto. Later, he taught English literature at York University. Like Tolkien and so many others, he knew the Western literary canon from the inside, as a university teacher. It almost was second nature when he came to write *The English Patient* that he should do what every other writer in the tradition has done, and that is to attempt to assimilate and to connect his own work with those prior masterpieces of the Western canon.

The English Patient is a wartime love story set in Italy. In that way, it is already aligning itself with Ernest Hemingway's classic *A*

Farewell to Arms. It also imbibes the northern Italian landscape of Stendhal's *The Charterhouse of Parma*. Why? Because Michael Ondaatje was actually at that Rockefeller villa in Bellagio, Italy, when he was writing *The English Patient*. In fact, there is a sort of weird movement of geography, or a sort of instability of geography: The villa in the novel is supposed to be set in Tuscany, but instead, his imagination keeps coming back to the place where he is writing, overlooking Lake Como. As a result, Stendhal becomes this wonderful sort of ghost presence and appears and disappears throughout the course of the novel.

The English Patient is also a lyric novel very much in the tradition of Virginia Woolf with *Mrs. Dalloway* and *To the Lighthouse* and *The Waves*. As a result, it has this sort of nonlinear, time-shifting motion. Ondaatje was better known as a poet before he became a novelist, and so this instinct toward the lyric novel came very naturally to him. In fact, it is so much a novel of sensation and observation and the emotional responses of characters that it was very, very hard for the screenwriter to adapt it for film later on, giving it that Aristotelian, clean narrative line. An important thing to appreciate about Michael Ondaatje, now, is he is Canadian, in fact a very important literary figure in his home nation of Canada. But this means that he is also aligning himself with the American literary tradition somewhat. Like *Moby-Dick*, *The English Patient* is brimming with this weird sort of technical information about desert mapmaking, even about bomb defusing—that sort of encyclopedic, technical, how-to information that would otherwise seem to be inappropriate for the novel. But within the American tradition, notably with a work like *Moby-Dick*, this sort of technical information almost is what we begin to expect.

At the heart of *The English Patient* is an adulterous love story, a classic sort of triangular relationship and a wonderful sort of moment in which the male character, the Hungarian archaeologist Count Almásy, falls in love with another man's wife, Katherine Clifton. And it happens one night when Mrs. Clifton is reading aloud around the campfire from Herodotus. She's reading a very particular story near the beginning of Herodotus's *The Histories*; it is a story about an earlier King of Lydia, his beautiful wife, and his head spearman.

And the story, in brief, would have the King of Lydia so proud of the beauty of his wife that he wanted to show it off secretly to his spearman, so he arranged the man to hide so he could watch as the wife undressed to go to bed. But she spotted him and confronted him and gave him two alternatives: one, that she would have to have him killed, or two, the two of them should kill her husband so that the spearman could become the new King of Lydia. Clearly, he chose plan B, but that is a lovely moment; it sort of reminds us how the platonic process of mimesis has functioned within Western literary theory for thousands of years—the idea that life imitates art, that people read a love story, a sort of forbidden passion, and then they are provoked to act it out in their own life.

We've seen this before, in Dante's *Inferno*. The traveler, Dante, with his spirit guide, Virgil, have come upon the Circle of the Lustful, and the individual they meet is Francesca da Rimini, and she tells the same story, that she and her adulterous lover Paolo were weakened and tempted because they, too, were reading a story about adulterous lovers, the Arthurian romance of Lancelot and Guinevere. And so this idea of reading about adulterous lovers and then enacting it in one's own life again connects Ondaatje's story in a beautiful way with a long tradition within the West.

Now the Hungarian archaeologist has a real passion for this book that Mrs. Clifton is reading from. He is constantly correcting and supplementing Herodotus's *Histories*, which he is using very much as a guidebook to the Egyptian desert. This suggests, in his process, the ways that European history itself is constantly open to being changed, crossed out, and rewritten by the outsider. Here he is rewriting Herodotus, the foundation of historical text in the entire Western tradition, but always open to revision.

Like Rushdie, then, Ondaatje operates as this transnational author schooled in books not originally his own. Now this isn't a disadvantage; this actually turns out to be a great boost for a writer aspiring to enter into this global marketplace. And again, Rushdie himself, as a critic, points out the advantage of using English on the part of these outsider authors. This is what Rushdie says:

> What seems to me to be happening is that those people who were once colonized by the language are now rapidly remaking it, domesticating it, becoming more and more relaxed about the way they use it—assisted by the English language's enormous flexibility and size.

It is one of the truisms about the English language that it has a huge vocabulary, and this is largely because the English language has always been willing to accept and assimilate foreign words. The whole history of the English language is importing French and Latin and Greek and Scandinavian words. The English language has this kind of open-endedness and plasticity that then makes it a really superb vehicle for writers coming from traditions wanting to draw upon their own kind of native literary methods, as well. However, the English language does not make its user or speaker or writer English.

That is very much the point, or kind of irony, that pervades Michael Ondaatje's *The English Patient*, because none of the main characters is actually English. Hana, the nurse, is Canadian; Caravaggio the spy, also Canadian; Kip, the British Army sapper who defuses bombs, is a Sikh from India; and the English patient himself is a Hungarian, the archaeologist László Almásy. If you look at this sort of profile and the continuing reception history of *The English Patient*, you'll see that Michael Ondaatje really is making, as I said, with Rushdie all the right moves. *The English Patient* won the Booker Prize in 1992. Ondaatje himself has been the subject of a book-long biography. *The English Patient* has become the subject of literary studies and even has a reader's guide dedicated to it. There is always a real mark of distinction when a single literary title gets a reader's guide. Also, the novel has been translated into multiple languages. All the way back to biblical times, it was so important to get the truly essential text translated into a language that a wider and wider audience could read and then appreciate the content, as well as the artistry, of the original work. *The English Patient* was also adapted as a really important, prize-winning movie; it garnered nine Oscars in its year of eligibility, including Best Picture for the year.

Michael Ondaatje continues to write and publish. He has a novel that has come out since *The English Patient*; it is called *Divisadero*, and part of the multiple storylines involves a now-forgotten World War I-era French writer named Lucien Segura. It's interesting that Ondaatje, who has tremendous popularity, notoriety, even celebrity status in our day should already be pondering the possibility that his current status is going to be short-lived. It is almost a sort of haunting obsession with him. Ondaatje coedited a collection entitled *Lost Classics*, lamenting the ruthlessness of the literary tradition at eliminating authors and works that really don't deserve to be consigned to oblivion. The subtitle really says it all: *[Writers on] Books Loved and Lost, Overlooked, Under-read, Unavailable, Stolen, Extinct, or Otherwise Out of Commission.*

But there is good news to this kind of relentless process of the Western canon and canon formation. Inclusion constantly operates throughout the tradition, and sometimes that inclusiveness is extremely benevolent and kind to the authors themselves. We are constantly in the process of retrieving those books loved and lost. Remember, for example, that the entire canon of the Greek classics was lost to the West for a thousand years, basically between the time of Boethius and the time of Sir Thomas More. It was in the Renaissance, through the works of humanists like Erasmus and the works of printers like the Venetian publisher of the Aldine Editions, that we now got back those classics for centuries known only by name, authors like Homer and Plato. Also, we've had the wonderful luck of discovering and reassimilating within our traditions these forgotten masterpieces like *The Epic of Gilgamesh* and *Beowulf*, totally forgotten for centuries. Scholars continue to piece together papyrus fragments from Egypt, looking for more poems by the great Greek lyric artist, Sappho.

Professor Harold Bloom has worried that we've, in fact, gained too many masterpieces—over 3,000 titles by his reckoning—as the Western canon opens itself out to become a true literature. That kind of openness and inclusiveness that Salman Rushdie sees as a kind of life blood of the Western tradition—now become the global tradition—is something that a traditionalist like Bloom finds unsettling.

I myself don't share Professor Bloom's anxiety about the Western canon, which, after all, has always been a work in progress. It has always generated itself backward in time. We've always made the decisions about what we want in and what we are willing to let gather dust on a library shelf (for example, now, the many, many novels of Edward Bulwer-Lytton). The Western canon is very much what Bloom describes: It's a survivors list, with an emphasis on surviving. There are works that we don't want to lose; there are works that we refuse to let go away, even if we do let them sometimes gather shelf dust at our own homes. Mostly I'm optimistic, because we remain a culture of readers in America and in the West. We continue to respect the classics, if only sometimes in the naming and the citing. We construct our own personal canons, and even national canons, around, and sometimes against, a traditional core—for example, Rushdie focusing on Charles Dickens, or Michael Ondaatje obsessed in *The English Patient* with Herodotus at the beginning of the tradition, and then Stendhal as a kind of cult classic love by other novelists.

We remain, then, the people of the book. We buy books; we stock our bookcases at home. We pack books to travel when we head to the airport. We have books piled up on our bedside tables; we are the people that continue to make summer reading lists year after year, and not only in America and the European homeland, but in any of these other parts of the world nearby and under the influence, where there's a sense that literacy matters. When I visited Istanbul, for example, on the west side of the Bosporus, I made a point of taking a kind of pilgrimage to the old book bazaar. And why? Because it is an absolutely amazing place. The old book bazaar is where the Byzantine Greeks for a thousand years were buying and selling books, just like their Athenian ancestors were trading in Homer and Herodotus. This was the marketplace in old Constantinople, where Venetian merchants in the 15th century came to buy used copies of Homer, Plato, and Euripides. These were the dusty, old, worn manuscripts that they, in turn, took home to Venice and made available for printing in those lovely Aldine editions and, in effect, brought us the European Renaissance. When I went to the old book bazaar, the book I ended up with was just a single page. It was a 200-year-old handwritten page of the poet Rumi, beautifully decorated in gold, colored, and with a picture of the poet Rumi himself surrounded by his disciples, the whirling dervishes.

The market there continues to function as a used bookstore for the nearby university in an interesting way. You have economics textbooks sitting next to these wonderful old books by Rumi and others. And in fact, the university built its library immediately next to the old book bazaar, as if making the transit easier, and this was the library in Istanbul where Erich Auerbach found the primary texts of the classics that he used for his book *Mimesis: The Representation of Reality in Western Literature*, in the 1930s.

Our culture, then, remains one organized around the marketing and consumption of books. Every mall and every shopping center has bookstores now with coffee shops for hanging out. Drugstores and even grocery stores have book sections. Airport bookstores sell the latest bestsellers and also the classics, like the newest translation of Virgil's *Aeneid*. We have libraries everywhere—public libraries in our communities, university libraries, even high school libraries, where I read Willa Cather's *Death Comes for the Archbishop*. We also have resources of the World Wide Web; Amazon.com makes a huge number of books available at a keystroke. There are online resources with e-books; Google Books is scanning and making available digitally complete collections of research libraries; and we have the classics as well as bestsellers available on CD, so that while commuting on the freeway or the subway, we can listen to *Pride and Prejudice* being read aloud just as Jane Austen read it aloud to her family.

And so I have tremendous confidence in the strength of the Western tradition. We do remain that culture of people of the book, and so when we get a reference in a movie (like Woody Allen's *Zelig*) to reading and not reading a classic like *Moby-Dick*, we get the joke. We continue to think that somehow it is a noble enterprise in the course of a lifetime to read a book like *Moby-Dick* or *War and Peace* or James Joyce's *Ulysses*. This is why I have tremendous optimism that the Western canon is alive and well in the 21st century.

Timeline

B.C.

c. 2700	Gilgamesh ruled in Uruk.
c. 1600	Earliest version of *The Epic of Gilgamesh* takes shape in Old Babylonian.
c. 1300	*Gilgamesh* written as "Standard Version" in Akkadian.
c. 1150	Troy destroyed by Mycenaean Greeks.
c. 700	Homer writes the *Iliad* and the *Odyssey*.
586	Babylonian exile of the Jews.
536–533	In Athens, Thespis develops the form of tragedy featuring a solo actor.
490–479	Greeks repulse Persian invasion at Marathon, Thermopylae, Salamis, and Plataea.
c. 440	Herodotus writes *The Histories*.
431	Euripides writes *Medea*.
431–404	Peloponnesian War between Athens and Sparta.
c. 427–347	Life of Plato, author of *Apology of Socrates*.
c. 426	Sophocles writes *Oedipus the King*.
c. 400	Thucydides writes *History of the Peloponnesian War*.
399	Trial and execution of Socrates.
384–322	Life of Aristotle, author of *Poetics*.
334	Alexander the Great defeats the Persian Empire.

264–146	The three Punic Wars, including Rome's final destruction of Carthage.
70–19	Life of Virgil, author of the *Aeneid*.
44	Julius Caesar assassinated at Rome.
43 B.C.–A.D. 17	Life of Ovid, author of the *Metamorphoses*.
31	Augustus defeats Antony and Cleopatra at Actium.

A.D.

43	Claudius makes Britannia a Roman province for the next four centuries.
50–100	The four Gospels of the New Testament are written.
325	The Council of Nicaea separates orthodox from heretical Christian doctrines.
330	Emperor Constantine moves the Roman imperial capital to Byzantium, renamed after himself as Constantinople (today called Istanbul).
331	Constantine commissions Eusebius of Caesarea to supply 50 Bibles for churches in his new capital.
367	Bishop Athanasius of Alexandria establishes a "canon" of books for the New Testament.
382	Pope Damasus I commissions Saint Jerome to undertake a revised translation of the Latin Bible.
387	Saint Augustine converts to Christianity.

391 ....Christianity becomes the official religion of the Roman Empire.

395–408......................................Split of Roman Empire into the Latin West and Greek East.

449 ....Coming of the pagan Anglo-Saxons to Britain.

524 ....Boethius writes *Consolation of Philosophy*.

Early 6th century ....Historical setting of *Beowulf*.

598 ....Christian missionaries arrive in England from Rome.

731 ....Bede completes his *Ecclesiastical History of the English People*.

9th century..................................Probable date for the writing of *Beowulf*.

899 ....Death of Alfred the Great, king of the West Saxons.

1066 ....Norman invasion of England; the French language is imposed on the Anglo-Saxons.

1215 ....The Fourth Lateran Council convened in Rome by Pope Innocent III.

c. 1220...Danish historian Saxo Grammaticus writes the earliest version of *Hamlet*.

c. 1301–1321...............................Dante writes the *Divine Comedy*.

1337–1453...................................The Hundred Years' War between England and France.

1348–1349...................................The bubonic plague reaches Europe.

1353 ....Boccaccio writes the *Decameron*.

1380s...*Sir Gawain and the Green Knight* is composed by an unknown author.

1390s	Two Wycliffite translations of Bible into English are created.
c. 1400	Chaucer writes the *Canterbury Tales*.
1405	Tamerlane's death leaves a power vacuum in Asia.
1453	Constantinople falls to Turks, and Byzantine scholars migrate westward with Greek manuscripts.
1455	Gutenberg prints the Latin Bible on a movable-type press.
1488–1513	Aldine editions of Greek classics by Homer, Aristotle, Sophocles, and Plato are printed in Venice.
1492	Ferdinand and Isabella capture the last Muslim stronghold at Grenada; Columbus discovers America.
1514–1522	The five-volume Polyglot Bible is produced in Spain as the first original-language texts of the Scriptures.
1515	Erasmus edits the Greek New Testament at Cambridge University.
1516	Sir Thomas More writes *Utopia*.
1532	Machiavelli writes *The Prince*.
1534	Henry VIII of England breaks with the Church of Rome; Martin Luther completes his German translation of the Bible.
1539	Franciscan missionaries first enter the territory later called New Mexico.
1540	Death of the historical Dr. Faust, magician and charlatan.

1546	Council of Trent confirms the canonic contents of Saint Jerome's Latin Bible.
1547–1616	Life of Miguel de Cervantes, author of *Don Quixote*.
1588	Spanish Armada attempts to invade England, outfitted by funds partly raised by Cervantes.
1564–1616	Life of William Shakespeare, author of *Hamlet* and *The Tempest*.
1607	English found the Jamestown colony in Virginia; the first recorded performance of *Hamlet* is performed on a ship off Sierra Leone; *Don Quixote* is performed as an amateur skit in Peru.
1610	Spanish found Santa Fe in New Mexico; *Historia de la Neuva México* is published in Madrid.
1611	King James Bible published.
1619	Start of the African slave trade in North America.
1620	English Puritans arrive in Massachusetts.
1623	First Folio of Shakespeare's plays published seven years after his death.
1649	Charles I of England executed.
1649–1660	Puritans rule England.
1660	Restoration of Charles II and the English monarchy.
1667	John Milton publishes *Paradise Lost*.

1680	Pueblo Revolt in New Mexico, leading to the reconquest in 1692.
1755	Novelist Tobias Smollett translates *Don Quixote* into English; Lisbon earthquakes kill 30,000.
1756–1763	Seven Years' War involving nine European powers.
1759	Voltaire publishes *Candide* anonymously.
1789	French Revolution begins with the *Declaration of the Rights of Man*.
1798	Napoleon's invasion of Egypt begins the West's long-term involvement in the Middle East.
1803–1815	Napoleonic Wars, including the 1812 invasion of Russia.
1808	Goethe writes *Faust*, Part I.
1810–1821	Mexican War of Independence from Spain.
1813	Jane Austen writes *Pride and Prejudice*.
1815	Battle of Waterloo.
1832	Goethe writes *Faust*, Part II.
1839	Stendhal writes *The Charterhouse of Parma*.
1846–1848	Mexican American War cedes southwest lands to the United States.
1848	Marx and Engels write the *Communist Manifesto*; uprisings occur across Europe.
1851	Herman Melville writes *Moby-Dick*.
1861–1865	American Civil War.
1868–1869	Leo Tolstoy writes *War and Peace*.

1871 ....Unification of Germany following the Franco-Prussian War.

1872 ....George Smith decodes the cuneiform language of the *Gilgamesh* tablets unearthed by Austen Layard at Nineveh.

1904 ....June 16, "Bloomsday," setting for James Joyce's *Ulysses*.

1914–1918...................................First World War.

1920 ....Gandhi starts India's independence movement.

1922 ....James Joyce's *Ulysses* and T. S. Eliot's *The Waste Land* are written.

1924 ....Thomas Mann writes *The Magic Mountain*.

1925 ....Virginia Woolf writes *Mrs. Dalloway*.

1927 ....Willa Cather writes *Death Comes for the Archbishop*.

1929 ....William Faulkner writes *The Sound and the Fury*.

1935 ....Sir Thomas More is canonized as a Catholic saint.

1936 ....J. R. R. Tolkien's British Academy lecture boosts *Beowulf* into the canon.

1939–1945...................................World War II.

1943 ....T. S. Eliot writes *Four Quartets*.

1945 ....Discovery of the long-lost Gnostic Gospels at Nag Hammadi in Egypt.

1947 ....Independence, then partition, of India and Pakistan.

1954–1955......................................J. R. R. Tolkien writes *The Lord of the Rings*.

1980 ....Salman Rushdie writes *Midnight's Children*.

1992 ....Michael Ondaatje writes *The English Patient*.

2003 ....The United States begins the occupation of Iraq, homeland of *Gilgamesh*.

Glossary

allegory: A literary mode, meaning "to say one thing and mean another"; that includes parables, personification, irony, and sarcasm.

Amadis de Gaule: Don Quixote's favorite chivalric quest-romance, read also by the Spanish conquistadors in Mexico.

Andalusía: Ancient Islamic homeland in southern Iberia, containing the great cities Granada and Córdoba; the area where Don Quixote heads on his quest.

Babylonian Captivity: Period during the 6th century B.C. when Hebrew scholars used the new alphabet to compile the earliest books of the Old Testament.

canon: An official list of books and authors.

catharsis: Of Greek origin; Aristotle's term for the purging or purifying of powerful emotions such as fear and terror.

chivalric quest-romance: Narrative of the knightly hero who sets out from the court on a quest, encounters dangerous adventures in the wilderness, and returns victoriously to the court afterward.

codex: A leaf-form book, bound at the spine, with pages that can be turned; the plural is *codices*.

deus ex machina: Of Latin origin; literally "god out of the machine," referring to the crane used to lower some supernatural character onto the stage, as well as a quick, artificial means for ending a drama, deplored by Aristotle.

dystopia: A very bad society, the opposite of **utopia**.

fetish: Inanimate object, like a book, revered because it is believed to possess magical powers; in Freud's sense, an erotic object; this definition was adopted by Mann in *Magic Mountain*.

hubris: Of Greek origin; the blind arrogance of man's ambition.

in medias res: Of Latin origin; means "into the middle of things" and describes the chronology of the epic from Homer through Virgil and to John Milton.

kolossal: Of German origin; aesthetic of something "colossal" creating a sense of the spectacular and the sublime.

liberal: Champion of political freedom and individual rights against tyranny, supporter of ideals of American and French revolutions extended to Italy (Stendhal) and Russia (Tolstoy).

lollardy: Early Christian reform movement in England, started by followers of Wyclif (d. 1384), with sympathizers like Chaucer, laying foundations for the Tudor Reformation of the 16th century.

mimesis: Of Greek origin; "imitation," either art imitating the reality of life or human beings imitating the examples preserved in literary texts.

nemesis: Of Greek origin; the divine force undercutting human greatness and ambition.

novella: Of Italian origin; "new story" or fictional narrative, usually short, typically comical, like those collected by Boccaccio in his *Decameron*.

parchment: Named after the Greek city of Pergamum, a writing surface made from animal skin; used instead of Egyptian papyrus.

Pentateuch: The first five books of the Old Testament.

picaresque: Describes a novel with a "hero" who is a rogue, deadbeat, or comic simpleton stumbling through a series of misadventures.

pietas: Of Latin origin; the sense of Roman duty and responsibility that takes precedence over personal desires, exemplified by Virgil's Aeneas.

postcolonial writer: An author in a previously colonized country who responds to the prior invaders by writing in his own native language (Chaucer) or using the intruder language in nontraditional ways (Salman Rushdie).

Septuagint: The Greek translation of the Hebrew Scriptures produced in Alexandria beginning in the 3rd century B.C., adopted by early Christians in the Greek-speaking eastern Mediterranean.

Sophists: Athenian rhetoric specialists trained to "make the worst case appear the best"; the first lawyers.

teleology: From the Greek work for "target," concerns the aims and conclusions of events in a plotline.

theodicy: Trust in God's goodness despite evil and injustice in the world.

translatio imperii: Of Latin origin; the "transition of power" from one country to another.

translatio studii: Of Latin origin; the "transition of culture" from one country to another.

utopia: More's made-up name, mixing Greek *eu topia* ("good place") with *ou topia* ("no place"); origin of the adjective *utopian*.

vellum: Named after the word for "calf," a writing surface made from cow or other animal skin; used throughout most of the Middle Ages.

Biographical Notes

Aeschylus (525–456 B.C.): The first great tragic playwright with surviving works, including *Prometheus Bound, The Persians*—which contains his eye-witness account of the Athenian naval victory at Salamis—and his only surviving trilogy, *The Oresteia.*

Alcibiades (450–404 B.C.): Athenian nobleman and student of Socrates; backed the invasion of Sicily and betrayed his homeland during the Peloponnesian War; a memorable character in Plato's *Symposium.*

Aldo Manuzio (1449–1515): Italian humanist and publisher; printed "Aldine editions" of Greek classics in Venice and invented *italic* type.

Alexander of Macedonia (356–323 B.C.): Student of Aristotle; united Greece, conquered the Persian Empire (including Egypt), and spread Greek culture throughout his domain.

Alfred the Great (849–899): King of the West Saxons; held back Viking Danes and ordered books such as Boethius's *Consolation* and Bede's *Ecclesiastical History* translated into Old English.

Ambrose, Saint (339–397): Bishop of Milan, one of the Four Doctors of the Church; served as an example to Saint Augustine for interpreting the Bible allegorically.

Amerigo Vespucci (1454–1512): Florentine navigator; published accounts of his voyages to the New World between 1499 and 1502, influenced More's *Utopia*, and had America named after him.

Aristophanes (c. 456–c. 386 B.C.): Athenian comic playwright who satirized Socrates in *The Clouds*; also a character in Plato's *Symposium.*

Aristotle (384–322 B.C.): Student of Plato; lectured on dozens of fields of knowledge, including *Poetics*, but had his treatises published only long after his death.

Ashurbanipal (7th century B.C.): The Assyrian king whose library at Nineveh preserved tablets of *Gilgamesh* discovered by Austen Layard and decoded by George Smith.

Athanasius (293–373): Bishop of Alexandria; proclaimed the "canon" of 27 books for the New Testament and wrote the *Life of St. Anthony* that facilitated Saint Augustine's conversion.

Auerbach, Erich (1892–1957): German literary scholar and Jewish refugee from the Nazis; wrote his classic study *Mimesis* using only the primary canonic texts available to him in Istanbul during World War II; died as a professor at Yale.

Augustine, Saint (354–430): Bishop of Hippo and author of the *Confessions*; established official Church theology and fixed the canon of 46 books of the Old and New Testaments.

Augustus Caesar (63 B.C.–A.D. 14): The first Roman Emperor; commissioned Virgil to write the *Aeneid* as the national epic proclaiming Rome's manifest destiny to rule the world.

Austen, Jane (1775–1817): Wrote six well-loved novels, including *Pride and Prejudice*, which she published anonymously; her last two novels, including *Northanger Abbey*, were published posthumously.

Averroës (1126–1198): Muslim scholar, physician, and scientist working mostly in Spain; produced an Arabic version of Aristotle's *Poetics* that was later translated into Latin for European readers.

Barlaam of Calabria (1290–1348): A Greek from southern Italy and Constantinople-based theologian; assisted Italians at translating Homer, Euripides, and Aristotle into Latin.

Bede, Saint (672–735): Monastic scholar; wrote *Ecclesiastical History of the English People* (731) describing the Anglo-Saxon invasions and later conversion of Britain to Christianity; honored among the most brilliant theologians in Dante's *Paradiso*.

Bloom, Harold (b. 1930): Yale English professor; author of *The Western Canon*, which centers on Shakespeare; *The Anxiety of Influence*, which examines generational competition between great authors; and *The Story of J*, which suggests that early books of the Old Testament were written by a woman; read *Moby-Dick* at age 16.

Boccaccio, Giovanni (1313–1375): Florentine author of the *Decameron*, *Falls of Great Men* (which uses Boethian tragedy as pattern for world history), and *Genealogy of the Pagan Gods*, preserving ancient mythologies based on newly discovered Greek manuscripts.

Boethius (c. 480–524): The last great Roman; translated Greek philosophical texts into Latin and authored *Consolation of Philosophy* while awaiting execution by the Ostrogoth king; his relics lie in the same church as Saint Augustine's outside Milan.

Bulwer-Lytton, Edward (1803–1873): English novelist, once extremely popular for works like *Paul Clifford* and *Last Days of Pompeii*, now fallen out of the canon; has a "bad writing" contest named after him.

Campbell, Joseph (1904–1987): Scholar of comparative mythologies, champion of James Joyce, and commentator on *Sir Gawain*; interviewed in a celebrated PBS series *The Power of Myth*.

Cather, Willa (1873–1947): American author best known for Nebraska novels like *O Pioneers!*; also wrote the New Mexico classic *Death Comes for the Archbishop*; now studied largely as a lesbian writer.

Cervantes, Miguel de (1547–1616): Spanish adventurer and author; wrote Oriental plays like *Great Sultana*, pastoral novel *Galatea*, and *Don Quixote* Part I (1605) and Part II (1615); died on the same date as Shakespeare.

Chaucer, Geoffrey (c. 1340–1400): Author of the *Canterbury Tales* whose kinship with Lancastrian kings helped his status as Father of English Literature, edging out William Langland and the anonymous *Gawain* poet.

Cicero, Marcus Tullius (106–43 B.C.): Roman politician and philosopher whose long-lost letters, discovered by Petrarch, revised Latin prose style for Renaissance authors such as Erasmus, Thomas More, and John Milton as well as the Italian prose of Boccaccio's *Decameron*.

Constantine I (c. 272–337): Roman Emperor; ended the persecution of Christians, converted, summoned the Council of Nicaea to settle doctrines of faith, moved the capital to the old Greek city of Byzantium, and ordered 50 Bibles for the churches in the new capital Constantinople in 331.

Cotton, Sir Robert (1571–1631): English courtier and antiquarian; after the dissolution of monastic libraries in Britain, compiled a massive collection of medieval manuscripts that included unique copies of *Beowulf* and *Sir Gawain and the Green Knight*, almost lost in a fire in 1731.

Demetrius of Phaleron (c. 350–c. 280 B.C.): Athenian follower of Aristotle; exiled to Egypt, he is credited with organizing the great Library of Alexandria as a center for preserving, copying, editing, and studying books.

Díaz del Castillo, Bernal (1496–1584): Conquistador with Cortés against the Aztecs; author of *The True History of the Conquest of New Spain*.

Du Bois, W. E. B. (1868–1963): African American writer and civil rights leader whose *The Souls of Black Folk* (1903) announced "the problem of the color line" as the chief challenge of the 20th century; became a citizen of Ghana at age 95.

Eliot, T. S. (1888–1965): American poet, dramatist, and critic; published three poems charting his spiritual quest: *The Waste Land*, *Ash Wednesday*, and *The Four Quartets*, as well as the church drama *Murder in the Cathedral* and the comic poems made into the musical *Cats*.

Erasmus, Desiderius (1469–1536): Dutch scholar, friend of Sir Thomas More, and author of *The Praise of Folly*; produced a Greek edition of the New Testament in 1515.

Euripides (c. 484–406 B.C.): Last of the three great tragic playwrights; won third prize for edgy dramas like *Medea*, but has more surviving plays than any other tragic poet.

Eusebius (c. 263–339): Bishop of Caesarea; influential at the Council of Nicaea, he sorted out "acknowledged" books of the New Testament and wrote *History of the Church*.

Faulkner, William (1897–1962): American writer; produced short stories and novels like *The Sound and the Fury* and *Absalom! Absalom!* concerned with South's race relations; honored as a "regional writer" when awarded the Nobel Prize for Literature in 1950.

Fletcher, John (1579–1625): English playwright, educated at Cambridge; collaborated with Shakespeare on *Henry VIII*, the lost *Cardenio*, and the Bard's last play, *The Two Noble Kinsmen*.

Forster, E. M. (1879–1970): English writer whose *Aspects of the Novel* contains brilliant critical insights; his novel *A Passage to India* (1924) provided an example for Postcolonial novelists like Salman Rushdie; his novel *Maurice*, written in 1913 but published posthumously in 1971, became a classic in the gay literary canon.

Foucault, Michel (1926–1984): French social historian and public intellectual; published *Birth of the Clinic* and *Discipline and Punish* examining how modern institutions create a "carceral society" using *matrix* to render people "docile and capable"; taught at Berkeley and died of AIDS.

Freud, Sigmund (1856–1939): Austrian psychiatrist and writer; introduced the "Oedipal complex" as a way to understand *Hamlet* in *Interpretation of Dreams* (1900), as well as studies of phallic images and erotic fetishes, influencing writers like Thomas Mann.

Geoffrey of Monmouth (1100–1155): Welsh, Oxford scholar whose *History of the Kings of Britain* introduced King Arthur to English literature, popularized belief that Trojan refugees colonized Britain, and told the earliest version of *King Lear*.

Goethe, Johann Wolfgang von (1749–1832): The first great German-language author; studied law, became court official in Weimar, began as an 18th-century writer with *Sorrows of Young Werther*, ended as a 19th-century Romantic with *Faust*, Parts I and II, and did research on plant morphology that influenced Darwin.

Gregory of Tours, Saint (538–594): Refers to Beowulf's uncle Hygelac in his *History of the Franks*.

Heaney, Seamus (b. 1939): Irish poet, winner of the Nobel Prize for Literature, roaming academic, and bestselling translator of *Beowulf*.

Herodotus (c. 484–c. 420 B.C.): Authored *The Histories* as the first major prose work examining the cultures of Egypt and Persia, including Xerxes's invasion of Greece and the confrontation with the Spartans at Thermopylae.

Hobbes, Thomas (1588–1679): English political philosopher, Royalist contemporary of John Milton, translator of Thucydides's *Peloponnesian Wars*, author of *Leviathan*, and first scholar to point out that Moses did not write the Pentateuch.

Innocent III (c. 1161–1216): Pope and author of *On the Misery of the Human Condition*; launched the Albigensian Crusade in southern France, convened the Fourth Lateran Council (1215) with sweeping religious reforms, and oversaw the Fourth Crusade while setting the stage for the Fifth Crusade.

Jerome, Saint (c. 347–c. 420): Traveled throughout Europe and the Middle East, rendered an official translation of the Bible into Latin by order of Pope Damasus I, and died as a hermit outside Bethlehem.

Johnson, Dr. Samuel (1709–1784): English critic and man of letters; educated at Oxford, compiled the *Dictionary*, edited Shakespeare in eight volumes, wrote *Lives of the Poets* outlining the English literary canon since the Renaissance, and gave critical support for the novel as a distinctive English genre.

Jones, Terry (b. 1942): Welsh, Oxford-trained scholar of medieval literature, political commentator, and writer/director of *Monty Python and the Holy Grail*, in which he played Sir Bedevere.

Joyce, James (1882–1941): Irish writer; defined the Modernist movement with *Ulysses* (1922) and spent the rest of his career in Paris working on the experimental novel *Finnegans Wake*.

Jung, Carl Gustav (1875–1961): Swiss psychologist and scholar of world religions; introduced the notion of the "universal unconscious" as the source of artistic creativity and promoted "archetypal" criticism; instrumental in the history of Alcoholics Anonymous.

Lachmann, Karl (1793–1851): German philologist; pioneered new editorial methods for the New Testament as well as Homer, Latin poets, and medieval German literature.

Langland, William (c. 1330–c. 1400): Credited with authorship of *Piers Plowman*, the first national bestseller in English and the founding text of the Puritan literary tradition.

Leibniz, Gottfried Wilhelm (1646–1716): German mathematician, philosopher, and polymath whose *Théodicée* (1710) proposed "the best of all possible worlds" satirized by Voltaire's *Candide*; he invented calculus and discovered the binary number system that would become the basis for modern computers.

Leontius Pilatus (d. 1366): Taught Greek to Boccaccio, translated the *Iliad* and the *Odyssey* into Latin, and was struck by lightning while sailing to visit Petrarch in Venice.

Lewis, C. S. (1898–1963): Oxford scholar of medieval and Renaissance literature, Christian apologist, and friend of J. R. R. Tolkien, whose fantasy fiction inspired his "Chronicles of Narnia."

Longinus (probably fl. 1st century A.D.): Classical literary critic whose *On the Sublime* emphasized the artist's "genius" and the spectacular effect of "sublimity."

Mann, Thomas (1875–1955): German novelist and political exile; started *Magic Mountain* as a companion piece to the homoerotic classic *Death in Venice*, won the Nobel Prize for bestseller *Buddenbrooks*, and later wrote his own *Doctor Faustus*.

Marcion of Sinope (110–160): Rejected the Old Testament and established an early "canon" of the New Testament comprising only the Gospel of Saint Luke and the 10 letters of Saint Paul.

Marx, Karl (1818–1883): German economic historian whose *Communist Manifesto* announced a "world literature" spread by global trade; in 1849, he settled in London to continue his research at the British Library.

Melville, Herman (1819–1891): American author; won his reputation as a sex symbol with his early Polynesian novels *Typee* and *Omoo* before publishing *Moby-Dick*, which he dedicated to his friend Nathaniel Hawthorne.

Milton, John (1608–1674): English humanist scholar; educated at Cambridge, became a civil servant in the Puritan Commonwealth, and, after going blind, composed *Paradise Lost* by dictating to his daughters.

More, Sir Thomas (1478–1535): English courtier under Henry VIII, friend of Erasmus, Catholic martyr, and author of *Utopia*; his biography was written by son-in-law William Roper.

Nietzsche, Friedrich (1844–1900): German Classical scholar and philosopher, early champion of Wagner's operas; wrote *The Birth of Tragedy*, distinguishing creative Apollonian and destructive Dionysian strains, as well as *Thus Spoke Zarathustra* and *The Will to Power*; retired to Italy and died of syphilis.

Ondaatje, Michael (b. 1943): Canadian writer born in Sri Lanka of Dutch-Portuguese parentage whose lyrical novel *The English Patient* won the Booker Prize and was made into an Oscar-winning film.

Origen of Alexandria (c. 185–c. 254): Greek scholar and author of 6,000 theological works; improved the text of Septuagint and combined the Hebrew and Christian scriptures in a single codex.

Ovid [Publius Ovidius Naso] (43 B.C.–A.D. 17): Assimilated Greek and Roman mythology in the *Metamorphoses*, was exiled by Emperor Augustus for the immorality of *Art of Love*, and influenced every later European artist from Chaucer, Botticelli, and Shakespeare to Franz Kafka, Salvador Dalí, and Ted Hughes.

Petrarch, Francis (1304–1374): First-ever international literary celebrity, friend and senior colleague of Boccaccio; he invented the sonnet sequence, pioneered rediscovery of the Classics, was crowned as Poet Laureate for his Latin epic *Africa*, and was the first to dismiss the medieval period as the "Dark Ages."

Plato (c. 427–c. 347 B.C.): Student of Socrates; authored the 25 dialogues, as well as *The Apology of Socrates*, that serve as the foundation of Western philosophy.

Radcliffe, Ann (1764–1823): English novelist whose *Mysteries of Udolpho* (1794) popularized Gothic fiction; influenced Sir Walter Scott and Mary Shelley, but was lampooned by Jane Austen in *Northanger Abbey*.

Richard II (1367–1400): King of England, patron of the *Gawain* Poet and Geoffrey Chaucer, and subject of a tragic history by Shakespeare.

Rushdie, Salman (b. 1947): Indian-born writer educated at Cambridge whose *Midnight's Children* became a landmark Postcolonial novel and whose *Satanic Verses* earned him a death sentence for blasphemy against Islam.

Sappho (c. 610–c. 570 B.C.): The greatest of the early Greek lyric poets; her works were almost completely lost, perhaps because Christians objected to their erotic content or because her obscure Aeolic dialect forced dropping her poems from the Byzantine curriculum; the term "lesbian" derives from her home island of Lesbos.

Saxo Grammaticus (c. 1150–c. 1220): Danish historian whose *Gesta Danorum* provided the earliest version of the Hamlet story.

Schliemann, Heinrich (1822–1890): German businessman and amateur archeologist; led early excavations at Mycenae and Troy to demonstrate the historical basis for Homer's epics.

Shakespeare, William (1564–1616): English playwright and theater professional; wrote successful tragedies, histories, and comedies during the reigns of Elizabeth I and James I, but his collected plays were only published seven years after death in the First Folio.

Smollett, Tobias (1721–1771): Scottish writer; translated *Don Quixote* (1755) and pioneered the "picaresque" novel with *Peregrine Pickle* and *Humphrey Clinker*.

Sophocles (c. 496–406 B.C.): Greek playwright; added the third actor and brought Athenian tragedy to its apex with *Oedipus the King*, Aristotle's favorite.

Stanley, Sir Henry (1841–1904): Welsh explorer and journalist; found Dr. David Livingston in 1871 and returned to Africa with 180 pounds of books, including Shakespeare, to advance Belgium's colonial ambitions in the Congo.

Stendhal (1783–1842): One of many pen-names of the writer Marie-Henri Beyle, author of travel writings, biographies, and criticism, as well as the "Romantic realist" novels *The Red and the Black* and *The Charterhouse of Parma*.

Tacitus (56–c. 117): Roman historian; wrote *Germania* as an ethnography describing the pagan practices of Germanic barbarians.

Thespis (fl. c. 530 B.C.): Legendary founder of Athenian tragedy; made the protagonist a solo performer with the chorus.

Thucydides (c. 460–c. 395 B.C.): Athenian historian; wrote *Peloponnesian War*, concerning the long period of warfare between Athens and Sparta that spilled over to Sicily.

Tolkien, J. R. R. (1892–1973): Oxford English professor and fantasy writer; championed *Beowulf* as a literary masterpiece, edited *Sir Gawain and the Green Knight*, and wrote his own heroic epic *The Lord of the Rings*, which became one of the top-selling publications in Western history.

Tolstoy, Leo (1828–1910): Russian aristocrat and writer whose classic novels *War and Peace* and *Anna Karinina* were followed by spiritual books like *Resurrection* and the early Postcolonial novel *Hadji Murád*, inspired by his military service during the Crimean War (1853–1856):

Virgil [Publius Virgilius Maro] (70–19 B.C.): Wrote pastoral poetry before being commissioned by Augustus to produce the *Aeneid* as a Homeric epic celebrating Rome's origins and future greatness; died while returning from a research trip to Greece.

Voltaire (1694–1778): Pen-name of François-Marie Arouet; author of hundreds of plays, histories, poems, philosophical and political tracts, and 20 satirical novellas, including *Candide*; made a fortune through shrewd financial dealings and box-office hits in Paris.

Woolf, Virginia (1882–1941): English novelist and critic; published lyrical novels *Mrs. Dalloway* and *To the Lighthouse*, which were printed by her husband Leonard's Hogarth Press; she was the inspiration behind Michael Cunningham's *The Hours*; her *Room of One's Own* (1929) became a feminist manifesto.

Wyclif, John (c. 1325–1384): Oxford theologian; condemned religious corruption and papal power, encouraged the Reformation movement, and championed two complete translations of the Bible into English during the 1390s.

Bibliography

Ackroyd, Peter. *T. S. Eliot: A Life*. New York: Simon and Schuster, 1984. The poet wanted no biography, and his estate did everything possible to hinder efforts at this first-rate attempt at connecting the author's life and works.

Aeschylus. *Prometheus Bound, The Suppliants, Seven Against Thebes, The Persians*, translated by Philip Vellacott. London: Penguin Books, 1961. This clean, agile translation is prefaced by a helpful introduction, play by play.

Alighieri, Dante. *The Divine Comedy*, translated by John Ciardi. London: NAL Trade, 2003. This is my favorite translation, faithful to the original, yet stunning as poetry, with just enough endnotes.

Alter, Robert, and Frank Kermode, eds. *The Literary Guide to the Bible*. Cambridge, MA: Harvard University Press, 1987. More than two dozen international specialists contributed to this introduction under the guidance of the eminent literary critic Kermode and biblical scholar Alter.

Ashcroft, Bill, Gareth Griffiths, and Helen Tiffin, eds. *The Empire Writes Back: Theory and Practice in Postcolonial Literatures*. New York: Routledge, 1989. This comprehensive study opens up debate about the relationships of emerging literatures of India, Africa, the West Indies, and Canada as context for the achievements of Rushdie and Ondaatji.

Auerbach, Erich. *Mimesis: The Representation of Reality in Western Literature*, translated by Willard R. Trask. Princeton, NJ: Princeton University Press, 1953. Fiftieth-anniversary edition, 2003. This text remains the single most respected volume of literary criticism from the 20th century, doing much to define the Western canon from Homer to Virginia Woolf, and is itself now a canonic masterwork.

Austen, Jane. *Pride and Prejudice*. 3rd ed. Edited by Donald Gray. New York: W. W. Norton, 2001. Contains family letters, biography, early writings, and selections from modern criticism.

Bayley, John. *Tolstoy and the Novel*. 2nd ed. Chicago: University of Chicago Press, 1988. This classic study sets *War and Peace* in the context of the European novel and elevates Tolstoy to the status of Shakespeare as supremely retrospective of writers.

Bell, Quentin. *Bloomsbury*. London: Weidenfeld and Nicolson, 1973. Written by Virginia Woolf's nephew, her first biographer.

Beowulf: A Verse Translation, translated by Seamus Heaney, edited by Daniel Donoghue. New York: W. W. Norton, 2002. Includes the Nobel Laureate's bestselling translation, as well as J. R. R. Tolkien's landmark lecture "*Beowulf*: The Monsters and the Critics" (1936).

Bercaw, Mary K. *Melville's Sources*. Evanston, IL: Northwestern University Press, 1987. This indispensable volume includes reports of the original whale "Mocha Dick" and the sinking of the *Essex*.

Berlin, Sir Isaiah. *The Hedgehog and the Fox: An Essay on Tolstoy's View of History*. 1953. Reprint, London: Phoenix Books, 1999. Tries to categorize thinkers either as hedgehogs who know one big thing (Plato and Dante) or foxes who know many things (Herodotus, Aristotle, Shakespeare, Goethe, and Joyce).

Besterman, Theodore. *Voltaire*. 3rd ed. Chicago: University of Chicago Press, 1976. The most informative biography.

Bloom, Harold. *The Western Canon: The Books and School of the Ages*. New York: Riverhead Books, 1994. Views the European tradition as a father-son competition between powerful authors, over many centuries, centered on Shakespeare.

Boccaccio, Giovanni. *The Decameron*, translated and edited by Mark Musa and Peter E. Bondanella. New York: W. W. Norton, 1977. Selections, also including Petrarch's letters to Boccaccio, four early biographies, and Auerbach's chapter from *Mimesis*.

Boethius, Anicius Manlius Severinus. *The Theological Tractates and Consolation of Philosophy*, translated and edited by H. F. Stewart, E. K. Rand, and S. J. Tester. Loeb Classical Library, 74. Cambridge, MA: Harvard University Press, 1973. Facing Latin and English texts of the *Consolation* as well Christian treatises like *On the Trinity*.

Bowers, John M. *Chaucer and Langland: The Antagonistic Tradition*. Notre Dame, IN: University of Notre Dame Press, 2007. Asks why Chaucer became the "Father of English Literature" instead of his London contemporary, William Langland, author of the more influential and widely read *Piers Plowman*.

———. *The Politics of "Pearl": Court Poetry in the Age of Richard II*. Cambridge: D. S. Brewer, 2001. Asks why the author of *Sir Gawain and the Green Knight* remains anonymous and his brilliant poetry survives in a single modest manuscript.

Boyle, Nicholas. *Goethe: The Poet and the Age*. 2 vols. Oxford: Oxford University Press, 1991–2000. This biography received rave reviews even from the German literary establishment; a third volume is projected.

Brewer, Derek, and Jonathan Gibson, eds. *A Companion to the "Gawain"-Poet*. Cambridge: D. S. Brewer, 1997. Contains important studies of "Authorship," "Manuscript," and "Historical Background."

Brown, Peter. *Augustine of Hippo: A Biography*. Berkeley: University of California Press, 1967. Drawing richly upon the *Confessions*, this beautifully written biography has become a classic in its own right.

Burrow, John. *A History of Histories: Epics, Chronicles, Romances, and Inquiries from Herodotus and Thucydides to the Twentieth Century*. New York: Knopf, 2008. Uses the two Greek historians as the alternative models for all later history writers.

Butler, Marilyn. *Jane Austen and the War of Ideas*. Oxford: Clarendon Press, 1989. Hardly sheltered, Austen learned much about her era's political and philosophical controversies from other novels.

Calvino, Italo. "Guide to New Readers of Stendhal's *Charterhouse*." In *Why Read the Classics?*, translated by Martin McLaughlin. New York: Pantheon Books, 1999. This collection includes other lively, loving essays on the *Odyssey*, Ovid, *Candide*, and Tolstoy, as well as his exploration of *Charterhouse* as perhaps "the best novel ever written."

Cambridge Companions to Literature. Cambridge: Cambridge University Press, 1991–. Series includes excellent, up-to-date collections of essays on (in chronological order) the Bible, Plato, Virgil, Ovid, St. Augustine, *Beowulf*, Dante, Cervantes, Jane Austen, Goethe, Melville, Tolstoy, Joyce, Mann, Woolf, Eliot, Faulkner, Cather, and postcolonial literary studies.

Carpenter, Humphrey. *J. R. R. Tolkien: A Biography*. Boston: Houghton Mifflin, 1977. Written with family support by someone who knew Tolkien personally, this biography does a brilliant job of shedding light on the relation between the Oxford professor's life and the contents of his works.

Casson, Lionel. *Libraries of the Ancient World*. New Haven, CT: Yale University Press, 2002. This brief book provides a smart overview of the earliest libraries of Mesopotamia, ancient Greece, imperial Rome, and the early Middle Ages.

Cather, Willa. *Death Comes for the Archbishop*. New York: Vintage Classics, 1990. Bare text without introduction or annotations.

Cervantes, Miguel de. *Don Quijote*, translated by Burton Raffel and edited by Diana de Armas Wilson. New York: W. W. Norton, 1999. Contains "*Don Quijote* across the Centuries" and criticism by Carlos Fuentes, Harold Bloom, and Michel Foucault, plus Jorge Luis Borges's "Pierre Menard, Author of the *Quixote*."

Chadwick, Henry. *Boethius: The Consolation of Music, Logic, Theology and Philosophy*. Oxford: Clarendon Press, 1981. Discusses the career of Boethius as a Platonist who happened also to be a Christian.

Chaucer, Geoffrey. *The Riverside Chaucer*, edited by Larry D. Benson. 3rd ed. Boston: Houghton Mifflin, 1987. The standard scholarly edition containing the complete works, minus *Equatorie of the Planets*.

Dalley, Stephanie, trans. and ed. *Myths from Mesopotamia: Creation, the Flood, Gilgamesh, and Others*. Oxford: Oxford University Press, 2000. This affordable paperback provides background myths made more readable by advances in scholarship on the ancient languages.

Damrosch, David. *The Buried Book: The Loss and Rediscovery of the Great Epic of Gilgamesh*. New York: Henry Holt and Company, 2007. Telling the story backward to the historical king around 2700 B.C., Damrosch spins a captivating yarn of West meets East, with the Mosul-born archeologist Hormuzd Rassan as the key 19th-century figure.

Durant, Will and Ariel Durant. *The Age of Voltaire*. The Story of Civilization, IX. New York: Simon and Schuster, 1965. This bestselling overview of the man and his century, engagingly written, makes Voltaire come alive.

Edwards, Robert R. *Chaucer and Boccaccio: Antiquity and Modernity*. New York: Palgrave, 2002. Shows the two great authors as rivals (on Chaucer's end) but also collaborators inventing modern literature.

Eliot, T. S. *Collected Poems, 1909–1962*. New York: Harcourt, Brace & World, 1963. These 221 large-print pages show a poetic output that has become more valuable for containing so few major works.

————. *Selected Essays: New Edition.* New York: Harcourt, Brace & World, 1964. The author's poems are illuminated by these essays, such as "Tradition and the Individual Talent," "Hamlet and His Problems," "Dante," and "The Metaphysical Poets."

————. *The Waste Land*, edited by Michael North. New York: W. W. Norton, 2001. Contains a large number of sources for the poem, also a wide span of criticism from Virginia Woolf onward.

Ellmann, Richard. *James Joyce.* 1959. Reprint, New York: Oxford University Press, 1983. Perhaps the best literary biography of any modern author—truly magisterial.

Eusebius. *The History of the Church*, translated by G. A. Williamson and Andrew Louth. New York: Penguin, 1989. Pages 88–89 cover the canonic books of the New Testament as well as those excluded as non-canonic.

Faulkner, William. *The Sound and the Fury*, edited by David Minter. 2nd ed. New York: W. W. Norton, 1994. Contains important Faulkner background materials, as well as classic criticism by Robert Penn Warren, Ralph Ellison, Cleanth Brooks, and even Jean-Paul Sartre.

Fiedler, Leslie A. *Love and Death in the American Novel.* New York: Stein and Day, 1966. This book shocked its first readers by discovering "innocent homosexuality" as a central theme in classic American fiction.

Forster, E. M. *Aspects of the Novel.* 1927. Reprint, New York: Penguin Books, 2005. These lectures contain the seasoned wisdom and insights of a master fiction writer.

Foucault, Michel. *The Birth of the Clinic: An Archeology of Medical Perception*, translated by A. M. Sheridan Smith. 1963. Reprint, New York: Vintage Books, 1994. Explores the institutionalization of modern man in a "carceral society."

Gallagher, Joseph. *A Modern Reader's Guide to Dante's "The Divine Comedy."* Forward by John Freccero. Liquori, MO: Triumph Publishing, 1999. With a forward by the dean of Dante studies in America, this inexpensive volume was consistently awarded five stars by Amazon.com customers, one praising it as "arguably the finest introduction to Dante in English."

Garth, John. *Tolkien and the Great War: The Threshold of Middle-Earth.* Boston: Houghton Mifflin, 2003. Reads *The Lord of the Rings* in light of the author's experiences as a veteran of World War I.

Gibson, Margaret, ed. *Boethius: His Life, Thought, and Influence.* Oxford: Blackwell, 1981. Commemorating the 1500th anniversary of the author's birth, this collection starts with an expert introduction by Henry Chadwick and ends with Anthony Grafton on the Boethian legacy in the Renaissance; the biographical essay by John Matthews places the writer's career in context of his senatorial background.

Goethe, Johann Wolfgang von. *Faust: A Tragedy*, translated by Walter Arndt and introduction by Cyrus Hamlin. 2nd ed. New York: W. W. Norton, 2001. Contains important modern criticism from Stuart Atkins, Jaroslav Pelikan, Benjamin Bennett, Franco Moretti, and Jane K. Brown.

Grafton, Anthony, and Megan Williams. *Christianity and the Transformation of the Book: Origen, Eusebius, and the Library at Caesarea.* Cambridge, MA: Harvard University Press, 2006. This fascinating "archeology" of early biblical editing is especially helpful in the introduction "Scholars, Books, and Libraries in the Christian Tradition."

Graziosi, Barbara, and Emily Greenwood, eds. *Homer in the Twentieth Century: Between World Literature and the Western Canon.* Oxford: Oxford University Press, 2007. Taking exception to Harold Bloom's claim that every Western reader is a descendant of Homer, the editors assemble new essays on the "bumpy ride" that Homeric epics traveled to arrive in the contemporary world—and how difficult it is to see these literary works clearly through intervening texts like Joyce's *Ulysses*.

Greaves, A. E. *Stendhal's Italy: Themes of Political and Religious Satire.* Exeter: University of Exeter Press, 1995. This political reading of *Charterhouse* also manages to bring art and opera into the discussion.

Greenblatt, Stephen. *Will in the World: How Shakespeare Became Shakespeare.* New York: W. W. Norton, 2004. This mass-marketed publication contains a fascinating chapter, "Speaking with the Dead," on the Ghost in *Hamlet*.

Hardie, Philip. *Virgil's "Aeneid": Cosmos and Imperium.* Oxford: Clarendon Press, 1986. No longer a dark pessimist, Virgil is seen as optimist about the grandeur of Augustan Rome, marshalling religious tradition and natural philosophy to support the imperial agenda.

Hardie, Philip, Alessandro Barchiesi, and Stephen Hinds, eds. *Ovidian Transformations: Essays on the "Metamorphoses" and its*

Reception. Cambridge: Cambridge Philological Society, 1999. These 18 essays focus on current concerns like the poet's use of time and his self-fashioning as a poet of exile, with Hardie's especially fine discussion of Ovid's influence upon Petrarch.

Heller, Erich. *The Disinherited Mind: Essays in Modern German Literature and Thought*. New York: Barnes & Noble, 1976. Heller sums up Goethe's theological paradox: "What is Faust's sin? Restlessness of spirit. What is Faust's salvation? Restlessness of spirit."

Herodotus. *The Histories*, translated by Walter Blanco. New York: W. W. Norton, 1992. This volume contains Plutarch's essay "On the Malice of Herodotus" and Oswyn Marray on "Greek Historians." Interested readers should also consult *The Landmark Herodotus* (2008), with its maps and explanatory notes.

Hexter, Ralph. *A Guide to "The Odyssey": A Commentary on the English Translation of Robert Fitzgerald*. New York: Vintage Books, 1993. After introductory sections on archeology, geography, religion, and family organization, Hexter proceeds with succinct explorations, book by book through the epic.

Hill, Christopher. *Milton and the English Revolution*. New York: Viking, 1978. Puts Milton's career in context of the Puritan movement against England's royal government.

Hollander, Robert. *Boccaccio's Dante and the Shaping Force of Satire*. Ann Arbor: University of Michigan Press, 1997. The great scholar and translator explores Boccaccio's pervasive responses to his predecessor, Dante.

Holy Bible: King James Authorized Version, 1611. Translated during the age of Shakespeare, this English Bible also benefited from the latest advances in textual editing during the Renaissance.

Jones, John. *On Aristotle and Greek Tragedy*. Oxford: Oxford University Press, 1962. Debunks the Neoclassical notion that Aristotle defined the tragic hero, "fatal flaw," and three unities of time, place, and action.

Joyce, James. *Ulysses*, edited by Hans Gabler, introduction by Richard Ellmann. New York: Vintage, 1993. Critical edition more correct than the text supervised by the author in the first edition of 1922.

Kernan, Alvin B. "The King and the Poet: *The Tempest*, Whitehall, Winter 1613." In *Shakespeare, the King's Playwright: Theater in the*

Stuart Court, 1603–1613. New Haven, CT: Yale University Press, 1995. Places the play in the precise context of its original performance at James I's court.

Knox, Bernard M. W. *Oedipus at Thebes: Sophocles' Tragic Hero and His Time.* New Haven, CT: Yale University Press, 1998. Clears away Freudian interpretations to understand what this play meant in ancient Athens and why it was singled out for praise by Aristotle.

Knox, Peter E., ed. *Oxford Readings in Ovid.* Oxford: Oxford University Press, 2006. Twenty of the most influential studies published in the last 30 years, but expensive, so get it from the library.

Ladenson, Elisabeth. *Dirt for Art's Sake: Books on Trial from "Madame Bovary" to "Lolita."* Ithaca, NY: Cornell University Press, 2007. Contains a lively chapter entitled "Leopold Bloom's Trip to the Outhouse."

Lee, Hermione. *Virginia Woolf.* New York: Knopf, 1997. The best-regarded biography.

————. *Willa Cather: A Life Saved Up.* New York: Little, Brown and Company, 2008. Sees the author as a Modernist whose novels contain camouflaged desires and suppressed sexuality.

Levenback, Karen L. *Virginia Woolf and the Great War.* Syracuse, NY: Syracuse University Press, 1999. Discusses the author as a civilian "war novelist" and places *Mrs. Dalloway* in context of post-war England.

Lewis, C. S. *The Discarded Image.* Cambridge: Cambridge University Press, 1964. Based on a series of Oxford lectures, this posthumously published book provides a fascinating survey of the ancient and medieval concepts of the world, its creatures, and the encompassing universe—with a good chapter on Boethius.

————. *A Preface to "Paradise Lost."* 1942. Reprint, London: Oxford University Press, 1961. Still the most useful, clear-headed, and entertaining introduction to Milton's Christian epic.

Luraghi, Nino, ed. *The Historian's Craft in the Age of Herodotus.* Oxford: Oxford University Press, 2007. International experts put *The Histories* in the context of late archaic and early classical Greece.

Mann, Thomas. *The Magic Mountain*, translated by John E. Woods. New York: Everyman's Library, 2005. Awarded the Helen and Kurt

Wolff Prize for translation as replacement for the longstanding but problematic 1927 version by H. T. Lowe-Porter.

Maude, Aylmer. *The Life of Tolstoy*. 2 vols. Oxford: Oxford University Press, 1987. Originally published in 1908–1910 with assistance from Tolstoy and his wife.

Mazzotta, Giuseppe. *The World at Play in Boccaccio's "Decameron."* Princeton, NJ: Princeton University Press, 1986. Scrutinizes the Italian masterpiece not only as a story about people playing but as a book itself playing with medieval conventions of religion, morals, medicine, law, and human romance.

McDermott, Emily A. *Euripides' Medea: The Incarnation of Disorder*. University Park, PA: Pennsylvania State University Press, 1989. Helps explain why the Athenian judges were so upset that they awarded the playwright only third prize.

Melville, Herman. *Moby-Dick*, edited by Hershel Parker and Harrison Hayford. 2nd ed. New York: W. W. Norton, 2002. The most reliable text, accompanied by background materials on Melville's reading and his whaling sources, as well as a survey of criticism from the first, mostly hostile newspaper reviews to the most recent critics like Camille Paglia.

Milton, John. *Paradise Lost*, edited by Gordon Teskey. New York: W. W. Norton, 2005. Includes biblical sources as well as criticism by Dr. Johnson, T. S. Eliot, and C. S. Lewis.

More, Sir Thomas. *Utopia*, edited by Robert M. Adams. New York: W. W. Norton, 1992. Contains Erasmus's word-portrait of More, G. R. Elton's "The Real Thomas More?", and C. S. Lewis's comments from *English Literature in the Sixteenth Century*.

The Nag Hammadi Library in English, edited by James M. Robinson. San Francisco: Harper & Row, 1988. These texts provide a striking look into the lost early world of Christian books and readers.

Nobel Prize Library: William Faulkner, Eugene O'Neill, John Steinbeck, edited by Alexis Gregory. New York: Helvetica Press, 1971. Contains presentation addresses, Faulkner's acceptance speech, and Joseph Blotner's "Life and Works of William Faulkner."

Norton Anthology of Theory and Criticism, The, edited by Vincent B. Leitch. New York: W. W. Norton, 2001. Contains canonic criticism by Plato, Aristotle, Longinus, Dante, Dr. Johnson, Shelley, Marx,

Nietzsche, Freud, Du Bois, Jung, Woolf, Eliot, Frye, De Beauvoir, Bloom, Foucault, Said, and Greenblatt.

Norton Anthology of World Literature, The, edited by Sarah Lawall. 2nd ed. Vols. A–F. New York: W. W. Norton, 2002. Provides texts of *Gilgamesh*, the *Odyssey*, *Oedipus*, *Medea*, *The Apology of Socrates*, the *Aeneid*, the *Metamorphoses*, *Confessions*, *Beowulf*, *Inferno*, *Sir Gawain and the Green Knight*, *Don Quixote*, *Hamlet*, and *Paradise Lost*.

Ondaatje, Michael. *The English Patient*. New York: Vintage, 1996. Just the original text, warts and all, like the misspelling of Stendhal's name on page 273.

Ondaatje, Michael, Michael Redhill, Esta Spalding, and Linda Spalding, eds. *Lost Classics: Writers on Books Loved and Lost, Overlooked, Under-Read, Unavailable, Stolen, Extinct, or Otherwise Out of Commission*. New York: Anchor Books, 2001. Ondaatje writes about *Bringing Tony Home* (1996) by the Sri Lankan filmmaker Tissa Abeysekara.

Orchard, Andy. *A Critical Companion to "Beowulf."* Cambridge: D. S. Brewer, 2003. With a breadth of learning and insight, this books cuts through scholarly controversies to become an indispensible guide to newcomers and experts alike.

Ovid. *Metamorphoses*, translated by Charles Martin. New York: W. W. Norton, 2004. Lovely translation with a concise introduction and glossary of proper names.

Paulson, Ronald. *Don Quixote in England: The Aesthetics of Laughter*. Baltimore: Johns Hopkins University Press, 1997. Shows the Knight of La Mancha as the model for comic writing in England during the 18th century.

Quint, David. *Epic and Empire: Politics and Generic Form from Virgil to Milton*. Princeton: Princeton University Press, 1993. Uses *The Aeneid* as the starting point for reading epic literature as an argument for imperialism.

Reed, T. J. *Thomas Mann: The Uses of Tradition*. Oxford: Clarendon Press, 1996. Has established itself as the standard English-language book on Mann's thought and fiction.

Roper, William. *The Life of Sir Thomas More*, in *Two Early Tudor Lives*, edited by Richard S. Sylvester and Davis P. Harding. New Haven: Yale University Press, 1971. Written by More's son-in-law and member of the family household.

Rushdie, Salman. *Midnight's Children*. London: Penguin Books, 1991. Paperback reprint for mass-marketing the original 1980 text.

Sewell, Richard. *In the Theater of Dionysios: Democracy and Tragedy in Ancient Athens*. Jackson, NC: McFarland, 2007. Describes the parallel emergence of democracy and tragedy, with sporting competitions, speculative philosophy, and especially the fatal Athenian obsession with war.

Shakespeare, William. *Hamlet*, edited by Cyrus Hoy. New York: W. W. Norton, 1992. Contains the original story of Amleth by Saxo Grammaticus, plus classic criticism by Dr. Johnson, Goethe, T. S. Eliot, and C. S. Lewis.

———. *The Tempest*, edited by Peter Hulme and William H. Sherman. New York: W. W. Norton, 2004. Sources are grouped under the headings "Magic and Witchcraft," "Politics and Religion," and "Geography and Travel." Also contains several fine articles, including John Gillies's "Shakespeare's Virginian Masque."

Shippey, Tom. *J. R. R. Tolkien: Author of the Century*. Boston: Houghton Mifflin, 2002. A professional medievalist explains what is best and timeless in the writings of another medievalist, Professor Tolkien.

Stanley, Henry M. *Through the Dark Continent*. 2 vols. New York: Harper and Brothers, 1878. See 2:384–386 on Stanley's decision to burn Shakespeare instead of his notebook—or his Bible—at the insistence of the tribesmen.

Stendhal. *The Charterhouse of Parma*, translated by Richard Howard. New York: Random House Modern Library, 1999. Wonderful translation with thumbnail introduction, just enough notes, and Howard's engaging "Afterword."

Stock, Brian. *Augustine the Reader: Meditation, Self-Knowledge, and the Ethics of Interpretation*. Cambridge, MA: Harvard Belknap Press, 1998. Shows how Augustine redefines "reading books" as the means of spiritual self-discovery and personal redemption.

Strauss, Leo. *Xenophon's Socrates*. Ithaca, NY: Cornell University Press, 1973. Explores the "alternative" and perhaps more authentic Socrates described by his other student, Xenophon, instead of Plato.

Swift, John N., ed. *Willa Cather and the American Southwest*. Lincoln, NE: University of Nebraska Press, 2004. This collection explores the impact of landscape on the author's 1920s novels, especially *Death Comes for the Archbishop*.

Taylor, Gary. "*Hamlet* in Africa 1607." *Travel Knowledge: European "Discoveries" in the Early Modern Period*, edited by Ivo Kamps and Jyotsna G. Singh. New York: Palgrave, 2001. Pages 211–222 investigate the shipboard journals documenting the first-recorded performance of Shakespeare's play off the coast of Sierra Leone.

Thucydides. *The Peloponnesian War*, translated by Walter Blanco. New York: W. W. Norton, 1998. This volume includes selections from Machiavelli on political brinkmanship, Hobbes on war's brutality, Francis Cornford on the irrationality of "luck," and Walter Karp on Thucydides and the Cold War.

Tolkien, J. R. R. *The Lord of the Rings: Three-Volume Set*. Boston: Houghton Mifflin, 2003. With maps and end-matter, this edition provides a text superior to the Ballantine paperbacks.

Tolstoy, Leo. *Hadji Murád*, in *The Death of Ivan Ilych and Other Stories*, translated by Alyner Maude. Introduction by David Goldfarb. New York: Barnes & Noble, 2004. Praised as "the best story in the world" by Harold Bloom, also a forerunner of the Postcolonial novel.

———. *War and Peace*, 2nd ed. Translated by Aylmer Maude and Louise Maude, edited by George Gibian. New York: W. W. Norton, 1996. The Maude translation (1923) was endorsed by Tolstoy himself. Contains the author's comments on composition, including the 1868 essay "Some Words about *War and Peace*," plus valuable criticism by Nikolai Strakhov, Henry James, Boris Eikhenbaum, Isaiah Berlin, Kathryn Feuer, and Gary Saul Morson.

Tomalin, Claire. *Jane Austen: A Life*. Revised edition. New York: Penguin Books, 2000. Written with wit and intelligence, this biography offers everything that can be known about the novelist and her colorful family connections.

Voltaire. *Candide*, 2nd ed. Edited and translated by Robert M. Adams. New York: W. W. Norton, 1991. Contains Auerbach's classic essay from *Mimesis* as well as contemporary accounts by English visitors Edward Gibbon and James Boswell.

———. *The Portable Voltaire*, edited by Ben Ray Redman. New York: Penguin Books, 1977. In addition to *Candide* and *Zadig*, this collection includes portions of the author's *Philosophical Dictionary*, *English Letters*, and his poem *The Lisbon Earthquake* translated by Tobias Smollett.

Wegemer, Gerald B., and Stephen W. Smith, eds. *A Thomas More Source Book*. Washington, DC: Catholic University of America Press, 2004. Includes the play *Sir Thomas More*, written partly by Shakespeare.

Williamson, Joel. *William Faulkner and Southern History*. Oxford: Oxford University Press, 1995. Regional themes in the novels are explored through a blend of biography, family history, and Mississippi culture, with particular attention to sex, race, and community.

Wilson, Emily. *The Death of Socrates: Hero, Villain, Chatterbox, Saint*. Cambridge, MA: Harvard University Press, 2007. The philosopher's self-inflicted execution is placed in context of long-term Western views on citizenship and celebrity, heroism and religious conviction, and individual freedom and state control

Woolf, Virginia. *Mrs. Dalloway*. 1925. Introduction by Maureen Howard. Reprint, New York: Harcourt, 1981. First published by her husband's press in 1925, this is one of Woolf's best-known and most important novels. This edition contains a fine introduction by Maureen Howard discussing the impact of *Mrs. Dalloway* on the novel form.

Notes